Grasping the Democratic Peace

Grasping the Democratic Peace

PRINCIPLES FOR A POST–COLD WAR WORLD

Bruce Russett

WITH THE COLLABORATION OF
William Antholis
Carol R. Ember
Melvin Ember
Zeev Maoz

PRINCETON UNIVERSITY PRESS
PRINCETON, NEW JERSEY

Library of Congress Cataloging-in-Publication Data

Russett, Bruce M.
Grasping the democratic peace : principles for a
post–Cold War world / Bruce Russett ; with the collaboration
of William Antholis . . . [et al.].
p.   cm.
Includes bibliographical references (p.   ) and index.
ISBN 0-691-03346-3 (C : acid-free paper)
1. Democracy.   2. War.   3. Peace.   I. Title.
JC423.R824   1993
321.8—dc20   93-16274

This book has been composed in Adobe Sabon

Princeton University Press books are printed on
acid-free paper and meet the guidelines for permanence
and durability of the Committee on Production
Guidelines for Book Longevity of the
Council on Library Resources

Printed in the United States of America

10 9 8 7 6 5 4 3 2 1

In memory of

Kenneth Boulding

1910–1993

who understood stable peace,
in the world
and in his life

Contents

Acknowledgments

THIS RESEARCH was supported by grants from the John D. and Catherine T. MacArthur Foundation, the National Science Foundation (Program in Political Science and Program in Social/Cultural Anthropology), the United States Institute of Peace, and the World Society Foundation (Switzerland).

I am grateful to Adam Scheingate for research assistance on parts of chapters 1 and 6; to Allison Asotorino, Ann Gerken, and Soo-Yeon Kim for their help in data processing for chapter 4; and to Nate Gallon, Daniel Jacoby, and Kirsten Sadler for coding assistance for chapter 5. Marie-Elena Angulo, Ann Biteti, Marilyn Cassella, Sandra Nuhn, and Mary Whitney helped in many ways.

I also thank Bruce Bueno de Mesquita, Peter Dougherty, Paul Diehl, Michael Doyle, William Foltz, Charles Fornara, Aaron Friedberg, Isabelle Grunberg, Ted Gurr, Donald Kagan, Robert Keohane, Sheldon Levy, Gavin Lewis, David Lumsdaine, Irad Malkin, Edwin Mansfield, Alex Mintz, Ben D. Mor, Martin Ostwald, Solomon Polachek, James Lee Ray, Thomas Risse-Kappen, R. J. Rummel, Jack Snyder, Harvey Starr, Marc Trachtenberg, Eric Weede, and Alexander Wendt for their comments on various parts of the manuscript. As usual, only I (and my co-authors of chapters 3–5) bear the responsibility.

Parts of this book were published earlier, notably most of chapter 3 in *Journal of Peace Research* 29,4 (1992), and most of chapter 5 in *World Politics* 44,4 (1992). Both chapters, however, contain a good deal of new material. More important, although I felt it desirable to get some portions into the public debate that has emerged over the basic proposition that democracies rarely fight each other, the book was conceived as an integrated product, in the form presented here.

B.R.

Hamden, Connecticut
December 1992

Grasping the Democratic Peace

CHAPTER 1

The Fact of Democratic Peace

> We have no quarrel with the German people. . . . It was not
> upon their impulse that their government acted in entering this
> war. It was not with their previous knowledge or approval. It
> was a war determined upon as wars used to be determined
> upon in the old unhappy days when peoples were nowhere
> consulted by their rulers and wars were provoked and waged
> in the interest of dynasties or of little groups of ambitious men
> who were accustomed to use their fellow men as pawns and
> tools. Self-governed nations do not fill their neighbor states
> with spies or set the course of intrigue to bring about some
> critical posture of affairs which will give them an opportunity
> to strike and make conquest. . . . Cunningly contrived plans of
> deception or aggression, carried, it may be from generation to
> generation, can be worked out and kept from the light only
> within the privacy of courts or behind the carefully guarded
> confidences of a narrow and privileged class.
> —Woodrow Wilson's war message to Congress,
> April 2, 1917

SCHOLARS and leaders now commonly say "Democracies almost never fight each other." What does that mean? Is it true? If so, what does it imply for the future of international politics? Would the continued advance of democracy introduce an era of relative world peace? Can policymakers act so as to make that kind of peaceful world more likely, and, if so, how? Does the post–Cold War era represent merely the passing of a particular adversarial relationship, or does it offer a chance for fundamentally changed relations among nations?

During the Cold War, Soviet-American hostility was overdetermined. The very different political systems of the two superpowers, with their built-in ideological conflict, ensured a deadly political and military rivalry. So too did the systemic stresses of two great powers, each leading a big alliance in a bipolar confrontation, which ensured that each would resist any enhancement of the other's strength as a threat to its own security. But the end of the Cold War destroyed both those sources of hostility. The ideological conflict dissolved with the end of communism, and the bipolar confrontation collapsed with that of the Soviet alliance system and of the Soviet Union itself. Given the revolutionary changes both in the global system and in the states that comprise it, the old bases for evaluating the character of international relations have also collapsed.

The end of ideological hostility matters doubly because it represents a surrender to the force of Western values of economic and especially political freedom. To the degree that countries once ruled by autocratic systems become democratic, a striking fact about the world comes to bear on any discussion of the future of international relations: in the modern international system, democracies have almost never fought each other. This statement represents a complex phenomenon: (a) Democracies rarely fight each other (an empirical statement) because (b) they have other means of resolving conflicts between them and therefore do not need to fight each other (a prudential statement), and (c) they perceive that democracies should not fight each other (a normative statement about principles of right behavior), which reinforces the empirical statement. By this reasoning, the more democracies there are in the world, the fewer potential adversaries we and other democracies will have and the wider the zone of peace. This book will document, explain, and speculate about the implications of the phenomenon of democratic peace.

The vision of a peace among democratically governed states has long been invoked as part of a larger structure of institutions and practices to promote peace among nation-states. Immanuel Kant (1970) spoke of perpetual peace based partially upon states sharing "republican constitutions." His meaning was compatible with basic contemporary understandings of democracy. As the elements of such a constitution he identified freedom (with legal equality of subjects), representative government, and separation of powers. The other key elements of his perpetual peace were "cosmopolitan law" embodying ties of international commerce and free trade, and a "pacific union" established by treaty in international law among republics.

Woodrow Wilson expressed the same vision for the twentieth century. This normative political basis of Wilson's vision of world order, evident as early as 1894, grew naturally from his progressive inclinations in domestic politics (Knock 1992, 9ff.); and his Fourteen Points sound almost as though Kant were guiding Wilson's writing hand. They included Kant's cosmopolitan law and pacific union. The third point demanded "the removal, so far as possible, of all economic barriers and the establishment of an equality of trade conditions among all the nations consenting to the peace and associating themselves for its maintenance"; and the fourteenth point called for "a general association of nations . . . formed under specific covenants for the purpose of affording mutual guarantees of political dependence and territorial integrity to great and small states alike." He did not so clearly invoke the need for universal democracy, since at that time not all of America's war allies were democracies. But the suggestion of this principle is clear enough if one thinks about the domestic political conditions necessary for his first point: "Open covenants of peace, openly arrived at, after which there shall be no private international understandings of any kind but diplomacy shall proceed always frankly and in the public view." Moreover, his 1917 war message openly asserted that "a steadfast concert of peace can never be maintained except by a partnership of democratic nations."

THE EMERGENCE OF DEMOCRATIC PEACE BEFORE WORLD WAR I

The strong norm that democracies should not fight each other seems to have developed only toward the end of the nineteenth century. That time period provides a number of examples in which stable democracies engaged in serious diplomatic disputes that took them to the brink of war, without ever actually going over the edge. In this restraint of action between democracies, and in the subsequent evaluations of the crises by the peoples and elites involved, we can discern some important differences between the expectations and norms operating among democracies and those that became operative when a democracy entered into an adversarial relationship with an authoritarian state.

During the 1890s Britain was engaged in a dispute with Venezuela over the boundary between that country and British Guiana. Grover Cleveland, the American president, grew exasperated by British unwillingness to submit the matter to arbitration and, invoking the Monroe Doctrine, threatened war. The British in turn took four months to reply—and then rejected the United States' position. Cleveland sought and obtained a congressional appropriation of funds for a boundary commission—in effect, enforced arbitration by the United States. In subsequent discussion, however, the United States offered to exclude from arbitration areas settled by British subjects for at least two generations, or sixty years. Charles Campbell (1974, 185) says this "unexpected reversal virtually ensured an early termination of the controversy." With it the British in turn backed down, and agreed to arbitration that ultimately decided the issue by a compromise that generally favored Venezuela. In doing so, "Great Britain made almost all the concessions, and all the important ones" (A. E. Campbell 1960, 27); and the United States then pressured the Venezuelans to accept the decision.

Clearly the British prime minister, Lord Salisbury, misjudged the American government's determination, and he was not willing to fight a war. Of Cleveland's intention we cannot be certain, but his actions look more like that of a poker player who expected his bluff to work, and not to be called. Both sides "blinked" in some degree—especially the British, at a time when their relations with Germany were deteriorating and they did not need another enemy.

Although important in preventing an Anglo-American war over this bagatelle, British strategic interests do not deserve all the credit for avoiding war. Stephen Rock, who has examined this and other international relationships during this time, has some illuminating comments on the public and official discourse. Describing the milieu of the Anglo-American relations—both during the crisis and over the next few years as the participants stepped back from the brink and considered what they might have done—he explains that "The reform bills of 1867 and 1884, which extended the franchise in England, had largely dissolved" the American image of England as feudal and aristocratic. "Anglo-Saxonism emerged as a major force" in relations between two nations toward the end of the nineteenth century, and burst forth in the war crisis. Feelings of Anglo-Saxon kinship contained strong elements of racialism and social Darwinism, but they held a serious political component as well. Richard Olney, Cleveland's secretary of state during the Venezuelan crisis, declared in 1896, "If there is anything they [Americans] are attached to, it is to ideals and principles which are distinctly English in their origin and development. . . . Nothing would more gratify the mass of the American people than to stand . . . shoulder to shoulder with England" (all from Rock 1989, 49–56). Consider how different these sentiments were from what Americans were saying about Spain in 1898.

From the other side, British Colonial Secretary Joseph Chamberlain had already praised the "common laws and common standards of right and wrong" of the two countries. Later he declared that Americans' "laws, their literature, their standpoint on every question are the same as ours; their feeling, their interest, in the cause of humanity and the peaceful development of the world, are identical with ours." Arthur Balfour claimed that America's "laws, its language, its literature, and its religion, to say nothing of its constitution are essentially the same as those of English-speaking peoples elsewhere, [and] ought surely to produce a fundamental harmony—a permanent sympathy." According to Rock, this feeling of homogeneity of societal attributes

> lay behind the initial outpouring of pacifist sentiment during the Venezuelan boundary controversy and was a central element in popular and official desires for the settlement of that and other issues. . . . First, it colored the perceptions of both Englishmen and Americans, causing them to underestimate the importance of the conflict of geopolitical and economic interests between the two countries and to discount the significance of the concessions necessary to

achieve an understanding. Second, it led many persons to conclude that the benefits of avoiding a fratricidal war with "racial" kin outweighed the costs of the sacrifices required for this to be accomplished. (All from Rock 1989, 49–56)

In effect, an Anglo-American security community was becoming established; "the last serious threat of war between the two powers passed" (Russett 1963, 5). Allen (1955, 540) concludes that "the British public never looked like accepting war, the American public after the first fine careless rapture drew back from the prospect of making it." In the Spanish-American war shortly thereafter, British sympathies were overwhelmingly with the United States (C. S. Campbell 1957, chap. 2).

Meanwhile and subsequently, British and then American relations with Germany deteriorated, and ended ultimately in war. Kennedy (1980, esp. 399) contrasts Britain's attitudes toward Germany with its new "special relationship" with the United States. Rock (1989, 56) declares, "These effects were devastatingly absent—or reversed—in the Anglo-German and German-American cases."

While turn-of-the-century Britain was an industrial-capitalist, liberal, parliamentary democracy, imperial Germany was an autocratic, bureaucratic, authoritarian state. . . . These differences were appreciated, and even exaggerated, on both sides of the North Sea, and they colored the attitudes and perceptions of important segments of popular opinion as well as governmental leaders themselves. Englishmen, who could agree on practically nothing else, were in fact almost unanimous in their distate for the German political system, its ideology, and its methods. . . . Both of these nations [Germany and the United States] were rising imperial powers with growing navies. Both threatened British interests in various regions of the globe. Yet Britons, while they detested and feared Germany, almost universally admired the United States and felt minimal apprehension at her ambitions. Part of this was geographic. . . . But a large portion was ideological and cultural as well. Imbued as they were with a sense of Anglo-Saxon solidarity, the vast majority of Englishmen simply did not believe that Americans could wish or do them serious harm." (Rock 1989, 86–87)

The Fashoda crisis of 1898, however, which pitted Britain against France, poses a harder case. British and French interests had been advancing toward the Sudan, with Britain increasingly determined to control the area as protection for its major stake in Egypt. But French forces occupied the small fortress of Fashoda before the British could get there. When a much larger British force arrived, government leaders had to decide what to do. The French were in no position to fight. Their forces at Fashoda were far weaker, they had their hands full on the Continent with Germany, and Britain held unquestioned naval superiority. The premier, Théophile Delcassé, admitted that "the problem is how to combine the demands of honor with the necessity of avoiding a naval war which we are absolutely incapable of carrying through" (quoted in Sanderson 1965, 359). Thus he offered compromise in several forms, ultimately offering to quit the area in return for commercial concessions. The British, however, would have none of it. They refused to negotiate so long as French forces were in the area, and the British prime minister, Lord Salisbury, seemed ready to go to war if the French would not concede totally. Ultimately they did.

The most recent scholarly work on the crisis (Bates 1984, 153) concludes that "there is really no evidence in the archives in London and Paris that either government seriously considered going to war over Fashoda." The French gave in because of their military weakness and the need to avoid isolation in their far graver quarrel with Germany. In addition, their hand was weakened by governmental instability resulting from the Dreyfus affair (Albrecht-Carrié 1970). Salisbury wanted good relations with France to counter the growing threat he felt from Germany, and generally preferred diplomacy to force. In this crisis Salisbury was the poker player. He had to play a "two-level game" (Putnam 1988) with imperialist hawks in domestic politics as well as with the French. While he might have been willing to fight if he had to, he did not want war and knew how weak the French really were.

Considerations of any norm that these two nations should not fight each other were well in the background on both sides; war was avoided primarily for other reasons. Nevertheless, sober reflection on the crisis brought the norms forward: "Both Britain and France possessed a commitment to liberalism and representative government and were opposed to autocracy and absolutism. During the period of reconciliation, numerous references were made to this effect, and to the role of this similarity in drawing the two countries together." A Liberal party leader, H. C. G. Matthew, said: "Most Liberals regarded the Entente with France as the natural result of common democratic impulses." Though they played little role in settling the crisis itself, these feelings were catalyzed by Fashoda and fed directly into the emerging Anglo-French entente (Rock 1989, 117–18).

Thus the feeling of common liberal and democratic values played its part in moderating power conflicts between the United States and Britain, and Britain and France. Between the United States and Germany, on the other hand, the feelings were very different. The German and American political-economic systems involved "two essentially different conceptions of the state: that of the economically liberal laissez-faire state, in which one from the German side saw only disorder, egoism, and corruption, and the half-absolutist, neofeudalistic, bureaucratic state, which in American eyes destroyed the freedom of the individual and lacked democratic legitimation through the 'voice of the people'" (Christof 1975, quoted in Rock 1989, 141). For Americans, an earlier vision of Germany became "replaced by the picture of an increasingly repressive, militaristic, authoritarian, and autocratic society" (Rock 1989, 143). Such views were strengthened by the subsequent German war with Britain. Relationships based on type of political system reinforced strategic considerations. The ground was prepared for Wilson's vision of a world that could be at peace if and only if it were democratic.

THE SPREAD OF DEMOCRATIC PEACE

At the time of Kant, and even of Wilson, the hope for a world of democratic nation states was merely that: a hope, a theory perhaps, but without much empirical referent. Certainly in Kant's time, Europe was hardly an area in which republics flourished. By the time of Wilson's Fourteen Points there were more, in the New World as well as the Old, but the dozen or so democracies of that time still were substantially in a minority.

Wilsonian "idealism" was widely regarded as discredited by the outbreak of World War II. True, the principles of collective security, as embodied in the League of Nations, failed to contain aggression by the Axis powers. In that sense, the element of international law in the Kantian and Wilsonian vision failed. But the elements of trade and democracy were never given a fair chance. International trade was damaged first by the imposition of war reparations on defeated Germany—with some of the effects forecast by Keynes (1919)—and then by the round of "beggar my neighbor" trade restraints imposed with the collapse of the world economy in the Great Depression (Kindleberger 1973). Not coincidentally, democracy also was lost in many countries; first in Russia, then Italy, Germany, Central Europe, Japan, and elsewhere. Thus the Kantian prescription once again had little basis on which to work.

Largely unnoticed, however, was the empirical fact that democracies had rarely if ever gone to war with each other during this period. Since there were few democracies, often at a distance from each other, it is hardly surprising that their failure to fight each other was little noticed. States need both an opportunity and a willingness (Most and Starr 1989) to go to war with each other. Noncontiguous democracies, unless one or both were great powers, had little opportunity to fight each other. States cannot fight unless they can exert substantial military power against each others' vital territory. Most states, if not great powers with "global reach" (large navies in this era; Modelski and Thompson 1988) could exert such power only against contiguous states or at least near neighbors. Furthermore, the willingness of states to fight depends in large part on issues over which they have conflicts of interest. Territorial disputes (over borders, or rights of ethnic groups whose presence is common to both) are rare in the absence of proximity (Diehl and Goertz 1992). Since relatively few of the democracies bordered each other in the 1920s and 1930s, it is not surprising that they generally avoided war with each other. Thus the empirical fact of little or no war between democracies up to this time could be obscured by the predominance of authoritarian states in the international system, and the frequent wars involving one or more such authoritarian states. One could still see the international system as not only anarchic, but in principle threatening the "war of all against all."

Following World War II the situation changed, again, ironically, with a vision of war prevention geared primarily to the last war. The post–World War II era began with the founding of the United Nations, dedicated—as was the League—to the general principle of collective security as carried out by Franklin Roosevelt's "four (ultimately five) policemen" with the power of permanent representatives on the Security Council. But with the Cold War and Soviet-American deadlock in the Security Council arising almost immediately, attention shifted to the more traditional means of collective security through alliance. Despite rhetorical statements like the Universal Declaration of Human Rights and the fact that most—but not all—members of the newly formed North Atlantic Treaty Organization were democracies, democracy was seen more as a binding principle of the Cold War coalition against communism than as a force actively promoting peace among democracies themselves. Moreover, many members of the wider Western alliance system (in Latin America, the Middle East, and Asia) certainly were not democratic.

But by the 1970s, with the increasing numbers of democracies in the international system, the empirical fact of peace among democracies became harder to ignore. There were at one time by various counts thirty-five or so democratic states, and more of them were proximate to one another. Still there was little war, or even serious threats of war, to be found in relationships among those democracies. And more clearly than before, the phenomenon of democratic peace extended beyond the North Atlantic area, and beyond merely the rich industrialized countries belonging to the OECD. The phenomenon began then to be more widely recognized, and by the end of the 1980s it had been widely accepted in the international relations literature, though not so easily explained. This research result is extremely robust, in that by various criteria of war and militarized diplomatic disputes, and various measures of democracy, the relative rarity of violent conflict between democracies still holds up.[1] By early 1992 it even had passed into popular political rhetoric, with the international zone of "democratic peace" invoked in speeches by then

Secretary of State James Baker and President George Bush, and by Bill Clinton during his presidential campaign.[2]

Wide recognition is not, however, synonymous with universal acceptance. It became confused with a claim that democracies are *in general*, in dealing with all kinds of states, more peaceful than are authoritarian or other nondemocratically constituted states. This is a much more controversial proposition than "merely" that democracies are peaceful in their dealings with each other, and one for which there is little systematic evidence.[3] Especially in the Vietnam era of U.S. "imperial overreach," it was a politically charged and widely disbelieved proposition. In that light, both academic observers and policymakers refused to accept even the statement that democracies are peaceful toward each other as a meaningful empirical generalization without some kind of theoretical explanation indicating that it was not merely a coincidence or accident.

Furthermore, some variants of the proposition took the form of statements like "democracies never go to war with each other," or even "democracies never fight each other." The latter statement, applied to relatively low-level lethal violence, is demonstrably wrong as a law-like "never" statement even for the modern international system. The former, limiting the statement to the large-scale and typically sustained form of organized international violence commonly designated as war, nonetheless tempts the historically minded reader to come up with counterexamples. And, especially with the key terms still largely undefined, it is not hard to identify candidate counterexamples.

DEMOCRACY, WAR, AND OTHER AMBIGUOUS TERMS

This book will establish the following: First, democratically organized political systems in general operate under restraints that make them more peaceful in their relations with other democracies. Democracies are not necessarily peaceful, however, in their relations with other kinds of political systems. Second, in the modern international system, democracies are less likely to use lethal violence toward other democracies than toward autocratically governed states or than autocratically governed states are toward each other. Furthermore, there are no clearcut cases of sovereign stable democracies waging war with each other in the modern international system. Third, the relationship of relative peace among democracies is importantly a result of some features of democracy, rather than being caused exclusively by economic or geopolitical characteristics correlated with democracy. Exactly what those features are is a matter of theoretical debate, which we shall explore.

At the risk of boring the reader, further discussion requires some conceptual precision. Without it everyone can—and often does—endlessly debate counter-examples while by-passing the phenomenon itself. We need to define what we mean by democracy and war, so as to be able to say just how rare an occasion it is for two democracies to go to war with each other. When we do so it will be evident that those occasions virtually never arise. We then shall spend the rest of the book trying to understand the reasons for that rarity, and its implications for international politics in the post-cold war era.

Interstate war. War here means large-scale institutionally organized lethal violence, and to define "large-scale" we shall use the threshold commonly used in the social scientific literature on war: one thousand battle fatalities (Small and Singer 1982). The figure of one thousand deaths is arbitrary but reasonable. It is meant to eliminate from the category of wars those violent events that might plausibly be ascribed to:

1. "Accident" (e.g., planes that may have strayed across a national boundary by mistake, and been downed).
2. Deliberate actions by local commanders, but not properly authorized by central authorities, as in many border incidents.
3. Limited, local authorized military actions not necessarily intended to progress to large-scale violent conflict but undertaken more as bargaining moves in a crisis, such as military probes intended to demonstrate one's own commitment and to test the resolve of the adversary.
4. Deliberate military actions larger than mere probes, but not substantially resisted by a usually much weaker adversary. The Soviet invasion of Czechoslovakia in 1968, which was met with substantial nonviolent resistance but not force of arms and resulted in less than a score of immediate deaths, is such an example, and contrasts with the Soviet invasion of Hungary in 1956 which produced roughly seventeen thousand Hungarian and Soviet dead.

A threshold of one thousand battle deaths rather neatly cuts off the above kinds of events while leaving largely intact the category of most conflicts that intuitively satisfy the commonsense meaning of war. (Not, of course such rhetorical examples as the "war on poverty" or "war on drugs," or for that matter the boat seizures and very limited exchange of gunfire [no casualties or intent to inflict casualties (see Habeeb 1988, chap. 6)] between Britain and Iceland in the 1975 "Cod War" over fishing rights.) It is also convenient that the one thousand-battle-death threshold provides a neat empirical break, with few conflicts between nation states very near it on either side. The most questionable case is probably that between Britain and the Argentine military dictatorship in 1982, over the Falkland Islands/Islas Malvinas. The battle-death count is customarily given as about 950, or just below our numerical threshold. But not to count it would be splitting hairs. It was deliberate, authorized, and involved some fierce land, naval, and air engagements and two invasions (first by Argentina, and then when the British returned to expel the Argentine invaders). It should count as a war, without apology.

The U.K.-Argentine war was unusual in that it inflicted very few civilian casualties. Most wars are not so limited, with civilian deaths frequently far outnumbering those of combatants. Deaths from hunger and disease may also far outnumber battle-inflicted casualties, as surely happened in many nineteenth-century wars and may well have been the case with the Iraqis after Operation Desert Storm. But the number of such deaths may be difficult or impossible to estimate reliably and may be as much a consequence of inadequate medical and public-health capabilities as of military actions. Without minimizing the human consequences of such civilian deaths, it is simply less ambiguous to limit the definition to battle deaths. Similarly, the definition omits wounded and military personnel missing in action, figures commonly included in "casualty" totals but of lower reliability.

A related problem is that of deciding which political units are to be listed as fighting in a war. Sometimes in coalition warfare most or all of the deaths in a particular coalition will be borne by one or a few members with other members formally but not practically engaged in combat. For the latter, especially in circumstances where a nominal combatant suffers few or *no* identifiable deaths, it seems forced to include it among war participants. Small and Singer (1982, chap. 4) use a criterion requiring a state either to commit at least one thousand troops to battle, or to suffer at least one hundred battle fatalities, in order to count as a participant.

This definition also excludes, on theoretical grounds, covert actions in which one government secretly undertakes activities, including the use of lethal violence and the support of violent actors within the other government's territory, either to coerce or to overthrow that government. Such activities may not involve deaths on the scale of "wars," and when they do the foreign intervention is by its very covert nature hard to document (though one can often, if perhaps belatedly, discover the metaphoric "smoking gun"). But these activities, precisely because they are denied at the time by the government that undertakes them, imply very different political processes than does a war publicly and officially undertaken. Because they may be undertaken under circumstances when overt war is not acceptable they will, however, receive attention at a later point in the book.

For purposes of theoretical precision in argument yet another qualification is required, and that is a definition of "interstate" war. Here that term means war between sovereign "states" internationally recognized as such by other states, including by major powers whose recognition of a government typically confers de facto statehood. Some such definition focusing on organized independent states is common in the social science literature, and is important for the analysis of this book. It is meant to exclude those "colonial" wars fought for the acquisition of territory inhabited by "primitive" people without recognized states, as practiced by nineteenth-century imperialism, or for the twentieth-century liberation of those people. War it may certainly be, but interstate it is not unless or until both sides are generally recognized as having the attributes of statehood. Applying this definition may well display a Western cultural bias, but it is appropriate to the behavior of states which, in the period, also are defined as "democratic" by the admittedly Western standards spelled out below. Nonstate participants would not meet those standards.

Wars of liberation—with one or both parties not yet recognized as a state—are in this respect similar to those civil wars in which one or both parties to the conflict fights precisely so as to be free of sharing statehood with the other. Such wars are fought to escape from the coercive institutions of a common state, and to include them would confuse rather than clarify the generalization that democracies rarely go to war with each other. As will be clear in the next chapter, a crucial element in that generalization often depends upon the role of democratic institutions and practices in promoting peaceful conflict resolution within states. Intrastate conflicts that become so fierce that lethal violence is common often indicate that the institutions of the state have become the problem rather than the solution. For example, the United Kingdom and the Republic of Ireland have lived in peace with each other, as separate states, since 1922; the conflict in Northern Ireland arises precisely because many people there emphatically do not wish to be governed as part of the existing common political structure. Democracies are only slightly less likely than other kinds of states to experience civil war (Bremer 1992b).

Democracy. For modern states, democracy (or polyarchy, following Dahl 1971) is usually identified with a voting franchise for a substantial fraction of citizens, a government brought to power in contested elections, and an executive either popularly elected or responsible to an elected legislature, often also with requirements for civil liberties such as free speech.[4] Huntington (1991, 7, 9) uses very similar criteria of "a twentieth-century political system as democratic to the extent that its most powerful collective decision makers are selected through fair, honest, and periodic elections in which candidates freely compete for votes and in which virtually all the adult population is eligible to vote." In addition, he identifies a free election for transfer of power from a nondemocratic government as "the critical point in the process of democratization." Ray (1993) similarly requires that the possibility for the leaders of the government to be defeated in an election and replaced has been demonstrated by historical precedent.

A simple dichotomy between democracy and autocracy of course hides real shades of difference, and mixed systems that share features of both. Moreover, the precise application of these terms is to some degree culturally and temporally dependent. As we shall see, democracy did not mean quite the same to the ancient Greeks as it does to people of the late twentieth century. Even in the modern era the yardstick has been rubbery. Nineteenth century democracies often had property qualifications for the vote and typically excluded women, while the United States—democratic by virtually any standard of the day—disenfranchised blacks. Britain, with its royal prerogatives, rotten boroughs, and very restricted franchise before the Reform Act of 1832, hardly could be counted as a democracy. Even that reform brought voting rights to less than one-fifth of adult males, so one might reasonably withhold the "democracy" designation until after the Second Reform Act of 1867, or even until the secret ballot was introduced in 1872. By then, at the latest, Britain took its place with the relatively few other states commonly characterized as democratic in the parlance of the era. But if, before the late nineteenth century, we admit countries with as few as 10 per cent of all adults eligible to vote as democratic (a criterion used by Small and Singer 1976; Doyle 1983a uses a cutoff of 30 percent of all males), by the middle to late twentieth century nothing less than a substantially universal franchise will suffice.

The term "contested elections" admits similar ambiguities, but in practice it has come to require two or more legally recognized parties. States with significant prerogatives in military and foreign affairs for nonelected agents (e.g., monarchs) should be excluded as having nonresponsible executives, even in the nineteenth century.

By the middle to late twentieth century the matter of guaranteed and respected civil rights, including rights to political organization and political expression, also become a key element in any commonsense definition of democracy (Dahl 1989). The exercise of such civil rights tends to be highly correlated with the existence of democratic institutions as just elaborated, but not perfectly so. The institutions may be found without the regular widespread exercise of the rights; the opposite (civil liberties assured, but not democratic institutions) is rarer. For purposes of the discussion here we will nevertheless not use civil liberties per se as a defining quality, and we shall also ignore the matter of free-market economic liberties. While there is very likely a causal nexus between economic liberties and secure political freedom, the relationship is complex and, unlike some authors (Rummel 1983, Doyle 1983a) I will not build it into the definition.

In not including civil rights and economic liberty as defining qualities of democracy we are lowering the standards by which a country can be labeled a democracy. That is highly relevant to our next topic, an examination of conflicts alleged by some scholars to be wars between democracies. By lowering the standards we are making it more likely that some events will be labeled wars between democracies—events that I and many other writers contend are, at most, exceedingly rare.

Theoretical precision, however, requires one further qualification: some rather minimal stability or longevity. Huntington (1991, 11) emphasizes stability or institutionalization as "a central dimension in the analysis of any political system." To count a war as one waged by a democracy Doyle (1983a) requires that representative government be in existence for at least three years prior to the war. Perhaps that is a bit too long, yet some period must have elapsed during which democratic processes and institutions could become established, so that both the citizens of the "democratic" state and its adversary could regard it as one governed by democratic principles. Most of the doubtful cases arise within a single year of the establishment of democratic government.

By application of these criteria it is impossible to identify unambiguously *any* wars between democratic states in the period since 1815. A few close calls exist, in which some relaxation of the criteria could produce such a case. But to have no clearcut cases, out of approximately 71 interstate wars involving a total of nearly 270 participants, is impressive. Even these numbers are deceptively low as representing total possibilities. For example, as listed by Small and Singer (1982), 21 states count as participating on the Allied side in World War II, with 8 on the Axis side. Thus in that war alone there were 168 pairs of warring states. Allowing for other multilateral wars, approximately 500 pairs of states went to war against each other in the period. Of these, fewer than a handful can with any plausibility at all be considered candidates for exceptions to a generalization that democracies do not fight each other.

Some Alleged Wars between Democracies

To see what these criteria produce, consider the list in table 1.1 of wars that have sometimes been suggested as exceptions to the generalization that democracies do not go to war with each other.

Four should be dismissed because they fall outside the criteria established even for any kind of interstate war in the period. The first, the War of 1812, is easy to dismiss simply because it precedes the beginning date—1815—of the best-known compilation of all wars (Small and Singer 1982). That may seem like a cheap and arbitrary escape, but it is not. There simply were very few democracies in the international system before that date, and as we discussed with the British case above, though Britain had moved quite far from royal absolutism it just did not fit the criteria either of suffrage or of fully responsible executive.

The American Civil War and the Second Philippine War are also readily eliminated as plausible candidates by straightforward use of the defini-

TABLE 1.1
Some "Candidate" Wars between Democracies

War of 1812, U.S. and Great Britain
Roman Republic (Papal States) vs. France, 1849
American Civil War, 1861
Ecuador-Colombia, 1863
Franco-Prussian War, 1870
Boer War, 1899
Spanish-American War, 1898
Second Philippine War, 1899
World War I, Imperial Germany vs. western democracies 1914 / 17
World War II, Finland vs. western democracies 1941
Lebanon vs. Israel, 1948
Lebanon vs. Israel, 1967

tions. Whatever it may be called below the Mason-Dixon line, the Civil War is rightly named, in that the Confederacy never gained international recognition of its sovereignty; as a war for separation or to prevent separation it comes under our rubric of wars induced by the frictions of sharing common statehood. The Philippine War of 1899 was a colonial war, in which the United States was trying to solidify control of a former Spanish colony it had acquired. The Philippine resistance constituted an authentic war of resistance against colonialism, but not on the part of an elected democratic government. This is not in any way to denigrate the resistance, but merely to insist on a distinction that will be important throughout the book: especially by the standards of Western ethnocentric attitudes at the time, the Philippine resistance was not widely regarded as "democratic" in a way that would induce either normative or institutional constraints on the United States.

The Boer War, begun in 1899, also fails to fit the requirements for an interstate war. Small and Singer (1982) identify it as an extrasystemic war because the South African Republic—by far the larger of the two Boer combatants, the other being the Orange Free State—was not generally recognized as an independent state. Britain recognized only its internal sovereignty, retaining suzerainty and requiring it to submit all treaties to the British government for approval. This, too, is properly an unsuccessful war for independence. Moreover, the two Boer republics strained the definition of democracy, then as for almost a century subsequently. Not only was suffrage restricted to the white male minority (roughly 10 percent of the adult population) in the South African Republic, but the electorate was further reduced, perhaps by half, by a property qualification and long-term residence requirements (Lacour-Gayet 1978, 168, 170, 182, 194).[5]

Two other conflicts can be dismissed because they fall short of the casualty levels required for a "war." These are Finland's participation in World War II on the "wrong" side and Lebanon's involvement in the Six-Day War of 1967. Finland was actively at war only with the Soviet Union, in an attempt to wrest back the territory taken from it in the Winter War of 1939–40. Although it was nominally at war with the Western allies, there is no record of combat or casualties between Finland and democratic states that would even approach the rather low threshold specified above. In the Six-Day War of 1967 Lebanon (then still an at least marginally democratic state, as it was not when invaded by Israel in 1982) participated in "combat" only by sending a few aircraft into Israeli airspace; the planes were driven back with, apparently, no casualties at all.

In the remaining six cases one or both of the participants fails the test for democracy. Lebanon's participation in the 1948 war was well above the criterion used for a belligerent. Israel, however, had not previously been independent, and had not yet held a national election. While the authenticity of Israel's national leadership was hardly in question, Lebanon—itself not fully democratic—could not have been expected to accredit it as a democratic state.

The 1863 war between Ecuador and Colombia also fits the criteria for war, but neither regime meets any reasonable requirement for democratic stability. Both governments came to power through revolution. Colombia's president governed with a new federal constitution promulgated only in May 1863; Ecuador's Gabriel García Moreno became president two years earlier, but is described as heading an "autocratic regime" (Kohn 1986, 150) and governing "with absolute authority" (Langer 1972, 852). As for France against the Roman Republic, both parties were but ephemerally democratic. Following the revolution of early 1848, presidential elections took place under the new French constitution only in December of that year. The notion of a democratic Papal States sounds oxymoronic. The pope introduced a constitution with an elective council of deputies in 1848, but reserved veto power to himself and the College of Cardinals. After an insurrection in November, he fled and the Roman Republic was proclaimed in February 1849. Within two months the republic was at war with France.

The Franco-Prussian War can be eliminated simply by looking at France. Reforms ratified in the plebiscite of May 1870 could be interpreted as making the empire into a constitutional monarchy, but war began a mere two months later. In Prussia/Germany the emperor appointed and could dismiss the chancellor; a defeat in the Reichstag did not remove the chancellor from office. The emperor's direct authority over the army and foreign policy deprives the state of the democratic criterion of "responsible executive" on war and peace matters; Berghahn (1973, 9) calls the constitutional position of the monarchy "almost absolutist." Doyle (1983a) rightly excludes Imperial Germany from his list of liberal states. Such a decision removes World War I from the candidate list.

The most difficult case is the Spanish-American War of 1898. Spain after 1890 had universal male suffrage, and a bicameral legislature with an executive nominally responsible to it. But the reality was more complex. The ministry was selected by the king, who thus remained the effective ruler of the state. Nominally competitive elections were really manipulated by a process known as *caciquismo*. By mutual agreement, the Liberal and Conservative parties rotated in office; governmental changes preceded rather than followed elections. Through extensive corruption and administrative procedures the king and politicians in Madrid controlled the selection of parliamentary candidates and their election. Election results were often published in the press before polling day. The meaningless elections were thus manipulated by the king and his close advisers; the system lacked the democratic quality of a responsible executive (Carr 1980, 10–15). May (1961, 97) describes the system as "preserving the appearance of a parliamentary democracy with none of its suspected dangers." None of the published large-scale analyses of the question of democracies fighting each other puts Spain among the democratic countries (Small and Singer 1976, Doyle 1983a, b; Chan 1984; Maoz and Abdolali 1989; Bremer 1992a), nor do most major long-term political surveys. (Vanhanen 1984; Banks 1971; Gurr et al. 1989 code it as sharing democratic and autocratic characteristics.)

It seems, therefore, best to treat it as a close call but probably not a refutation even of the strong statement that democracies *never* make war on each other. Equally important, as we shall see later in the book, is the matter of perceptions. The Spanish political situation was at best marginal enough that key United States decisionmakers could readily persuade themselves and their audiences that it was not democratic. Consider, for example, the remarks of the two Republican senators from Massachusetts. Senator Henry Cabot Lodge: "We are there because we represent the spirit of liberty and the spirit of the new time, and Spain is over against us because she is mediaeval, cruel, dying." Senator George Hoar: "The results of a great war [on which the U.S. was embarking] are due to the policy of the king and the noble and the tyrant, not the policy of the people" (*Congressional Record*, April 13, 1898, p. 3783 and April 14, 1898, p. 3831).

Subsequent to my writing the above, Ray (1993) has presented a thorough review of these and other alleged cases of wars between democracies, and concludes that the generalization of no wars between democracies remains true. Whether or not one holds to the lawlike "never" statement may not really be very important. Almost all of the few near misses are in the nineteenth century. Since that was an era of generally very imperfect democracy by modern criteria, it is no surprise to find most of the near misses then.

Depending on the precise criteria, only twelve to fifteen states qualified as democracies at the end of the nineteenth century. The empirical significance of the rarity of war between democracies emerges only in the first half of the twentieth century, with at least twice the number of democracies as earlier, and especially with the existence of perhaps sixty democracies by the mid-1980s. Since the statistical likelihood of war between democracies is related to the number of pairs of democracies, the contrast between the two centuries is striking: by a very loose definition, possibly three or four wars out of roughly sixty pairs before 1900, and at most one or two out of about eighteen hundred pairs thereafter.[6] As twentieth-century politics unfold, the phenomenon of war between democracies becomes impossible or almost impossible to find.

Even with the differing definitions of democracy and of war, this generalization is exceedingly robust. Long-term rival states, with many conflicts of interest between them, have gone to war or had substantial fatal clashes only when one or both of them was not governed democratically. For example, in the case of the Greek-Turkish dispute over Cyprus, by far the worst violence erupted in 1974 under the most dictatorial government either country experienced since 1945, when the Greek colonels overthrew the elected Cypriot government of Archbishop Makarios. Faced with the prospect of forcible *enosis* between Greece and Cyprus, Turkey replied by invading the island and occupying nearly a third of its territory. By contrast, the 1963–64 clashes—when democratic Greek and Turkish governments supported their protégés during outbreaks on the islands— were much more easily contained, largely by an American warning and UN peacekeeping action. And confrontations later in the 1970s, between democratic governments, were restrained short of any fatalities (Markides 1977; Rustow 1987; Stearns, ed., 1992). India and Pakistan have of course fought repeatedly and sometimes bloodily during their history as independent states. Yet no fatalities are recorded in disputes between them during Pakistan's most democratic periods of 1962–64 and 1988– 92 (Burke 1973; Thomas 1986; Tillema 1991).

Even the kind of crisis bargaining that uses military force in a threatening manner becomes, in the twentieth century, rare between democracies, even if not quite absent. And if there is crisis bargaining, it does not escalate to the point of war.

Table 1.2 illustrates these facts in data on all militarized diplomatic disputes over the period from 1946 to 1986. "Dyad" means a pair of states; for the table we count each year of existence separately, thus Brit-

TABLE 1.2
Dispute Behavior of Politically Relevant Interstate Dyads, 1946–1986

Highest Level of Dispute	Both States Democratic	One or Both Nondemocratic	Total Dyads
No dispute	3,864	24,503	28,367
Threat of force	2	39	41
Display of force	4	116	120
Use of force	8	513	521
War	0	32	32
TOTALS	3,878	25,203	29,081
Escalation Probabilities			
To threat of force	0.05%	0.16%	
To display of force	85.7%	94.4%	
To use of force	57.1%	77.9%	
To war	0.0%	4.6%	

Sources: See chapter 4 for sources and definitions.

ain and France in 1946 constitute one observation, and another in 1947. The highest level of conflict reached in the dispute between that pair of states is identified. (Disputes that spill over into two or more years are counted only in the year they began or were escalated to a higher level.) The phrase "politically relevant dyads" refers to all pairs of states that are contiguous or at least fairly close to each other, or where one of the states in the pair is a major power and hence has military "global reach." This recognizes, as noted above, that the majority of states in the international system lack the means or the interest to engage in militarized disputes with each other, and hence are irrelevant to a serious analysis. Further information on definitions and sources can be postponed for much more detailed analysis in chapter 4.

The information in this simple table has several rich theoretical implications, and we shall return to it in subsequent chapters. There were no wars between democracies, and even though the number of democratic dyads is relatively small, if they had fought wars as frequently with each other as one finds in the second column, there would have been five wars between democracies. Note also that in this period there were only fourteen instances of disputing pairs involving the threat, display, or use of military force by one democracy against another. The odds that any pair of politically relevant democratic states would have a militarized dispute, at any level, in a year during this period were only 1 in 276. By contrast, if one or both states in the pair was not a democracy, the odds were as short as 1 in 36—eight times greater. Surely this is a very dramatic difference in behavior. The actual use of military force involved trivial occasions like the "Cod War"; very minor fire by Israel against Britain during the 1956 Suez intervention, in which the British and Israelis were in fact accomplices; brief conflict between British and Turkish forces during a 1963 peacekeeping operation on Cyprus; and Turkish sinking of a Greek boat in 1978.

One can also use the tabular information to calculate "escalation probabilities" for militarized disputes that do occur. For democracies, the chances that any militarized dispute would progress up the scale of force were consistently lower, at every level, than for pairs in which one or both states were not democracies. For example, only a little more than half of the few disputes between democracies resulted in the actual use of force, whereas nearly 80 percent of all disputes by other kinds of pairs of states escalated at least to the use of force. For earlier periods (the nineteenth century, and 1900–1945) the relationships for conflict-proneness and escalation appear to be in the same direction—democratic pairs of states dispute less—but much weaker than in the post-1945 era (Maoz and Abdolali 1989; Bremer 1992a).

It is tempting to believe that a norm against the use of force between democracies, and even the threat of use of force, has emerged and strengthened over time. To pursue the matter of norms, however, becomes a subject for much further analysis. The emergence of norms against democracies fighting each other is traceable, and by many theories it did indeed become a powerful restraint. Other theories, however, attribute the relative absence of lethal violence between democracies to many other influences. The next chapter lays out these partly competing, partly complementary theories in detail.

Consideration of the evidence then begins—in a historically problematic context, the world of ancient Greek city-states—with a detailed analysis of who fought whom during the Peloponnesian War. Whereas a number of examples of warring democratic pairs of states emerge during that era, there are hints in the historical record of restraints as well as of the instances when the restraints failed.

We then examine the explanatory power of the competing theories during the post–World War II era—the time when by far the largest number of democracies and hence of possible warring democratic pairs existed. We will grasp the meaning of the democratic peace by establishing that the rarity of lethal violence between democracies is not due to any apparent confounding influence, but to something in the nature of the democratic-to-democratic state relationship itself, and then begin to identify what that is.

In an effort to widen the empirical net further beyond the modern Western experience, we then look at the experience of preindustrial ethnographic units—societies as studied by anthropologists. This will provide still further evidence that such polities, when governed according to democratic "participatory" principles, do not often fight similarly governed polities.

Finally, the concluding chapter considers all this evidence, and the discourse of late twentieth-century international relations, in search of glimpses into the future. It addresses the emerging policy debate about whether further democratization, in addition to being a "good thing" for people in their relations within democratically governed countries, may be a major force to promote peace between countries. If so, by what principles can democracy best be advanced in a world of nationalism and ethnic hatred? What are the prudent possibilities for intervention— whether by economic means or by military force—to promote democracy? Can we grasp the possibility of a wider democratic peace? What are the prospects for building a world predominantly of democratic states that are able to live together—not without conflicts of interest, but without the large-scale lethal violence called war which has so blighted the human experience to date?

CHAPTER 2

Why Democratic Peace?

WHEN DEMOCRATIC states were rare, the Kantian perspective had little practical import, and power politics reigned. But if the Kantian perspective is correct, recent events replacing authoritarian regimes with democratic values and institutions in much of Asia, Eastern Europe, and Latin America[1] may have profound implications not just for governmental practices within states, but for worldwide peace among states. It may be possible in part to supersede the "realist" principles (anarchy, the security dilemma of states) that have dominated practice to the exclusion of "liberal" or "idealist" ones since at least the seventeenth century.

Politics within a democracy is seen as largely a nonzero-sum enterprise; by cooperating, all can gain something even if all do not gain equally, and the winners are restrained from crushing the losers. Indeed, today's winners may, as coalitions shift, wish tomorrow to ally with today's losers. If the conflicts degenerate to physical violence, either by those in control of the state or by insurgents, all can lose. In most international politics—the anarchy of a self-help system with no overall governing authority—these norms and practices are not the same. "Realists" remind us of the powerful norms of legitimate self-defense and the acceptability of military deterrence, norms much more extensive internationally than within democratic states. Politics among nations takes on a more zero-sum hue, with the state's sovereign existence at risk.

The principles of anarchy and self-help in a zero-sum world are most acute in "structural realist" theories of international relations. The nature of states' internal systems of government is seen as nearly irrelevant; their overall behavior is basically determined by the structure of the international system and their position in that structure. "Peace" is a fleeting condition, dependent upon deterrence and eternal vigilance. By this structural realist understanding the kind of stable peace that exists among democracies cannot last, because eventually democracies would be compelled, by the structure of the international system and their eternal security dilemma, to enter a state of war or at best of military deterrence (Waltz 1979, Mearsheimer 1990). Realism has no place for an expectation that democracies will not fight each other. To the degree we establish that peace between democracies is a fact, and are able to explain it theoretically, we build an alternative view of the world with great import for expectations and for policy. We begin with the theories.

If scholars are near consensus that democratically governed states rarely go to war with each other or even fight each other at low levels of lethal violence, this does not mean there is anything like consensus on why the phenomenon occurs. Nor can the same generalization be supported for relations among other kinds of political systems (for example, military or other dictatorships). Sharing common forms of political structure and political culture in general does not prevent war between independent states.[2] If similarity of form of government in general were enough, then we would have seen peace between the Soviet Union and China, between the Soviet Union and its formerly communist East European neighbors, and between China and Vietnam. Despite important differences in political values and organization among the communist countries, they were much more like one another in values and ideology than like the democracies or even like right-wing dictatorships. Yet war between these countries, and disputes that threatened to erupt in war, were commonplace.

Certainly some kinds of differences, if politically salient, can cause conflict. But that becomes virtually tautological unless one can specify what differences will be salient. For sixteenth-century Europe religious differences between Catholics and Protestants provided politically salient ideological reasons for killing each other; by the twentieth century those differences were irrelevant to violent conflict save in isolated pockets like Northern Ireland. Thus it seems likely that the reasons for "democratic peace" are either rooted somehow in the nature of democracy itself, or are correlated in the modern world with the phenomenon of democracy.

Some scholars vigorously question the causal inference that democracies are at peace with each other simply because they are democratic. They point instead to other influences that are correlated with democracy and hence create a spurious relation between democracy itself and general peace between democratic states. Without going into the vast range of hypotheses about the causes of war and peace, we need to consider some of the most important ones that might specifically account for the relationship between democratic states.

ALTERNATIVE EXPLANATIONS

Alternative hypotheses to explain the phenomenon include the following.

Transnational and international institutions make peace. The states in question are peaceful toward each other because they are bound by common ties in a network of institutions crossing national boundaries. Democracies often do share many common institutions. Analysts may emphasize the role of the European Community (EC), for example, and certainly one of the major motivations of the founders of the institutions that evolved into the EC was to bind together previously hostile states so that they would be unable to make war on each other. Some international organizations clearly have this intention. Others, not primarily addressed to war prevention, help to resolve many troublesome conflicts of interest that might feed suspicion and hostility. But states and ethnic groups typically share common institutions just because they have major interests in conflict as well as in common; institutions are supposed to provide a means to resolve those conflicts peacefully. If the common institutions cannot do so, or if one party is coerced into unwillingly sharing common institutions with another, the institutions exacerbate conflict and may become the occasion for civil war.[3] Hence the existence of common intergovernmental or supranational institutions cannot so plausibly be invoked as a prior reason for the absence of war. Peaceful relations must in some degree precede the institutions.

An influential variant of the institutional approach focuses on transnationalism: individual autonomy and pluralism within democratic states foster the emergence of transnational linkages and institutions—among individuals, private groups, and governmental agencies. Those linkages can serve to resolve transnational conflicts peaceably and, by forming transnational alliances into other states, inhibit their national governments from acting violently toward each other. This perspective derives from classics both of international integration theory and of bureaucratic politics and foreign policy.[4] It is not, however, completely separable from the matter of democracy. Democracies foster, and are fostered by, the pluralism arising from many independent centers of power and influence; autocracies do not. Democracies are open to many private and governmental transnational linkages; autocracies rarely are. (Recall the late and unlamented Iron Curtain.) Thus transnationalism cannot easily be considered separately from the distinction between democracies and other kinds of states. Since it is substantially correlated with the "open" institutions of democratic politics, it cannot be treated analytically or empirically as an independent cause.

Distance prevents war. Most wars are fought between physically adjacent states, thanks to their combination of capability and willingness (reasons) to fight neighbors.[5] Likewise, individuals are most likely to be murdered by friends and close relatives with whom they are are in constant contact. But until after World War II democracies tended to be relatively few and far between. Hence the absence of murderous quarrels between democracies was not too surprising, and may need—at least for the pre-1945 era—little further explanation. Even for much of the post-

1945 period, the rarity of contiguous democratic states outside of Western Europe might explain much of the absence of violent conflict between democracies.[6] Yet the more recent one's snapshot of the international system, with many contiguous democracies in Europe and the Western Hemisphere, the less conclusive the distance argument seems.

Alliances make peace. Allies may be presumed to choose each other because of their common interests, and hence to be already peacefully inclined toward each other. Moreover, their common interests are likely to concern security against a common enemy. If so, they are not likely to fight each other. Many democracies have shared common interests in presenting a unified alliance front. NATO and the Western alliance system provide the most recent example, but in both world wars the democracies found themselves ranged together (with some nondemocracies alongside, to be sure) against the nondemocratic Central/Axis powers.[7] So of course democracies won't fight each other.

One trouble with this hypothesis is that it begs the question. Did they not fight each other because they were allied, or did they ally because they feared a common foe (and hence did not fight each other)? And if the latter, did they fear a common foe because they were united in a desire to preserve their common democratic institutions? If the latter, then democracy, not alliance, accounts for the peace among them.

A related hypothesis accounts for peace among members of multilateral alliances not by the alliance per se, but by the active policy of a dominant major power to keep peace within the alliance. Such a hegemonic power may make it very clear to the small powers that in the interest of common security against a major power rival it simply will not tolerate violence among them. Surely in the Western Hemisphere (Rio Pact) and in NATO the United States played such a role, with threats to withhold economic and military assistance to the culprits.[8]

The trouble with this variant of the hypothesis, however, is that as a generalization it is empirically backward. Repeated systematic analyses, beginning with Bueno de Mesquita's (1981), affirm that allies are in general more likely to fight each other, even while still formally allied, than are nonallies. Again, the reasons are not so mysterious: the apparently "common" interests may be enforced by a big power with the capability and will to keep straying allies in the fold. Military action by the Soviet Union against Hungary in 1956 provides an example. Consistent with this interpretation, Bremer (1992a) finds allied states likely to fight each other when both states are militarized. But democratic allied states are different; they are not likely to have violent conflicts with each other (Siverson and Emmons 1991; Bueno de Mesquita and Lalman 1992, 166–67).

Wealth makes peace.   Since democracies are often wealthy, it can be hard to separate their effects. Several variants of this argument persist. One is that for politically stable, economically advanced, and rapidly growing countries the cost/benefit ratio of any war fought on or near their home territories with another advanced state looks extraordinarily unpromising. Historically many wars have been fought to acquire territory; the value of acquiring as war booty the territory of an advanced industrial country would rarely compensate for the costs of wartime destruction and the problems of pacifying newly incorporated peoples (Mueller 1989; Shepherd 1986). The disincentives would be magnified for highly interdependent economies, which suffer even from damage inflicted on each other's territory that destroys investments, markets, or sources of imports. Interdependence also creates groups with vested interests in continuing economic exchange (Rosecrance 1986; Milner 1988).

The wealth-makes-peace argument is thus closely related to the one that transnational interests of trade and investment make peace. Writers as various as the nineteenth-century liberal Richard Cobden, the Marxist Karl Kautsky, and Joseph Schumpeter argued that the web of economic interdependence would promote international peace. Yet Lenin and other theorists of imperialism opined otherwise. Economic interdependence, for example between the United States and Japan, provides both glue and friction. Even where a relationship between trade and peace can be demonstrated, there may be a chicken-and-egg problem. Weak economic ties within the industrialized world during the Depression help explain the political tensions that produced World War II, but after that war peaceful relations were largely established before high levels of economic interdependence were reached in the 1970s (Russett and Starr 1992, 385–92). Some systematic evidence indicates that trade diminishes political conflict, with the party receiving greater benefits from trade acting on greater incentives (Gasiorowski and Polacheck 1982; Polachek 1980). But if one party perceives the benefits as markedly asymmetrical against it, the effects are not pacific. Trade between rich and poor states may concentrate on raw materials, with the threat of military action by the rich state in the background or forefront. Other research (Pollins 1989a, b) points the primary causal arrow from political relations to economic ones ("trade follows the flag") rather than the other way. As with other generalizations, the conclusions are often context-dependent or indeterminate (Russett 1967; Bueno de Mesquita and Lalman 1992, 289).

Yet another variant of the wealth-makes-peace view emphasizes growth. Many democracies have experienced fairly consistent rapid economic growth during the past half-century. Rapidly growing states may generally be less inclined to initiate conflict. The reasons are similar to those regarding the connection between wealth and lack of conflict. A special case, however, may be made regarding growth in democracies. States often engage in international conflict to divert attention and anger from domestic problems (Levy 1989). Democratic governments are not immune to such temptations. They often initiate international disputes during economic slowdowns or recessions, or if in economic difficulty respond more aggressively when others initiate disputes (Ostrom and Job 1986; Russett 1990, chap. 2; Russett and Barzilai 1991; Mintz and Russett 1992). But rapidly growing democracies would not have such an incentive for conflict between them.

Political stability makes peace. The diversionary effects of economic instability are related to those of political instability. States with stable and durable political systems will lack incentives to externalize domestic discontent into conflict with foreign countries. They will be even more reluctant to engage in conflict against other states that are politically stable. If they see the government of the would-be opponent as possessing substantial legitimacy, they will expect the population at large, and those sectors of society that have ensured domestic stability, to back it in international conflict (Huth and Russett 1993, Maoz 1989). Unstable governments have more to gain from scapegoating and diversion, and are more likely to do so when they confront an adversary that faces substantial domestic political problems.

If stable governments are less likely to initiate international disputes, especially against other stable governments, it is important to note that twentieth-century European and Anglo-American democracies were generally more stable—more durable and adaptable—than were nondemocracies (Gurr 1974). The more years a given type of political system lasts, the better its odds of surviving another year. Perhaps the inherent stability that characterizes many democratic political systems accounts for their low rate of conflict with other democracies. In fact, the combination of variables denoted as stable democracy becomes a component of the theory to be developed and tested in this book.

Conceptually and empirically the competing explanations overlap somewhat and reinforce each other. Some of them are quite plausible. The network of international institutions has been strongest in the past half-century among the democratic, allied, prosperous, and politically stable states of Western Europe. Yet counterexamples can be cited for each proffered explanation. There have not been wars even between poor but democratic states, yet World War II is an obvious example of a war pitting advanced capitalist states against each other. Argentina and Britain fought in 1982 despite their common alliance with the United States. The Soviet Union, after achieving apparent stability by the early 1920s, nevertheless fought four wars. Later we will analyze the incidence of wars and less violent conflicts between states in the post-1945 era, with proper statistical controls to test many of the above alternative hypotheses. Even when controls for physical distance, alliance, wealth, economic growth, and political stability are incorporated into the analysis, an independent explanatory role for democracy remains.[9] Nevertheless, no merely empirical relationship can be compelling without a powerful theoretical explanation. Nor can it be clear how widely, in different historical and cultural contexts, the relationship may apply. Two kinds of theories, one stressing norms and the other stressing political structures, offer explanations to which we now turn.

DEMOCRATIC NORMS AND CULTURE?

We should begin with the common assertion that democracies are *inherently* more peaceful or "dovish" internationally because of the political culture favoring the peaceful resolution of disputes, or because democratic processes produce restraint by the general populace which will have to pay the price of war in blood and money (Schumpeter 1955; Snyder 1991). Individual examples of the operation of these factors can easily be found. Over the course of a long war democratic governments may experience seriously eroding domestic support for the war effort, and may feel constrained, if they do go to war, to pursue strategies designed to minimize their own costs, especially in casualties. (U.S. strategy against Iraq in 1991 immediately comes to mind.)

This is a strong assertion, however, and, overall, the evidence for it as a generalization is not very compelling.[10] It ignores the evidence for the familiar "rally 'round the flag effect" typically induced by the threat or use of force by democracies against other countries. Hostility especially to certain kinds of foreigners—those seen as governed autocratically—can often be mobilized to support military actions by democracies (Geva, DeRouen, and Mintz 1993; Mintz and Geva 1993). Elites can even feel impelled by popular pressures to act militarily (Russett 1990, chap. 2). Also, so long as this explanation focuses on the characteristics of single states, it cannot explain the consistent evidence that democracies are about as war-prone and disputatious in general (not toward other democracies) as are other kinds of states (recently, Maoz and Abdollali 1989; Bremer 1992a; chapter 4 of this volume). Nor can it explain the pattern of nineteenth- and twentieth-century imperialism by democracies. (On Snyder's 1991 effort see Zakaria 1992.) And it would have us believe that the United States was regularly on the defensive, rarely on the offensive, during the Cold War. Though there are elements of plausibility in the argument that democracies are inherently peaceful, it contains too many holes, and is accompanied by too many exceptions, to be usable as a major theoretical building block.

A more plausible theoretical strain, however, yields a more limited assumption. It focuses on powerful norms within democratic states against the use of lethal force under certain conditions—namely, "dovishness" in relations between democracies, though not necessarily in their relations with other kinds of states. Several authors offer a perspective emphasizing social diversity, perceptions of individual rights, overlapping group memberships, cross-pressures, shifting coalitions, expectations of limited government, and toleration of dissent by a presumably loyal opposition. The basic norm of democratic theory is that disputes can be resolved without force through democratic political processes that in some balance ensure both majority rule and minority rights. A norm of equality operates both as voting equality and certain egalitarian rights to human dignity. Democratic government rests on the consent of the governed, but justice demands that consent not be abused. Resort to organized lethal violence, or the threat of it, is considered illegitimate, and unnecessary to secure one's "legitimate" rights. Dissent within broad limits by a loyal opposition is expected and even needed for enlightened policy-making, and the opposition's basic loyalty to the system is to be assumed in the absence of evidence to the contrary.[11]

All participants in the political process are expected to share these norms. Even though all these images may be founded to a large extent on myth as well as on reality, they may operate as powerful restraints on violence between such systems. In practice the norms do sometimes break down, but the normative restraints on violent behavior—by state and citizens—are fully as important as the state's monopoly on the legitimate use of force in keeping incidents of the organized use of force rare. The norms themselves may be more important than any particular institutional structure (two-party/multiparty, republican/parliamentary) or formal constitutional provision. If institutions precede the development of norms in the polity, the basis for restraint is likely to be less secure.

By this hypothesis, the *culture, perceptions, and practices* that permit compromise and the peaceful resolution of conflicts without the threat of violence within countries come to apply across national boundaries toward other democratic countries. In short, if people in a democracy perceive themselves as autonomous, self-governing people who share norms of live-and-let-live, they will respect the rights of others to self-determination if those others are also perceived as self-governing and hence not easily led into aggressive foreign policies by a self-serving elite. The same structures and behaviors that "we" assume will limit our aggression, both internally and externally, may be expected similarly to limit similarly governed people in other polities. Those who claim the principle of self-determination for themselves are expected to extend it to others. Within a transnational democratic culture, as within a democratic nation, others are seen as possessing rights and exercising those rights in a spirit of enlightened self-interest. Acknowledgment of those rights allows us to mitigate our fears that they will try to dominate us. That acknowledgement also prevents us from wishing to dominate them; a norm that it would be wrong to do so in effect raises the "costs" to us of doing so.

By contrast, these restraints do not apply toward a country governed by very different and nondemocratic principles. According to democratic norms, authoritarian states do not rest on the proper consent of the governed, and thus they cannot properly represent the will of their peoples— if they did, they would not need to rule through undemocratic, authoritarian institutions. Rulers who control their own people by such means, who do not behave in a just way that respects their own people's rights to self-determination, cannot be expected to behave better toward peoples outside their states. "Because non-liberal governments are in a state of aggression with their own people, their foreign relations become for liberal governments deeply suspect. In short, fellow liberals benefit from a presumption of amity; nonliberals suffer from a presumption of enmity" (Doyle 1986, 1161). The essence of America's Cold War ideology was that it had no quarrel with the Russian people, but only with the atheistic communist elites who repressed them. A vision of the other people as not in self-governing control of their own destiny justified a hostile policy. Authoritarian states are expected to aggress against others if given the power and the opportunity. By this reasoning, democracies must be eternally vigilant and may even need to engage in defensively motivated war or preemptive action anticipating an immediate attack.

Whereas wars against other democratic states are neither expected nor considered legitimate, wars against authoritarian states may often be both. Thus an international system composed of both democratic and authoritarian states will include both zones of peace (actual and expected, among the democracies) and zones of war or at best deterrence betwen democratic and authoritarian states. And by this reasoning democracies may fight wars and other lethal conflicts as often as authoritarian states do—which is what most of the systematic empirical evidence indicates. They just will not fight each other.

The presumption of enmity from and toward nondemocracies was exemplified by American determination to root out aggressive fascism and Nazism in Japan and Germany after World War II, and to establish the basis for democratic government there. It took more dubious forms in many Cold War interventions (including covert operations, which we shall consider later) and in the 1989 invasion of Panama. Elihu Root's

(1917) wartime rhetoric, in his presidential address to the American Society of International Law, expressed the tradition vividly:

> So long as military autocracy continues, democracy is not safe from attacks, which are certain to come, and certain to find it unprepared. The conflict is inevitable and universal; and it is *à l'outrance*. To be safe democracy must kill its enemy when it can and where it can. The world can not be half democratic and half autocratic. It must be all democratic or all Prussian. There can be no compromise. If it is all Prussian, there can be no real international law. If it is all democratic, international law honored and observed may well be expected as a natural development of the principles which make democratic self-government possible.

These assumptions lead to the following propositions about democracies' external relations. The norms of regulated political competition, compromise solutions to political conflicts, and peaceful transfer of power are externalized by democracies in their dealing with other national actors in world politics. On the other hand, nondemocracies may not externalize these norms. Hence, when two democracies come into a conflict of interest, they are able to apply democratic norms in their interaction, and these norms prevent most conflicts from mounting to the threat or use of military force. If they do go that far, at least they will not go to all-out war. By contrast, when a democracy comes into conflict with a nondemocracy, it will not expect the nondemocratic state to be restrained by those norms. It may feel obliged to adapt to the harsher norms of international conduct of the latter, lest it be exploited or eliminated by the nondemocratic state that takes advantage of the inherent moderation of democracies. Similarly, conflict between nondemocracies may be dominated by the norm of forceful conduct and search for decisive (noncompromise) outcome or elimination of the adversary.

Axelrod's (1984, 1986; also Behr 1980; Dacey and Pendegraft 1988) work on the evolution of cooperation and norms shows how norms of behavior depend heavily on the environment in which they are applied. When a player employing a conditionally cooperative strategy like tit-for-tat is confronted by someone playing a consistently noncooperative strategy, noncooperation dominates. Short of teaching cooperation to "meanies"—which takes a long time—noncooperative strategies typically force cooperative strategies to become noncooperative.[12]

Legal systems in democratic states seem to make distinctions between democratic and authoritarian states when deciding whether to enforce in their own courts the laws of other nations. Other democratic states are recognized as within a "zone of law," a legal community defined by various institutional and ideological similarities. Courts in democracies share enough common values to recognize and enforce each other's law in accord with pluralist principles of tolerance and reciprocity. They do not, however, recognize the legal systems of nondemocratic states as equal partners; they are seen as lacking the political autonomy of democratic legal systems, and hence not appropriate as providing norms for conflict resolution (Burley 1992).

Governments and political institutions can change rapidly after a revolution, but norms take time to develop. Laws can change faster than the practices in which norms are embedded. Formal norms such as one of nonrecourse to war can be written into a constitution, but become effective only with the repeated practice of bargaining and conciliation (Kratochwil 1991). Thus if violent conflicts between democracies do occur, we would expect them to take place between democratic states that are relatively young in terms of the tenure of the democratic regime. That is, they would occur between states in at least one of which democratic norms have not matured to a degree that is expressed in moderate and dependable strategies of peaceful conflict management. Democratic governments in which democratic norms are not yet fully developed are likely to be unstable, or to be perceived by other states as unstable, so they may be unable to practice norms of democratic conflict resolution internationally. Equally important, the democratic states with whom they develop conflicts of interest may not perceive them as dependable in their practices. Newness and instability cloud others' perceptions.

Of course, democracies have not fought wars only out of motivations of self-defense, however broadly one may define self-defense to include anticipation of others' aggression or to include "extended deterrence" for the defense of allies and other interests. Many of them have also fought imperialist wars to acquire or hold colonies, or to retain control of states formally independent but within their spheres of influence. Here is another aspect of perception and misperception, of cases where democracies have fought against people who on one ground or another could be characterized as not self-governing.

The nineteenth-century objects of colonial expansion were peoples who in most instances were outside the European state system. They were in most instances not people with white skins, and whose institutions of government did not conform to the Western democratic institutional forms of their colonizers. Europeans' ethnocentric views of those peoples carried the *assumption* that they did not have institutions of self-government. Not only were they available for imperial aggrandizement, they could be considered candidates for betterment and even "liberation"— the white man's burden, or *mission civilatrice*. They could be brought the benefits not only of modern material civilization, but of Western principles of self-government. If they did not have such institutions already, then by definition they were already being exploited and repressed. Their governments or tribal leaders could not, in this ethnocentric view, be just or consensual, and thus one need have few compunctions about conquering these legitimate candidates for "liberal" imperialism.[13] Later, when Western forms of self-government did begin to take root on a local basis in many of the colonies, the extremes of pseudo-Darwinian racism lost their legitimacy. Decolonization came not only because the colonial governments lost the power to retain their colonies, but because in many cases they lost confidence in their normative right to rule.

We can now summarize all this discussion about restraints on violent conflict among democracies in a set of propositions as follows.

THE CULTURAL/NORMATIVE MODEL

1. In relations with other states, decisionmakers (whether they be few or many) will try to follow the same norms of conflict resolution as have been developed within and characterize their domestic political processes.
2. They will expect decisionmakers in other states likewise to follow the same norms of confict resolution as have been developed within and characterize those other states' domestic political processes.

A. Violent conflicts between democracies will be rare because:

3. In democracies, the relevant decisionmakers expect to be able to resolve conflicts by compromise and nonviolence, respecting the rights and continued existence of opponents.
4. Therefore democracies will follow norms of peaceful conflict resolution with other democracies, and will expect other democracies to do so with them.
5. The more stable the democracy, the more will democratic norms govern its behavior with other democracies, and the more will other democracies expect democratic norms to govern its international behavior.
6. If violent conflicts between democracies do occur, at least one of the democracies is likely to be politically unstable.

B. Violent conflicts between nondemocracies, and between democracies and nondemocracies, will be more frequent because:

7. In nondemocracies, decisionmakers use, and may expect their opponents to use, violence and the threat of violence to resolve conflict as part of their domestic political processes.
8. Therefore nondemocracies may use violence and the threat of violence in conflicts with other states, and other states may expect them to use violence and the threat of violence in such conflicts.
9. Democratic norms can be more easily exploited to force concessions than can nondemocratic ones; to avoid exploitation democracies may adopt nondemocratic norms in dealing with nondemocracies.

The numbered propositions are part of the deductive structure, and whereas it will be useful further to illustrate their application and plausibility, we will not subject most of them to rigorous empirical testing. The basic empirical statements A and B, however, will be so tested, in the form that *violent conflicts between democracies should be observed much less frequently than between democracies and nondemocracies.* Indeed, because of the susceptibility of democratic norms to exploitation, we may well find *violent conflicts between democracies and at least some kinds of nondemocracies to be more frequent than would be expected* if conflicts were distributed around the international system totally by chance. Proposition 6, that *if violent conflicts do arise between democracies at least one of the democracies is likely to be politically unstable,* also is empirically testable. As such, it can provide some extra empirical content to the basic hypothesis about the relative frequency of violent conflict of democracies with other democracies and with nondemocracies.

Propositions 5 and 6 therefore incorporate into the cultural/normative theoretical structure the point about political stability that was initially treated as one of several alternative perspectives on the phenomenon of peace between democracies. They do not yet, however, indicate just why force might be used when one democracy in a pair is politically unstable.

As noted in the discussion about the possible role of economic growth or its absence, increasing evidence is accumulating that democracies are more likely to use or threaten to use military force, in general, when the economy has been doing badly. Most of the studies cited there also indicate that democracies are more likely to use or threaten to use military force in the year or months immediately preceding an election.[14] The motivation, of diverting hostility toward foreigners and of producing a "rally 'round the flag" effect for the party in power, is similar. If we expand the notion of political instability to include domestic political threats to the government because of its economic policy shortcomings, or competition in a close election, this gives us a temporal context for the possible use of military force by democracies. It suggests that the "unstable" state will initiate, or escalate, the use of force in a diplomatic dispute. But it does not tell us against whom it may direct that force.

To do that, we can elaborate the hypothesis as suggesting that the threat or use of *force will be directed against states that a democracy perceives as politically unstable.* At least two possible reasons for this come to mind: The state may see an unstable democratic regime as under these political pressures, and hence as a real danger needing to be forcibly constrained or deterred. Alternatively, an unstable democratic regime may seem a publicly more legitimate and acceptable object for diverting hostility and provoking a 'rally effect. That is, the government may truly feel itself threatened in some degree by such a regime, or, if not, it may believe that the public will at least accept perception of a threat. If the adversary is perceived as a stable democracy, by contrast, the cultural/normative argument suggests little political benefit in trying to invoke a rally against it. Thus instability may work both as encouraging the use or threat of force by the "unstable" regime, and in selecting an "unstable" object for the exercise of force.

Empirically it will be very difficult to sort out the mechanism systematically. Even in the 1946–86 period with many democracies in the international system, table 1.2 showed only fourteen militarized disputes between democracies. In their manifestation of threat or use of force all of them were extremely localized, typically an air incursion or shelling in the general direction of a boat lasting a single day. None were reciprocated uses of military force, in which the attacked party made any military reprisal, and nearly all of them were bloodless. Most could plausibly have been unauthorized acts by local commanders. In most instances it is hard to show that they were deliberate and considered governmental acts of the sort plausibly included under the rubric of politically motivated incidents just discussed. And while one can identify who actually used force or first threatened to use it, it is not so easy to say which side played the greater role in provoking the incident. Thus one should not expect to find a systematic pattern of motivation in such low-level incidents. In near-wars, however—where the level of violence may be greater, and the degree of central control and deliberate act may be stronger—we may find some such evidence.

We should also, by extension, expect such events to occur *between states where one or both states' status as a democracy leaves some basis for doubt.* Perceptions of instability may be based on the recency and immaturity of experience with democratic processes and norms: a new democracy will not yet have developed wide experience in practices of democratic conflict resolution. Perceptions of instability may also be based on a high degree of violent opposition to the democratic government: a democracy under siege of domestic terrorism, insurgency, or civil war is one in which the ostensible norms of peaceful conflict resolution simply are not working well. If a government's practice of democratic forms of government is very recent and subject to violent domestic challenge, or its practice of democracy is incomplete or imperfect by the standards of the day, it may be imperfectly constrained by the norms of democratic government that are supposed to keep conflict nonviolent. Or uncertainty about the commitment to democratic norms by the state with which one has a conflict of interest may lead to perceptions and expectations that it will practice those norms imperfectly.

The list of numbered propositions above often implies a dichotomy between democratic and nondemocratic states. But in the real world such a dichotomy masks degrees of democratic practice. Therefore if we find militarized disputes between democracies we should typically find that one party or both is only recently democratic, is subject to violent domestic challenge, or is toward the center of a democratic to nondemocratic continuum. We should also, in a revised version of proposition 6, look for evidence that one party, correctly or not, *perceives* the other as not really democratic.

STRUCTURAL AND INSTITUTIONAL CONSTRAINTS?

As with the normative and cultural argument, it is best to avoid assuming that democracies are dovish or peaceful in all their relations. Rather, a plausible argument can be constructed on the strategic principles of rational action; that is, about how states, in interactions of threat and bargaining, behave in anticipation of how their bargaining adversaries will behave. Decisionmakers develop images of the government and public opinion of other countries. They regard some governments or peoples as slow to fight, or as ready and eager to do so. In forming these images leaders look for various cues: in other leaders' and countries' past behavior in diplomatic or military disputes, and in other countries' form of government. Perhaps other governments will see a democracy as culturally (normatively) dovish on the above grounds, but Kant's own view argued that *institutional constraints*—a structure of division of powers, checks and balances—would make it difficult for democratic leaders to move their countries into war.

Democracies are constrained in going to war by the need to ensure broad popular support, manifested in various institutions of government. Leaders must mobilize public opinion to obtain legitimacy for their actions. Bureaucracies, the legislature, and private interest groups often incorporated in conceptualizations of the "state" must acquiesce. The nature and mix of institutions varies in different kinds of states (for example, "strong" states and "weak" states, parliamentary and presidential systems) but it is complex. Popular support in a democracy can be built by rhetoric and exhortation, but not readily compelled.

The complexity of the mobilization process means that leaders will not readily embark on an effort to prepare the country for war unless they are confident they can demonstrate a favorable ratio of costs and benefits to be achieved, at acceptable risk.[15] Moreover, the complexity of the process requires time for mobilization, as the leaders of various institutions are convinced and formal approval is obtained. Not only may it take longer for democracies to gear up for war, the process is immensely more public than in an authoritarian state. Democratic governments can respond to sudden attack by using emergency powers, and by the same powers can even strike preemptively in crisis. But in normal times they are ill suited to launching surprise attacks.[16] Apparently for these reasons, major-power democracies seem never to have launched preventive war (a deliberate attack not under immediate provocation) against another major power (Schweller 1992). The greater the scale, cost, and risk of using violence, the more effort must be devoted to preparations in public, and of the public.

Even if two states were totally ignorant of each other's form of government, structural delays in the process of mobilization for war in both states would provide time to elapse for negotiation and other means of peaceful conflict resolution. Yet perceptions matter here too. If another nation's leaders regard a state as democratic, they will anticipate a difficult and lengthy process before the democracy is likely to use significant military force against them. They will expect an opportunity to reach a negotiated settlement if they wish to achieve such a settlement. Perhaps most importantly, a democracy will not fear a surprise attack by another democracy, and thus need not cut short the negotiating process or launch a preemptive strike in anticipation of surprise attack.

If democratic leaders generally consider other democracies to be reluctant and slow to fight because of institutional constraints (and possibly because of a general aversion of the people to war), they will not fear being attacked by another democracy. Two democratic states—each constrained from going to war and anticipating the other to be so inhibited—likely will settle their conflicts short of war. Bueno de Mesquita and Lalman (1992, chap. 4) provide a deductive argument that two such states, each with perfect information about the other's constraints, will always settle their conflicts by negotiation or by retaining the status quo. In the real world perfect information is lacking, but the presence of democratic institutions provides a visible and generally correct signal of "practical dovishness"—restraints on war in the form of institutional constraint if not of inherent disposition. Reading that sign, democracies will rarely if ever go to war with each other.

Leaders of nondemocratic states may also anticipate that a democratic country will be slow to go to war. But if they are themselves aggressive, they may be more likely to threaten or bully a democracy to make concessions. In turn, that would raise the threshold of provocation facing the democracy, and perhaps overcome its initial inhibition against fighting. That would explain why the overall frequency of war fighting by democracies is no different from that of nondemocratic states.[17] But leaders of two nondemocratic states, neither encumbered by powerful structural constraints, are more likely than two democratic states to escalate to war.

This argument can be summarized as follows.

THE STRUCTURAL/INSTITUTIONAL MODEL:

A. Violent conflicts between democracies will be infrequent because:
    1. In democracies, the constraints of checks and balances, division of power, and need for public debate to enlist widespread support will slow decisions to use large-scale violence and reduce the likelihood that such decisions will be made.
    2. Leaders of other states will perceive leaders of democracies as so constrained.
    3. Thus leaders of democracies will expect, in conflicts with other democracies, time for processes of international conflict resolution to operate, and they will not fear surprise attack.

B. Violent conflicts between nondemocracies, and between democracies and nondemocracies, will be frequent because:
    4. Leaders of nondemocracies are not constrained as leaders of democracies are, so they can more easily, rapidly, and secretly initiate large-scale violence.
    5. Leaders of states (democracies and nondemocracies) in conflict with nondemocracies may initiate violence rather than risk surprise attack.
    6. Perceiving that leaders of democracies will be constrained, leaders of nondemocracies may press democracies to make greater concessions over issues in conflict.
    7. Democracies may initiate large-scale violence with nondemocracies rather than make the greater concessions demanded.

DISTINGUISHING THE EXPLANATIONS

The cultural/normative and institutional/structural explanations are not neatly separable. Institutions depend on norms and procedures. For example, stability, which we treated as a measure of normative acceptance of democratic processes, is also an institutional constraint if political structures are not subject to overthrow. States may also consider the dominant norms in other states, as well as their institutions, as signals; thus both explanations also depend in part on perceptions. Great emphasis on reading signals of the other's intention, however, slights the importance of self-constraint. Institutions may slow or obstruct one's own ability to fight. Perhaps more importantly, a norm that it is somehow not "right" to fight another democracy raises the moral and political cost, and thus limits one's own willingness to do so. Bueno de Mesquita and Lalman (1992) neglect this, as well as the opposition a democratic government might find among its own population against fighting another *democratic government* (Geva, DeRouen, and Mintz 1993). Within democracies, structural impediments to using force are less strong than within autocracies; normative restraints must bear the load. So we should not assume that normative constraints are unimportant in relations between democracies. Both norms and institutions may contribute to the phenomenon of peace between democracies; they are somewhat complementary and overlapping. But they are also in some degree distinctive and competing explanations, allowing us to look for greater impact of one or another in various contexts.

Other influences, such as trade and the network of international law and organizations as suggested by Kant, likely also play a role in directly supplementing and strengthening that of democracy. Further elaboration of the theoretical arguments is probably needed. Certainly, detailed empirical work is necessary on how institutions operate, and on how perceptions toward other countries evolve, so as to make it possible to weigh the relative power of institutional and normative explanations. So too is the creation and application of systematic empirical tests to differentiate between the two kinds of explanations for violence in the modern interstate system. One such test, distinguishing between measures of democracy as stability (normative) and of democracy as the adoption of particular institutions, will be performed later in this book. The prediction about stable democracies being less likely than unstable ones to use military force against each other is embedded in the normative model, and more tenuously so in the structural one.

Another way of differentiating between the two is to look for other hypotheses that may be derived from either, and tested. One such hypothesis for the normative model is represented in work by Dixon (1993, also 1992). He postulates that *democracies, with norms of using third-party intervention for peaceful and non-coercive resolution of conflicts internally, will carry those norms into management of their international conflicts with other democracies*. Dixon then looks at how international conflicts have been settled in the post–World War II era. Not only does he confirm our results from table 1.2 that conflicts between democracies are much less likely to escalate to lethal violence and to be settled peacefully, but he finds that they are much more likely to be settled by some means of third-party conflict management, such as the use of good offices, mediation, and intervention. Also, all conflicts between democracies were ended either by agreement or by stalemate; none terminated in a settlement imposed by one of them or by a third party. Such a pattern is much more readily explicable by common norms than by characteristics of internal democratic institutions acting as constraint. Leng (1993) similarly infers support for the normative argument from evidence that in interstate crises democracies are much more likely to use strategies of reciprocating the escalatory or de-escalatory moves of other states than are authoritarian regimes. He argues that reciprocation is an engrained democratic norm, as constrasted with behavior like bullying, appeasing, or stonewalling.

Another test can be derived from the patterns of strategic interaction as discussed in the model of structural constraints. By that argument, two democracies engaged in a conflictual bargaining process with each other can reasonably expect each other not to escalate the dispute to the point of war or serious violence. Therefore, many bargaining models predict there would be few strategic restraints on escalating the conflict up to, but not beyond, the point of an exchange of lethal violence. In fact, each state might have strong incentives to go that far for the purpose of showing resolve; perhaps even escalating to the first (limited) use of force in confidence that the other would be unlikely to reply in any substantial military manner. Such behavior is implicit in the bargaining "game" of chicken, which is widely applied to crisis negotiation (Brams and Kilgore 1988; Brams 1990; Poundstone 1992). This reasoning, therefore, leads to the prediction that disputes between democracies should commonly escalate to the display and even limited use of force, though not to war. But as table 1.2 showed, that is not the case. Democracy/democracy pairs are less likely to enter into militarized disputes at all than are other pairs of states, and less likely to escalate them at any level up the escalation ladder—not just at the top to war.[18]

Rather, this suggests that *to use or threaten to use force is not usually normatively acceptable behavior in disputes between democracies*, even in the form of symbolic, ritualized bargaining behavior. Relations between democracies therefore fit into the category of "stable peace" (Boulding 1979) or a "security community" (Deutsch et al. 1957) in which states not only do not fight each other, they do not expect to fight each other, or significantly prepare to fight each other. In such relationships disputes are routinely settled without recourse to threat and military deterrence. Dependent as the definition of security community has been on expectations, it has been a difficult phenomenon to observe reliably; here, in the relative absence of militarized dispute and escalation, is a reasonably objective measure.

We shall continue to juxtapose the normative and structural models for their relative explanatory power throughout the book. It is also important to explore the outer limits of the empirical domain to which the proposition about lack of war between democracies may apply. All the systematic empirical work to date has employed modern and Westernized definitions of both war and democracy. Careful relaxation of these definitions, in ways appropriate to other times and contexts, may also produce insights about the relative importance of normative and institutional constraints.

CHAPTER 3

The Imperfect Democratic Peace of Ancient Greece

With William Antholis

As a basis for understanding better the sources and nature of peace among modern democracies, we begin with the only other well-documented state system with a large number of democratic regimes—the city-state system in Greece during the late fifth century B.C. That examination allows us to consider influences that restrained, or failed to restrain, democracies from fighting each other in a political and cultural context very different from the modern state system. Doing so may help give insights into the role that related yet quite different institutions and perceptions have played in restraining such conflict more recently.

We first establish some definitions, appropriate to the conditions of ancient Greece, by which to identify autonomous states, democracies, and wars. Next we look at the aggregate evidence of who fought whom, and find that support for the proposition that democracies fight one another less often than they fight other states is mixed and inconclusive. We then show why the aggregate evidence is misleading—largely exaggerating the disposition of democracies to fight each other—by looking in detail at the cases that deviate from the hypothesis. Finally we discuss the fragile emergence, during the Peloponnesian War era, of some norms that democracies should not fight each other, and briefly address some alternative hypotheses.

DEMOCRACY, AUTONOMY, AND WAR IN ANCIENT GREECE

Anyone familiar with the Peloponnesian War will surely recall instances of democracies fighting one another—most notably the great clash between Athens and Syracuse. Many scholars have speculated on the incidental causes and meanings of such conflicts (Ste. Croix 1954–55, 1972; Bradeen 1960; Gillis 1971; Legon 1968; Pope 1988; Quinn 1964; Sabin 1991), but no one has conducted a systematic examination of the frequency and causes of wars between Greek democracies.[1]

To examine this more systematically we compiled political and military histories of independent Hellenic states (excluding, for example, the Sicels and Persia) for which we have record from 434 to 405 B.C. The period runs from the early battles of the Archidamian War—the first of the series of conflicts known as the Peloponnesian War—to the destruction of the Athenian fleet at the Hellespont, which forced the Athenians to capitulate to the Spartans.[2] We included all states known to have participated in wars during this period, and those few others that did not fight but about whose political systems we know something. In doing so we paid close attention to definitions and meanings—both ours and the Greeks'—of democracy, autonomy, and war. These terms were as loaded in ancient Greece as in contemporary analysis.

Greeks knew a great deal about how each other's city- states were governed; they especially knew about their major friends and enemies. Bonds of commerce, travel, common religion, and common language (with different dialects of course) usually ensured this knowledge. This fact is essential to any explanation of Greek war-fighting behavior that depends upon perceptions and the ties, in some instances, of a common democratic culture. On occasion, when one democracy fought another it did so because its people were in some ignorance of how the other was currently governed; for example, not realizing that the *dēmos* had recently seized power from oligarchs. In such cases, perceptions may have been more important than reality.

As we shall see, the *dēmos* could be fully as impulsive and warlike as could oligarchs and generals. Democracies were not necessarily more peaceful in general than were oligarchies. Moreover, Greek democracies lacked the institutional and structural complexities of democracies in modern nation states. They had relatively few full-time public officials save for judges and generals, and certainly no bureaucracies. Their governing popular assemblies could make war rapidly, without structural checks and balances. Thus while we shall employ institutional criteria for identifying democracies, this does not mean that we apply, from the modern debate about the determinants of democracies' foreign policies, the argument that stresses structures and institutions. With institutional restraints in the modern sense so weak, we will attend more to the role of perceptions and norms as the apparent basis for whatever restraints on war between democracies we find.

Democracy

Democracy is a highly contentious term. Attempts to characterize the democratic politics that appeared more than two millennia ago require sifting through conceptual and empirical artifacts. Conceptually, the

Greek city-state democracies differed significantly from twentieth-century liberal representative democracies. Greek democracies were more participatory than their recent progeny, but more formally selective in granting citizenship. That is, direct involvement in most aspects of government—including the decision to go to war—was open to all citizens, but citizenship was generally restricted to the nonslave male population of citizen birth.[3] As we shall see, the citizens of most democratic cities probably did not think of democracy as a trans-Hellenic project, at least at the outset of the Peloponnesian War. The individual liberties central to liberal democracy were not so universalized in the ancient world.[4] To the degree that these normative differences—in addition to the limited institutional restraints—apply, we should not expect to encounter all the norms of restraint that may be characteristic of modern democracies. The test of democratic restraint on warmaking decisions here will be a demanding one.

Thucydides' history of the war provides most of the empirical artifacts. Most extant information on fifth-century politics—both within and between the scores of city-states—comes from this narrative. As with most ancient and modern accounts of the period, our analysis begins with his description of regimes and events, and we generally trust the narrative's empirical content. We supplement it as much as possible with other ancient sources such as Aristotle, Diodorus, and Xenophon, and rely on secondary accounts as merited by each city's history. Unfortunately, Thucydides provides information about the local politics of city-states only as they affected inter-*polis* affairs. When such artifacts are presented, the discussion tends to be scattered and unsystematically organized.

In addition, Thucydides' many declarative statements and evaluative labels are often fused and do not clarify matters. Students of political philosophy have long debated Thucydides' personal political convictions and the effect they had on his description and evaluation of institutions. In such interpretive debates, his famous depiction of Athenian politics, for example (1954/1972, 2.65): "So, in what was nominally a democracy, power was really in the hands of the first citizen,"[5] becomes hotly contested. Scholars from various perspectives take this as a sign of Thucydides' distaste for democracy (Strauss 1963; Grene 1950, 41). But others emphasize his commitment to the Periclean party and moderate democracy, contrasting his position with that of his contemporaries (Ste. Croix 1972, 27; 1954–55, 40; Farrar 1989; Pope 1988).[6] Perhaps the least controversial statement about Thucydides' understanding of Periclean democracy is that Pericles showed the need for leadership in a democracy—which also proved the most identifiable threat to its representativeness and longevity. As a famous study (Ste. Croix 1954–55, 16) remarks, of the democratic nature of the Athenian alliance, "The partiality of Thucydides could scarcely have been exposed but for the honesty of Thucydides." To avoid the interpretive debate about what Thucydides meant by democracy, we instead focus on the evidence for various democratic institutions that can be culled from his text and other ancient sources.

While we accept the importance of ancient conceptual approaches to defining democracy, we rely on contemporary sources to provide the conceptual framework. Finley (1973, 72) provides a good starting point. Athens was distinct from nondemocratic regimes in at least three ways: (1) All citizens had a right to speak in the assembly, (2) The assembly chose (sometimes by lot) all public officials, including generals, (3) Leaders were constrained in their decisions by the assembly; that is, the assembly approved all broad policy directives to be implemented by officials.[7] Such democratic moments applied not merely to constitutional and momentous decisions (e.g., office selection procedures, criteria for citizenship, decisions of war and peace), but also to strategies chosen. By contrast (Manicas 1989, p. 19), in Sparta the assembly's power was tightly constrained: "Its members lacked the right to make speeches and to criticize and propose amendments (isēgoria), and not all decisions required the consent of the Assembly; . . . the decision making process never came close to what it was in Athens."

Athens probably exceeded most Greek city-states not only in the scope of policy questions left to popular control, but also in the proportion of its population that held the participatory rights of citizenship. Finley (1973, 82–87) emphasizes the role of the state in paying all citizens a wage when they performed public services, affording the poor requisite "leisure time" for politics. Many other democratic city-states—especially tribute-paying members of the Athenian alliance—could not easily afford such an extravagance. They either curtailed the scope of participation or sacrificed other endeavors to help maintain a democratic citizenship. Consequently democratic culture rarely developed to the degree known in Athens.

We will not, however, limit democracy to the extreme case. The Greeks did not. Nor today do we deny the label "democracy" to poor countries merely because they are poor, or to those with fewer elections than the myriad local, regional, and national elections in Western Europe and North America—the frequency and policy scope of which still falls far short of the Athenian model. Rather, we will simply look for basic democratic institutions and procedures.

In a number of regimes a great assembly of the dēmos made all public decisions—from the important to the mundane—and selected officials—from generals to jury members. Even when the scope was not so broad we classify as a democracy any city that had an established assembly of the dēmos and in which a party purporting to represent the dēmos held some power. This falls a bit short of Finley's demands. Since the evidence (in

Thucydides and other primary sources) is fragmentary on the detailed nature of assemblies and the selection of public officials in cities outside Athens, our analysis must be limited to general statements about institutions. Still, we must be cautious about calling any regime democratic merely if another scholar—ancient or modern—refers to it as a democracy. Thus we classify two groups of democracies: those that clearly met both of the above criteria, and those that did not but for which some evidence of democracy exists.

The full list of states and whom they fought is in the appendix to this chapter. Thirteen states met the strict criteria: Acanthus, Amphipolis from the time of its revolt against Athens, Argos save for a brief period, Athens except for the oligarchic regime of the Four Hundred in 413–12, Colophon most of the time, Corcyra, Mantinea, Megara from about 427 to 424 and later as a regime of democratic exiles, Mende, Miletus, Samos late in the war, Scione when resettled by Plataean exiles, and Syracuse. For these clear democracies, about whose governance there is little doubt, we will carry out some analyses of their war-fighting behavior alone. These clear democracies are identified by code (a) in the appendix to this chapter, and appear in column 1 in table 3.1, below.

Many other states exhibited certain elements of democratic government, but either more evidence is not available or these governments only partially met our criteria. Examples of borderline cases that did not quite make our cutoff include the ex-Messenians at Naupactus, where democratic parties were in power but there is little evidence of institutions, and Methymna, with similar characteristics and several different regimes. In addition to twenty-three cities that at some time met such less strict criteria, we extend the period of democracy for Amphipolis to before the revolt, and for Athens to include the Athenian navy which in exile was run by a democratic faction (but without the previous democratic institutional structure) and fought Aenia and Sparta. We label these states as democratic by one or more codes, used in the chapter appendix: (b) a democratic faction was in power;[8] (c) an assembly was called for some constitutional decision (such as to declare war or assert autonomy) but there is no evidence of a regular assembly; (d) they are called democratic without evidence by Thucydides or modern scholars; or (e) were called a democracy but without convincing evidence or were colonies of a democratic power, with some evidence of democratic practice.

These states, which appear in column 2 of table 3.1, will be analyzed as "other democracies." They include some often characterized as "moderate" democracies or having had "mixed" constitutions. Readers may surely dispute any of our criteria, but at least we have applied them consistently.[9] Moreover, the findings we report about states' behavior are not sensitive to a small number of classificatory changes.

We use each city-state regime as a unit of analysis. When a state changed political organization fundamentally, we consider it a new regime. Hence we follow Aristotle (1984, 3.3.7, 1276a–76b10), who said, in defining a city as "a partnership of citizens in a regime," that "if the regime becomes and remains different in kind, it might be held that the city as well is not necessarily the same." Argos illustrates a complicated application of Aristotle's criterion. It begins this historical period as a clear democracy, with a standing assembly and a popular party in power. But after fighting frequently on the Athenian side it experiences an oligarchic coup; under the oligarchs it fights Sicyon. It then undergoes a full democratic restoration and returns to war on the Athenian side. The exiled oligarchs settle at Orneae and fight against Athens. We combine both democratic periods as representing a single regime, and the Orneaan exiles as a continuation of the oligarchic regime. But when a democratic regime undergoes a substantial constitutional transformation while remaining democratic we count it twice when analyzing "clear" and "all other" democracies. For example, we treat the earlier regime in Amphipolis as distinct from the later regime for which we are more confident of its democratic nature.

Similar distinctions are necessary for the remaining states. Many, as evidenced in the historical record, clearly were not democracies (coded (n) in the appendix; column 4 in table 3.1). For the remaining cities we simply lack evidence. Some probably were democratic, and mixed or moderate regimes, but many probably were not. We put them in an "unknown" category between known "other" democracies and known non-democracies (not coded in the appendix; column 3 in table 3.1).[10] In one case, Sicyon, we distinguish an initial regime, probably not democratic but possibly mixed, from the subsequent oligarchy installed in 219 B.C. Sicyon is thus counted first for its actions when probably not democratic and then as definitely nondemocratic. Others are continuing regimes. As with the oligarchs of Argos, when the people of Aegina (Spartan ally and oligarchy) are moved to Thyrea, we treat them as continuing the initial regime, transplanted to other soil, until they are finally annhiliated.[11] (This is comparable, though with a different ultimate outcome, to treating Kuwait as an internationally recognized state, capable of some military action, even while Iraq occupied its territory.)

Autonomy

An equally contentious problem concerns identifying autonomous states in a world of cleruchies, colonies, mercenaries, and vassals (Smith 1986) (codes (kk), (k), (m), and (v) in the appendix). The most clearly dependent subject states are cleruchies: foreign cities run by resident Athenians

(Greenidge 1911, 201; Graham 1983). As on Imbros and Lemnos, Athens expelled non-Greek residents from these islands after defeating the Persians, and the islands were established as administrative units of Athens proper. The land was divided into lots and given to Athenians who, as new colonials, or cleruchs, retained legal status as Athenian citizens. Whenever the islands showed signs of independence, the mother city reinforced its control by settling more cleruchs. In the economically and strategically important cleruchies of Euboea, Athenian policy "was not to support democratic factions but to subject cities directly to the Athenian *dēmos*, as if they were outlying districts of Attica" (Lintott 1982, 101). Thus we cannot count cleruchies as autonomous state actors, and they do not appear in table 3.1.

Similarly, at least two states—Agraea and Astacus—were "vassals" of Athens for a part of this period, having lost autonomy in war-fighting decisions. We exclude them from table 3.1, and also units from several areas (e.g., Acarnarnia, Aetolians when fighting in Sicily, Arcadia, Crete) that participated as mercenaries, but not in the name of their home states.

At the other end of the scale are states that clearly fought independently. In his "war catalogue" for the Sicilian expedition, Thucydides (1954/1972, 7. 57–58) lists three such as allies of Athens: Chios, Corcyra, and Plataea. Two of these city-states are distinguished by having contributed ships. Others fought from mixed motives. But city-states that only sent troops were generally considered "subject" states by the Athenians. Such states lacked the resources for Thucydides' description of full autonomy.

Several major powers—Athens, Boeotia, Corcyra, Corinth, and Sparta—spawned colonies, many of which continued to pay tribute or commit forces to the mother city's alliance. Behind the rhetoric of formal autonomy in foreign affairs and the general reality of autonomy in local affairs, colonies were bound by ties of economics, culture, religion, and guest friendship (Herman 1987). When these were not sufficient, physical compulsion was institutionalized by garrisons from the mother city.

Still, we cannot dismiss all "subject" cities and colonies peremptorily as vassals. Some were not independent, but others effectively were. Were these particular smaller powers forced to go on this expedition while other Athenian allies were not? How could colonies play one great power off against another? How could colonies revolt if they lacked the potential for autonomy? Why did others choose not to do so when Athenian power declined? Throughout his account, Thucydides provides support for the formal autonomy of many cities which, in his "war catalogue," he summarily and uniformly describes as subjects. The logic of the latter assessment would see all garrisons as occupying forces. In fact, Athenian garrisons were often welcomed as defending colonies and allies from Persians, Spartans, and the *dēmos* from its own oligarchs. These city-states sacrificed some autonomy for enhanced security. While we do not imagine that garrisons had no effect on local politics, neither can we assume that the imperial powers controlled all decisions of war and peace.

The constitutional histories of these states—including their ethnic and economic ties to Athens—created powerful but not unbreakable bonds. The causal force of these relationships on the colonies' decisions to go to war usually fell somewhere in between the absence of effect perhaps implied in the formal autonomy of city-states and the more draconian compulsion implied by Thucydides' summary statement. Many city-states, especially in the islands, remained loyal to Athens even after the Syracuse debacle, when Athens could no longer compel their allegiance. We therefore treat small states and colonies as autonomous actors unless genuine and recurrent efforts of their governments to free themselves are habitually denied or repelled. Moreover, since war provides a moment of constitutional self-determination, we paid close attention to Thucydides' discussions of how and when states decided to engage in battle.[12] As with our discussion of regime type, we invite debate over our descriptions of city-state autonomy.[13] But we do not believe that our decisions, even if sometimes questionable, systematically affect our conclusions about states' warmaking patterns.

War

Finally, there is the matter of defining war, as distinct from single battles. War periods are, on the whole, fairly clearly demarcated. "Typically a war was announced, the forces gathered for the clash or a series of clashes, and the war ended with one side victorious, the other vanquished. Both the beginning and the end were signaled by highly ritualized and symbolic acts. . . ." (Manicas 1989, 27). Our standard requires that attacking states needed to know whom they were attacking, and defending states had to put up a fight. Thus we require some battle engagement, involving on both sides forces under state authorization. We do not try to count the number of such engagements for each pair; any engagement during the entire period of the regimes' existence makes the two such states a warring pair for purposes of our analysis. Wars may include sieges, but if a state's only involvement in hostilities was to serve as the site of pillaging and ravaging expeditions, or of a siege without fatalities, we do not count the events as a war. Indeed, such marginal involvement often indicated the absence of severe antagonism between the states at issue. A bloodless unopposed revolt against hegemonic alliance or colonial authority also does not count. Threatened or intended hostile acts count only if actually carried out.

To count as having fought in an alliance a state needed to have contributed ships or hoplites who actually fought; paying tribute or providing material resources alone were not sufficient. Often conflict was very localized, as when Athens alone fought a colony or other small state. In other circumstances (e.g. the war against Syracuse), many allies were involved on the Athenian side and all must be counted as having fought. We do not count allies unless they are explicitly mentioned in the narrative, or we know from earlier history that they were integral parts of the forces.

Who Fought Whom?

Before looking at the results it is worth bearing in mind how the numbers are derived. For several reasons the historical record is biased in a way that will tend to tilt the evidence away from our hypothesis that democracies rarely fight each other.

First, it is likely that wars between democracies were *relatively* rarer than simple (or simple-minded) "bean counting" might suggest. Such simple counting almost certainly undercounts the true number of wars between democracies and nondemocracies and especially between pairs of nondemocratic states. It rests implicitly on the assumption that we have examined the full population (or at least a representative sample) of Greek city-states and their wars—and that assumption is clearly false.

Recall that our catalogue of states is much less than the complete population of Greek city-states in the period. We are not dealing with a period, like the modern one, when it is fairly obvious, once terms are carefully defined, just how many states are in the system and there is essentially complete information on who fought whom when. Rather, what we have is the list of Greek city-states mentioned by Thucydides (usually because of their role on one side or the other in the Peloponnesian War) and a few others about which we have some record of warfare or political regime from other sources. Peripheral states, marginally relevant if at all to the main conflicts of the Peloponnesian War, may not be mentioned at all. Nor would a variety of states that, though not strictly at the physical periphery of the Greek world, were skillful or fortunate enough to stay at the political periphery of the main conflicts.

These reservations about the adequacy of reports of the existence of states apply even more strongly to the reporting of wars. Thucydides and other historians of the Peloponnesian War scrutinize the rivalry between Athens and its allies and Sparta and its allies. Many wars not closely related to this rivalry—either wars between aligned and nonaligned states, or entirely between nonaligned states—may not have been deemed worthy of those historians' attention. We might know of the existence of these states (they would contribute to the denominator), but not about most of their wars (in the numerator). Furthermore, such states, near the physical or political periphery, often not part of the Athenian empire, were unlikely to have been democratic. Finally, Thucydides usually was more interested in what Athens was doing than in Sparta. He chronicles in detail Athens's difficulty in holding together its coalition of democracies, but only suggests the common and disparate interests among oligarchies and the scope of the Peloponnesian alliance. Thus his book focuses substantially on the Athenian empire, and less on relations among the states allied with Sparta. Many Spartan allies in expeditions against Athens are not listed separately, and so escape our count.

With these cautions in mind we now can make a crude quantitative test of the hypothesis that democracies will fight each other less frequently than do other states, and less frequently than democracies fight nondemocracies. The top half of table 3.1 shows the relative frequency of war between all four types of regimes: clear democracies, all other democracies, states whose regime type is unknown, and states known not to be democratic. Each cell shows first the percentage (warring pairs out of all possible pairs), and below that the total number of pairs of states.

For example, the upper left-hand corner shows the behavior of the thirteen clear democracies toward each other. They fought a total of fourteen wars among themselves. Thus the numerator is 14 for wars and the denominator is $(13 \times 12)/2$. (Not 13×13 because a state cannot fight itself, and divided by 2 since in both terms we count each pair only once, e.g., Athens-Syracuse does not also appear as Syracuse-Athens. As in the data for table 1.2 we do not try to identify the instigator or initiator of each war.) The percentages would be the same in the symmetrical off-diagonal cells, so all the information can be put in the upper right-hand part of each matrix and the lower left part kept blank.

Our basic expectation was that the relative frequency of war (percentages) should increase fairly steadily as one moves from the upper left-hand portion of the table to the right; that is, from the clear democracies all the way to the states known to be nondemocratic. That is not entirely what we find; the results are more complex. The exception, against the hypothesis, is that clear democracies were slightly more likely to fight one another than to fight any other type of regime. Of all possible pairs in this cell, 17.9 percent actually did fight each other. Supporting the hypothesis, however, is that clear democracies were very much less likely to fight other democracies than to fight those either probably or certainly nondemocratic. Also, clear democracies were, as expected, less likely to fight the regimes we cannot identify (probably including some democracies and mixed regimes) than to fight those we know to have been nondemocratic—as note 10 suggests should happen. The second row sup-

TABLE 3.1

Percentage of Pairs Engaging in Wars, by Different Types of Political Systems

	(1) Clear Democracies	(2) All Other Democracies	(3) Unknown	(4) Not Democracies
	(13)	(25)	(65)	(32)
Clear Democracies	17.9% (78)	9.2% (325)	13.7% (845)	15.9% (416)
All Other Democracies		1.7% (300)	4.4% (1,625)	8.3% (800)
Unknown			3.2% (2,080)	4.9% (1,984)
Not Democracies				4.8% (496)

	(1) + (2) All Democracies (36)	(3) + (4) Other (96)
All Democracies	7.8% (630)	9.2% (3,456)
Other		4.1% (4,560)

Notes: Number of states is in parentheses at tops of columns; number of pairs is in parentheses under percentages.

The lower table eliminates double counting of states and wars as a result of regime changes within broad categories.

ports the hypothesis all the way, with other democracies very much least likely to fight one another and by far most likely to fight states known to us as nondemocratic.

We offered no predictions about whether nondemocracies would fight one another or democracies more often, so the small percentages in the three lower right cells as compared with those in the upper right four do not address our hypothesis at all. It is nonetheless surprising that wars in the lower right cells (nondemocracies combined) are generally rarer than in two of the upper left three (all democracies).

The very low incidence of war (only five) between "other democracies" deserves comment. These states are in this category partly because we are apt to know less about them; this may mean they were generally more peripheral to the conflicts of the day. The low rate may also reflect the power of hegemonic Athens to enforce discipline among the democracies of its alliance, perhaps preventing them from fighting one another. Thucydides gives no evidence of such actions, though the example Pericles made of Samos in 440 B.C., when it refused to accept Athenian arbitration of its quarrel with Miletus (Hammond 1986, 314–16), may well have lingered. But even if hegemonic discipline did operate to some degree, it could not overwhelm the textual evidence for normative constraint that we present below.

The bottom half of the table, combining all democracies into one category and all other states into a second, provides some modest support for the hypothesis. All democracies together fought each other relatively less often than they fought other states, but not by a wide margin. And again, wars among other states appear to be relatively the least frequent.

Interpreting these results is difficult. Overall, it seems most reasonable to say that aggregate quantitative analysis neither clearly confirms nor clearly disconfirms the hypothesis. Biases in the historical record make it impossible to determine whether this lack of clear result is a reflection of the true situation or of the biases that work against the hypothesis. The crude quantitative results, however, represent the beginning rather than the end of the story. The numbers must be used carefully for interpretation, not mechanically. They provide a baseline by which deviant case analysis can foster interpretation and understanding. One must look at the kinds of events to which they apply in context, and scrutinize textual evidence about how participants perceived their own and others' actions.

WHEN AND WHY DID DEMOCRACIES FIGHT EACH OTHER?

Beyond the simple count one must look in detail at just who fought in the wars among democracies. Eight of the fourteen wars among clear democracies were as part of the Athenian campaign against Syracuse, and not completely separate events.[14] In addition to Athens itself, the democratic allies included Argos, Corcyra, Mantinea, the democratic Megaran exiles, Miletus, Samos, and Scione (ex-Plateans). The wars of Athens and allies against Syracuse of course represent the glaring exception to any generalization that democracies rarely fight each other.

Of Athenian democracy in this historical context there can be no question. Whatever reservations one may have by modern standards, for the period Athens is the archetype of democracy. Regarding Syracuse there is some dispute. Ste. Croix quotes Aristotle, who regarded Syracuse as distinctly less democratic than Athens at the beginning of and during the Sicilian campaign, with a turn to radical democracy only after Syracuse's victory: "In Syracuse, the people, as the cause of victory in the war against the Athenians, effected a revolution from polity to democracy" (Ste.

Croix 1954–55; Aristotle 1984, 5. 4., 1304a27–29). Ste. Croix also cites a passage in which the generals terminate debate in Syracuse and make military decisions without approval of the assembly.

These arguments, however, are not persuasive. Thucydides shows Athenian generals to exert wide prerogative in limiting democracy in moments of crisis. Pericles "saw that for the moment the Athenians were being led astray by their angry feelings. So he summoned no assembly or special meeting of the people, fearing that any general discussion would result in wrong decisions, made under the influence of anger rather than of reason" (1954/1972, 2.22). In each case military leaders obstructed the full operation of existing democratic institutions without overthrowing them or fomenting disorder. It is true that the Syracusan generals ended debate so as to prepare for battle with a democratic city—of some relevance for us—while Pericles avoided beginning debate on a pressing domestic concern with potential external consequences (the plague). Still it would be hard, with a consistent definition of democracy, to exclude one of these democratic city-states for excessive executive prerogative without excluding the other. In this light, it is ironic that Aristotle's distinction between polity and democracy had less to do with institutions—as we have defined democracy here—than with the question in whose interest the government ruled. For him, polities ruled in the common interest (the *polis*), democracies in that of the *dēmos*.

Ste. Croix contends that Athens was popular with the Syracusan public, who regarded Athens as more democratic. A pro-Athenian faction did appear in Syracuse, and some Syracusan exiles fought with the Athenians. Ste. Croix attributes this to ideological class (democratic-oligarchic) conflicts within these cities, suggesting that Sicilian democracy was less radical than its Athenian cousin. (Also see Greenidge 1911, 57) Yet Ste. Croix's evidence for democratic sympathy in Syracuse works against his conclusions. Thucydides reports that the Athenians were frustrated in their unsuccessful attempts "to make use of a fifth column or to offer the prospect of a change in government as a means of gaining power over them" (1954/1972, 7.55). The *dēmos* ultimately is credited for victory over Athens. And whatever revolution did take place, Syracuse subsequently continued to fight Athens at sea, hence democracy was as belligerent toward Athens as was polity.

In the end, we affirm Thucydides' judgment on the Athenians' policy: "They wished all the more that the expedition had never been made. These were the only cities they had come up against which were of the same type as their own, democracies like themselves, and places of considerable size equipped with naval and cavalry forces" (1954/1972, 7.55). We accept the war of Athens—with its democratic allies—against Syracuse as cases when democracies really did fight each other. Yet it is less clear whether, before their attack, the Athenians themselves shared Aristotle's later perception of Syracuse as not equivalently democratic. Given the technology of the time and the great distance between Athens and Syracuse, communications were very poor. Misperception (perhaps motivated misperception, wishful thinking about a sympathetic democratic party) was entirely possible. We shall return to the possibility that misperception accounted for some wars between democracies that were not perceived as such.[15]

Athens fought five other wars against clear democracies. Mantinea may be regarded as less than a fully free agent in its campaigns against Athens. Landlocked on the Peloponnesus and largely surrounded by Spartan-allied oligarchies, it had little choice but to fight Athens when Sparta was strong. When Sparta was weakened after the Peace of Nicias, however, Mantinea repeatedly fought on the Athenian side. On one of the latter occasions Thucydides reports the Mantinean generals exhorting their troops that the battle would mean either "keeping the power which they had won or . . . relapsing again into the slavery of the past" (1954/72, 5.69). Yet some allowance must be made for rhetorical hyperbole. During their "slavery" on the Spartan side the Mantineans had conquered a large part of Arcadia, and they feared that "now that Sparta had the time to deal with other matters, she would not allow them to keep what they had won" (1954/72, 5.29). Thus, even if not quite freely chosen, Mantinea's participation in the alliance against Athens had certainly been consistent with a larger self-interest, as was its shift to the Athenian side.[16]

Megara, initially with a mixed constitution, became democratic around 427 B.C. Although their democratic constitution made them suspect among the oligarchic states, from then until 424 the Megarians were part of the Peloponnesian alliance against Athens. Yet there were no open clashes until 424, when a conspiratorial attempt by the democrats failed to bring the city over to the Athenian side. In attempting to penetrate the city, Athenian troops clashed with guards of the still formally democratic state, and a few soldiers were killed. While strictly consistent with our definition of "war," this was hardly a full-scale battle typical of most events in our catalogue of wars.

The three other Athenian wars with clearly democratic enemies were against rebels from the alliance. Mende had a democratic regime when it revolted from the Athenian empire—albeit at the prodding of a minority faction—and turned to Brasidas, the Spartan general, when he came to the area. Arms were distributed to the people, but with Athenian troops outside the gates the democratic faction refused to make war against Athens and turned against the Peloponnesian garrison. The Athenians nevertheless attacked, and sacked the town. We count this as a revolt approved by the people under democratic institutions, however reluctant majority assent might have been. The Athenians certainly saw it this way, and seem to have been unaware that the democrats later turned against the revolt. Thus they at first applied harsh sanctions against a people who, though democrats, had rebelled. Later, recognizing that the popular party wished to remain loyal to Athens, they told them "they might continue to govern themselves as before and should put on trial those whom they regarded as responsible for the revolt." We see here both some operation of norms against democracies fighting each other, and the fury of one side when it appeared that the other had broken those norms. Perceptions of intent of another democracy proved more potent than institutions. We also see suggestion of the importance of perceiving the other as an enduring and stable democracy—a perception the Athenians certainly lacked in this instance.

Miletus did not revolt until after the Athenians' defeat at Syracuse left them unable to hold much of the empire; when the Milesians switched sides they also fought against democratic Argos. Amphipolis is the hardest case for our hypothesis. It was an Athenian colony, organized on democratic principles. It revolted from Athens at about the same time as Mende, but apparently with full democratic institutions and with the approval of the multitude. Kagan (1971, 297–98), argues that "though Thucydides does not report the very important speeches during the debate . . . we need not wonder that there was a debate." Graham (1983, 27), holds that the circumstantial evidence points to democratic government. It was subsequently attacked by Athens to restore its colonial status—again with some savagery against a state, recognized as a democracy, with the temerity to rebel.

Amphipolis was one of several states to rebel and fight Athens with assistance from a Spartan garrison. Presence of a garrison might lead some to think that rebellious states were not autonomous. Indeed, in some cases Athens did not hold the *dēmos* responsible when the city was returned to the alliance. It would be too much, however, to assume that a democracy's decision to ally itself to an oligarchy was not autonomous, simply on the grounds that the latter provided a garrison.

Among the thirty wars between clear and other democracies, nine involved Syracuse as one of the combatants, and another ten involved Athens. Of the latter, all but Elis, Scione, and Thurii were Athenian colonies that revolted. Elis was in a geopolitical position little better than Mantinea's, and like Mantinea fought on the Athenian side when it had more latitude after the Peace of Nicias. An assembly was called in Scione, but its function is uncertain. We called it (and a few others) an "other democracy" on rather slight evidence. Thurii was an apparently democratic colony of mixed origins in Italy (Graham 1983, 36; Kagan 1969,

154–60). It fought alongside Athens against Sparta and Syracuse, but became part of Sparta's seagoing expedition about 411 B.C., fighting both Athens and radically democratic Samos. Its shifts in allegiance seem to have been largely a consequence of shifts in dominance of the various ethnic groups loyal to Athens and Sparta.

Some of Athens' democratic non-Ionic allies, including Methymna and Mytilene (Aeolian), Rhodes (Doric), and Thurii (mixed) turned against the Athenians after the defeat at Syracuse—in some cases (especially Rhodes) under heavy persuasion by large Spartan expeditions. Even then, save for Chios and Miletus, democratic Ionian colonies in the region remained remarkably loyal.[17] Not until the revolt of Miletus do we find Athens fighting another Ionian democracy. At that point the economic and security interests that—in addition to ideological ties—had originally bound them to Athens were no longer served, and some felt they had to make whatever arrangements with Spartan power that they were able. As Lintott puts it (1982, 119), "If we consider the events of 412–411, it appears from the evidence we possess that the majority of citizens in Aegean, Ionian, and Hellespontine cities were not involved in the decisions to secede. The revolts were arranged by small groups of people, and for the most part they took place under the threat of a Peloponnesian force. . . . The political behavior of the cities of the eastern Aegean suggests that they were still dominated by their wealthiest citizens, whatever their constitutions. . . ."

In addition, the analysis so far has assumed implicitly that no confounding influences might predispose certain kinds of states to certain kinds of wars, apart from the kind of structural or normative influences we attribute to democracy. That assumption misses far too much.

The nondemocratic states were disproportionately (but not exclusively) isolated and regional in their interests and contacts. They had neither the commercial causes, nor the physical opportunity, that would lead them to fight in a wider theater—and hence against the democracies. So they would in fact engage in fewer wars (not just have fewer of their wars be reported) than did the democracies—but not because form of government per se made the difference.

Most democracies were naval powers, with the capacity to exert at least some military power at what in the context of the time was great distance—among clear democracies only Mantinea was landlocked. Democracies, as naval powers, thus had greater opportunity to fight and the occasion of commerce-induced conflicts to fight about. The situation was analogous to that of Britain and the United States in the nineteenth and twentieth centuries, whose wide reach and interests led them into many violent conflicts.

Moreover, it is no mere coincidence that the democratic states were primarily seafaring states, populated by a seafaring people with a "rower" culture. Democracy was instituted or strengthened in substantial degree by the need for a large navy of relatively poor but free citizens, who were paid for their ship duty by the state. The democratic reforms of Periclean Athens, for example, shifted the domestic political and military balance of power toward the poor and the navy. To continue to support those citizens the state needed to expand and control trade routes. At the height of democratic government, trireme rowers were full citizens. With 170 rowers in each of at least 200 ships, no fewer than 30,000 supporters of democracy, generally from the lower classes, would find themselves committed to an expansive empire.[18] Thus democratic Athens fought more overall (with 66 other states) than even Sparta did (with 50 states).

NORMS AND PERCEPTIONS

Democratic states in ancient Greece sometimes did fight one another, despite the ties—often fragile—of democratic constitution and ideology that might have kept them at peace. We have seen how some of the restraints worked, and how they sometimes broke down. Certainly, they lacked the strength and effectiveness they more often attain in the modern world. Among the Greeks, democratic *institutions* in themselves at best provided weak constraint on democracies from fighting each other. Such institutions were not able to provide a generally effective limit or temporal restraint on warmaking decisions. The mere existence of institutions tells us little about the extent to which they are in harmony with the habits and daily customs of a people. More important is the degree to which one *dēmos perceived* its interests to coincide with those of another in a different city-state. The evidence about norms and perceptions is fragmentary and cannot be conclusive; it nevertheless is intriguing.

Athens never fought explicitly to extend democratic principles, and Sparta was allied at various times with different democratic regimes.[19] Yet a democratic ideology emerged swiftly and dramatically. Much textual evidence shows democratic states reluctant to fight each other, precisely because of their ties of constitution and ideology. "Both Athens and Sparta believed fervently in the excellence of their own political arrangements. Furthermore, the encouragement among neighbours of a government like one's own was, then as well as now, a defensive measure, rendering attacks on one's own constitution less likely" (Lintott 1982, 83).

Ties with democratic Athens similarly served the domestic political interests of the allies. According to the orator Isocrates (1929, 12.68), cities paid tribute "not to preserve Athens, but to preserve their own democratic polity and their own freedom and to escape falling into such great misfortunes, through the setting up of oligarchies, as were suffered under the decarchies and under the domination of the Lacedaemonians." Again and again Thucydides tells us how, in a city or colony, the *dēmos* sided with Athens and the oligarchs with Sparta: in Amphipolis, Antissa, Argos, Corcyra, Cythera, Eresus, Leontini, Megara, Mende, Mytilene, Platea, Samos, Torone, and some more ambiguous cases. States' pro-Athenian or pro-Spartan orientations were determined at least as much by whether the *dēmos* controlled the state as by abstract balance of power constraints.

Even Athenian oligarchs were prepared to accept democracy elsewhere, treating the *dēmos* of a conquered town as friends against their local oligarchs (Pseudo-Xenophon 1962, 633–43). In Thucydides' report, Diodotus argues from enlightened self-interest, with a hint of normative prescription as well, when he persuades the Athenians not to kill the populace of Mytilene after that city's revolt. Whatever the guilt in this particular case, it is in Athens' interest to preserve the *dēmos*, and to be seen by other democratic cities as doing so. Athens' imperial relations are at stake: "In all the cities the democracy is friendly to you; either it does not join with the oligarchies in revolting, or, if it is forced to do so, it remains all the time hostile to the rebels, so that when you go to war with them, you have the people on your side" (1954/1972, 3. 47). Moreover, "The right way to deal with free people is this—not to inflict tremendous punishments on them after they have revolted, but to take tremendous care of them before this point is reached, to prevent them even contemplating the idea of revolt" (1954/1972, 3. 46). One scholar calls this "an actual and uniform policy to maximize allied sympathy and cooperation, not merely a case-by-case expedient to return rebellious allies to Athenian control" (Cogan 1981, 56). Another characterizes it as "a new morality applied to the changing relations of states, which in Athens' case requires confederal rather than imperial policies" (Coby 1991, 89).[20]

Much of the scholarship of this period has focused on the popularity (or lack of it) of the Athenian empire, and only incidentally on the natural affections between democracies. Anecdotal attention to particular instances obscures the nuances of relations as they developed over time. Democratic government was a relatively new experience in the ancient world, and the desire for a democratic *polis* and the desire for an autonomous one frequently came into conflict. Relations developed over time. Athens actively courted the *dēmos* of other cities first in the Ionian islands and the cities that had suffered under direct oligarchic control (e.g., Corcyra, Messenia), and later in cities whose freedom was only partially restricted by neighboring oligarchic hegemony (e.g., Argos, Elis, Mantinea, and Megara). The *dēmos* in these places were willing to risk provoking civil disorder (*stasis*) so as to gain greater autonomy from the oligarchic neighbors to whom their local oligarchs were increasingly indebted. Athens's new alliances following the Peace of Nicias reflected and encouraged the growth of democratic friendship following domestic polarization.

Other democracies, however, later fled the Athenian alliance when doing so seemed consistent with both autonomy and internal order. Sparta sometimes convinced cities to fight Athens when it assured them they could keep their form of government. Whereas democracies near Spartan borders were reluctant to risk such assurances, some cities farther away (e.g., Acanthus, Chios, Miletus, Rhodes) became willing to take the risk. Their ties to Athens became less valuable as Athenian power waned, yet their distance from Sparta still gave them some security from that power. Even then, however, many democracies (e.g., Clazomenae, Cos, Samos) stayed loyal to Athens. Few revolted without Spartan prodding or oligarchic inspiration, with the *dēmos* often resisting the switch.[21] Thucydides records the disaffection when the troops of Chios suddenly found themselves fighting Athens: they "were far from being united among themselves. . . . The rest of the city was held down by an oligarchy, and the people were suspicious of one another and apathetic" (1954/1972, 3. 38). Similarly, the cities of Lesbos traded hands between Athens and Sparta twice in a very short period of time, with the complicity of internal factions.

Ties of common democratic culture therefore offered some restraint on wars between Greek democracies. That restraint, certainly rooted in self-interest, also exhibited elements of normative restraint. For the restraints to operate, however, it was necessary for states and peoples actually to perceive each other as democratic. If, because of motivated misperception, or poor or outdated information, one did not perceive the other as democratic, those restraints could not apply. Furthermore, it may have been important to perceive the other as in some degree stably democratic, with reasonable prospects that the democratic faction could retain power.

In contrast, alternative hypotheses such as those discussed in chapter 2 ignore states' mutual estimation of one another. It is impossible with the existing evidence to test these alternatives systematically, but they do not appear to work very well in the Greek case. The Athenian empire was the primary relevant institution crossing state boundaries (analogous to a modern *transnational institution*). Some member states nonetheless pursued independent courses in the face of Athens' hegemonic position. The decision to rebel was generally made because of the institution, not despite it, and oligarchs were more likely to rebel than were democrats. The institutional explanation is not readily distinguishable from that about states *allying against a common enemy*, and that explanation depends on the further question of why some states perceive another as a common enemy. The democratic-oligarchic distinction does help explain that, both for long-standing alliances and for cases where civil disorder changed the character of the ruling regime. As for the role of distance, this did not significantly inhibit wars between democracies; quite the contrary was true in a world where democracies were generally seafaring. Neighboring democracies rarely fought each other; the Athens-Megara skirmish was the sole exception among clear democracies. And Athens and Syracuse fought each other all over the Mediterranean.

Finally, the *wealth-makes-peace* explanation, in its modern form, is hard to apply to the Greek world. Under ancient conditions, some wars for colonial conquest surely paid, as did some to retain rebellious colonies. Other wars were a net loss. Some wars between democracies were encouraged by economic motivations; for example, Athens feared for its viability if Amphipolis and Miletus allied with a hostile power and cut off timber and grain transportation.

Each of these hypotheses thus needs to examine more clearly the reciprocal perceptions of peaceful and belligerent dyads, and how democratic politics affected them.

Thucydides is often regarded as the father of "realist" theories of international relations[22]—that is, of theories that regard states as the most important actors in world politics, and which postulate that states act as if they were unitary rational actors, seeking to maximize their power and a victim of those inevitable competitive pressures. By these assumptions, the domestic political structure of states makes little difference to their decisions for war and peace. But Thucydides' great book actually is a penetrating analysis of the role and weaknesses of democratic politics in formulating security policy, and of the linkages between the *dēmos* in one state and the *dēmos* of others. These influences, ignored in the realist paradigm, are more familiar in contemporary liberal-institutionalist and idealist paradigms that compete with realism.

To some degree the norms that "democracies should not fight each other" were just being born, and even when present were not fully effective due in part to misperception. In the end, Thucydides' plaint about Athenians' regret over making war against cities "of the same type as their own, democracies like themselves," evokes a normative tragedy as well as a material one.

GREEK CITY-STATES IN THE PELOPONNESIAN WAR: THEIR DOMESTIC
REGIMES AND WHO THEY FOUGHT

This appendix lists every named geographic unit or independently organized fighting group, including vassal states, cleruchies, and mercenaries, known to have fought in a war between 434 and 405 B.C. It also includes those states for which we could identify domestic political institutions, even if there is no record of their having fought in any wars. The numbers on the left identify states; gaps in the sequence are the result of dropping states to which we had originally assigned numbers, but about which we had no information, either for wars or for political institutions.

v = vassal (does not include cities paying tribute to Athens)
m = mercenaries
k = colony of a democracy
kk = cleruchy
x = exiles
a = clear democracy
b = democratic faction in power
c = an assembly called for constitutional decision (though no indication of daily administration)
d = called a democracy without evidence
e = called a democracy with less than convincing evidence
n = nondemocracy (clear evidence)
no code = insufficient or no information regarding local politics

n	1 Abdera	165, 181, 207n, 208, 221
	2 Abydos	46n
a	3 Acanthus	
m	4 Acarnanian mercenaries	14n, 29m, 47n, 51, 69n, 96, 103, 118, 121, 203, 205n, 207n, 213a
n	5 Aegina (and Thyrea I)	43a, 147a
k	6 Aegina	14n, 29m, 47n, 51, 69n, 96, 103, 118, 121, 203, 205n, 207n, 213a
	7 Aenos	14n, 29m, 47n, 51, 69n, 96, 100n, 103, 118, 121, 203, 205n, 207n 213a
	8 Aetolia	43a, 56, 232
m	9 Aetolia	14n, 29m, 47n, 51, 69n, 96, 103, 118, 121, 203, 205n, 207n, 213a
n	10 Agraea	36, 43a, 158b, 211

v	11	Agraea	162n, 204, 206
	12	Agrigentium	34a, 43a, 59bc, 71m, 127a, 134x, 190bce
n	14	Ambracia	4m, 6k, 7, 9m, 20kk, 34a, 36, 43a, 46n, 53kk, 54, 56, 57kk, 59bc, 68a, 71m, 75b, 92kk, 104k, 111kk, 116kk, 127a, 134x, 141, 142be, 147a, 158b, 159, 190bce, 196n, 200a, 206, 211, 212kk, 216d, 217, 225d, 232
k	15	Amphipolis	31b, 165, 207n, 208
a	16	Amphipolis	43a, 81k, 111kk, 116kk
n	17	Anactorium	43a, 68a, 158b, 206, 211
n	19	Anaia	43a, 45bc, 46n
kk	20	Andros	14n, 29m, 47n, 51, 69n, 96, 103, 118, 121, 203, 205n, 207n, 213a
n	23	Antandrus	43a
kk	25	Antissa	
b	26	Antissa	
m	29	Arcadian mercenaries	4m, 6k, 7, 9m, 20kk, 34a, 43a, 53kk, 54, 56, 57kk, 59bc, 68a, 71m, 75b, 92kk, 104k, 111kk, 116kk, 127a, 134x, 141, 142be, 147a, 158b, 159, 190bce, 196n, 200a, 212kk, 216d, 217, 225d, 232
n	30	Arcadian Federation	127a
b	31	Argilus	15k, 43a, 81b, 111kk, 116kk
a	32	Argos	47n, 69n, 84, 86, 102, 118, 125, 133n, 173, 174n, 204, 207n, 215
n	33	Argos	204
a	34	Argos	12, 14n, 29m, 47n, 51, 60c, 69n, 96, 99, 103, 107, 112, 118, 121, 125, 133n, 147a, 173, 174n, 190bce, 203, 205n, 207n, 213a, 226v
nx	35	Argos exiles (Orneae)	43a
	36	Argos (Amphilochia)	10n, 14n, 69n, 100n, 124, 127a, 207n
n	39	Astacus	43a, 68a, 158b
v	40	Astacus	69n
n	41	Astacus	
a	43	Athens	5n, 8, 10n, 12, 14n, 16a, 17n, 19n, 23n, 29m, 31b, 35x,

39n, 47n, 51, 60c, 69n, 72, 74n, 82e, 94, 96, 99,
100n, 102, 103, 107, 112, 113b, 118, 121, 122, 123,
124, 125, 127a, 131n, 132a, 133n, 135a, 138n,
140, 142be, 146, 147a, 150, 151, 152, 153, 156b,
162n, 165, 181, 190bce, 199c, 203, 204, 205n,
206, 207n, 208, 210, 213a, 215, 220n, 224, 225d,
227n, 228c, 229

n	44	Athens	
bc	45	Athens	19n, 207n
n	46	Athens	2, 14n, 19n, 48, 60c, 61n, 63, 67n, 69n, 70, 76, 83, 92kk, 99, 122, 133n, 173, 190bce, 203, 207n, 213a, 219n, 225d
n	47	Boeotia	4m, 6k, 7, 9m, 20kk, 32a, 34a, 43a, 53kk, 54, 56, 57kk, 59bc, 68a, 71m, 75b, 82d, 92kk, 104k, 111kk, 116kk, 127a, 134x, 141, 142be, 147a, 158b, 159, 190bce, 196n, 197a, 200a, 212kk, 216d, 217, 222n, 225d, 232
	48	Byzantium	46n
	51	Camarina	4m, 6k, 7, 9m, 20kk, 34a, 43a, 53kk, 54, 56, 57kk, 59bc, 68a, 71m, 75b, 92kk, 104k, 111kk, 116kk, 127a, 134x, 140, 141, 142be, 147a, 158b, 159, 190bcf, 196n, 200a, 212kk, 213a, 216d, 217, 225d, 232
kk	53	Carystos	14n, 29m, 47n, 51, 69n, 96, 103, 118, 121, 203, 205n, 207n, 213a
	54	Catana	14n, 29m, 47n, 51, 69n, 96, 103, 118, 121, 203, 205n, 207n, 213a
n	56	Cephallenia	8, 14n, 29m, 47n, 51, 69n, 96, 103, 118, 121, 203, 205n, 207n, 213
kk	57	Chalcis (Euboea)	14n, 29m, 47n, 51, 69n, 96, 103, 118, 121, 203, 205n, 207n, 213a
n	58	Chaonia	211
bc	59	Chios	12, 14n, 29m, 47n, 51, 69n, 96, 103, 107, 112, 118, 121, 135a, 138n, 199c, 203, 205n, 207n, 213a
c	60	Chios	34a, 43a, 46n, 64be, 66a, 70, 79, 128, 172, 183, 197a
n	61	Chios	46n, 70
d	62	Clazomenae	
	63	Clazomenae	46n
be	64	Clazomenae	60c, 69n, 99, 133n, 207n

	99	Hermione	34a, 43a, 46n, 64be, 66a, 70, 79, 128, 172, 183, 196n, 197a
n	100	Heraclea	7, 36, 43a, 78, 126, 148, 158b, 164, 206, 211, 222n
	102	Heraea	32a, 43a, 127a
	103	Himera	4m, 6k, 7, 9m, 20kk, 34a, 43a, 53kk, 54, 56, 57kk, 59bc, 68a, 71m, 75b, 92kk, 104k, 111kk, 116kk, 127a, 134x, 141, 142be, 147a, 158b, 159, 190bcf, 196n, 200a, 212kk, 216d, 217, 225d, 232
k	104	Histiae	14n, 29m, 47n, 51, 69n, 96, 103, 118, 121, 203, 205n, 207n, 213a
	107	Hyccara	34a, 43a, 59bc, 71m, 127a, 134x, 190bce
	108	Iasus	203, 207n, 213a
kk	111	Imbros	14n, 16a, 29m, 31b, 47n, 51, 69n, 94, 96, 103, 118, 121, 152, 153, 165, 203, 205n, 207n, 208, 210, 213a, 229n
	112	Inessa	34a, 43a, 59bc, 71m, 134x, 190bce
b	113	Lampsacus	43a
kk	116	Lemnos	14n, 16a, 29m, 31b, 47n, 51, 69n, 94, 96, 103, 118, 121, 152, 153, 165, 203, 205n, 207n, 208, 210, 213a, 229n
	117	Leontini	140, 151, 213a
	118	Lepreum (Neodamodes)	4m, 6k, 7, 9m, 20kk, 32a, 34a, 43a, 53kk, 54, 56, 57kk, 59bc, 68a, 71m, 75b, 82d, 92kk, 104k, 111kk, 116kk, 127a, 134x, 141, 142be, 147a, 158b, 159 190bce, 196n, 200a, 212kk, 216d, 217, 225d, 232
	121	Leucas	4m, 6k, 7, 9m, 20kk, 34a, 43a, 53kk, 54, 56, 57kk, 59bc, 68a, 71m, 75b, 92kk, 104k, 111kk, 116kk, 127a, 134x, 141, 142be, 147a, 158b, 159, 190bce, 196n, 200a, 212kk, 216d, 217, 225d, 232
	122	Locri	43a, 46n, 140, 189, 196n, 197a
	123	Locris (Opuntian)	43a
	124	Locris (Ozolian)	36, 43a, 148, 158b, 164, 176, 206, 211
	125	Maenalia	32a, 43a, 127a
	126	Malia	100n
a	127	Mantinea	12, 14n, 29m, 30n, 36, 43a, 47n, 51, 69n, 96, 102, 103,

			107, 118, 121, 125, 133n, 148, 158b, 164, 168, 173, 174n, 203, 204, 205n, 206, 207n, 211, 213a, 215
	128	Marthussa	60c, 69n, 99, 133n, 207n
v	129	Mecyberna	165
n	131	Megara	43a, 68a, 158b
a	132	Megara	43a, 178be
n	133	Megara	32a, 34a, 43a, 46n, 64be, 66a, 70, 79, 82e, 127a, 128, 172, 183, 196n, 197a
ax	134	Megara	12, 14n, 29m, 47n, 51, 69n, 96, 103, 107, 112, 118, 121, 203, 205n, 207n, 213a
a	135	Mende	43a, 59bc, 221n
n	138	Melos	43a, 59bc, 142be
kk	139	Melos	
	140	Messina	43a, 51, 117, 122, 159, 189, 213a
	141	Metapontine	14n, 29m, 47n, 51, 69n, 96, 103, 118, 121, 203, 205n, 207n, 213a
be	142	Methymna	14n, 29m, 43a, 47n, 51, 69n, 96, 103, 118, 121, 138n, 153, 203, 205n, 207n, 213a
	146	Methone	43a, 68a, 158b
a	147	Miletus	5n, 14n, 29m, 34a, 43a, 47n, 51, 69n, 74n, 96, 103, 118, 121, 203, 205n, 207n, 213a
	148	Molycrium	100n, 124, 127a, 207n
	150	Mycalessus	1, 43a
	151	Mylea	43a, 117, 189
	152	Myrcinus	43a, 81k, 111kk, 116kk
	153	Mytilene Federation	43a, 111kk, 116kk, 142be
b	154	Mytilene Federation	
kk	155	Mytilene	
b	156	Mytilene	43a
b	158	Naupactus (Ex-Messinians)	10n, 14n, 17n, 29m, 39n, 47n, 51, 69n, 82e, 96, 100n, 103, 118, 121, 124, 127a, 131n, 146, 203, 204, 205n, 206, 207n, 213a

	159	Naxos	14n, 29m, 47n, 51, 69n, 96, 103, 118, 121, 140, 203, 205n, 207n, 213a
kk	160	Naxos	
n	162	Oeniadae	11v, 43a, 206, 211
	164	Oeta	100n, 124, 127a, 207n
	165	Olynthos	1n, 15k, 43a, 80, 81k, 111kk, 116kk, 129v
	168	Parrhasia	127a, 207n
	172	Pele	60c, 69n, 99, 133n, 207n
	173	Pellene	32a, 34a, 46n, 82d, 127a, 183, 196n, 197a
n	174	Phlius	32a, 34a, 127a
	176	Phocis	124
be	178	Plataea	132a, 207n, 220n
	180	Polychitna	72
	181	Potidaea	1n, 43a
	183	Pteleum	60c, 69n, 99, 133n, 207n
kk	185	Pyrra	
b	186	Pyrra	
	189	Rhegium	122, 140, 151, 213a
bce	190	Rhodes	12, 14n, 29m, 34a, 43a, 46n, 47n, 51, 69n, 96, 103, 107, 112, 118, 121, 196n, 197a, 203, 205n, 207n, 213a
n	196	Samos	14n, 29m, 47n, 51, 69n, 86, 96, 99, 103, 118, 121, 122, 133n, 173, 190bce, 203, 205n, 207n, 213a, 225d
a	197	Samos	47n, 60c, 69n, 86, 99, 122, 133n, 173, 190bce, 203, 205n, 207n, 213a, 225d
c	199	Scione	43a, 59bc, 221n
a	200	Scione [x-Plataeans]	14n, 29m, 47n, 51, 69n, 96, 103, 118, 121, 203, 205n, 207n, 213a
	203	Selinus	4m, 6k, 7, 9m, 20kk, 34a, 43a, 46n, 53kk, 54, 56, 57kk, 59bc, 68a, 71m, 75b, 92kk, 104k, 108, 111kk, 116kk, 127a, 134x, 141, 142be, 147a, 158b, 159, 190bce, 196n, 197a, 200a, 212kk, 216d, 217, 225d, 232
	204	Sicyon	11v, 32a, 33n, 43a, 82d, 127a, 158b, 207n, 211
n	205	Sicyon	4m, 6k, 7, 9m, 20kk, 34a, 43a, 53kk, 54, 56, 57kk,

			59bc, 68a, 71m, 75b, 92kk, 104k, 111kk, 116kk, 127a, 134x, 141, 142be, 147a, 158b, 159, 190bce, 196n, 197a, 200a, 212kk, 216d, 217, 225d, 232
	206	Sollium	11, 14n, 17n, 43a, 68a, 69n, 100n, 124, 127a, 158b, 162n, 207n, 211
n	207	Sparta	1n, 4m, 6k, 7, 9m, 15k, 20kk, 32a, 34a, 36, 43a, 45bc, 46n, 53kk, 54, 56, 57kk, 59bc, 64be, 66a, 68a, 70, 71m, 75b, 79, 81k, 82d, 92kk, 104k, 108, 111kk, 116kk, 127a, 128, 134x, 141, 142bf, 147a, 148, 158b, 159, 164, 168, 172, 178be, 183, 190bce, 196n, 197a, 200a, 204, 206, 211, 212kk, 216d, 217, 221n, 222n, 225d, 232
	208	Spartolus	1n, 15k, 43a, 80, 81k, 111kk, 116kk
	210	Stagirus	43a, 111kk, 116kk
	211	Stratus [Acarnania]	10n, 14n, 17n, 58n, 69n, 100n, 124, 127a, 162n, 204, 206, 207n
kk	212	Stria	14n, 29m, 47n, 51, 69n, 96, 103, 118, 121, 203, 205n, 207n, 213a
a	213	Syracuse	4m, 6k, 7, 9m, 20kk, 34a, 43a, 46n, 51, 53kk, 54, 56, 57kk, 59bc, 68a, 71m, 75b, 92kk, 104k, 108, 111kk, 116kk, 117, 127a, 134x, 140, 141, 142be, 147a, 158b, 159, 189, 190bce, 196n, 197a, 200a, 212kk, 216d, 217, 225d, 232
	215	Tegea	32a, 43a, 127a
d	216	Tenedos	14n, 29m, 47n, 51, 69n, 96, 103, 118, 121, 203, 205n, 207n, 213a
	217	Tenos	14n, 29m, 47n, 51, 69n, 96, 103, 118, 121, 203, 205n, 207n, 213a
be	218	Thasos	
n	219	Thasos	46n
n	220	Thebes	43a, 178be
n	221	Therme [Perdiccas]	1n, 135a, 207n, 199c
n	222	Thessaly	47n, 100n, 207n
	224	Thronium	43a
d	225	Thurii	14n, 29m, 43a, 46n, 47n, 51, 69n, 96, 103, 118, 121, 196n, 197a, 203, 205n, 207n, 213a

CHAPTER 4

The Democratic Peace since World War II

With Zeev Maoz

IN THE MODERN WORLD, the phenomenon of democratic peace is real. In this chapter we find strong evidence of the relative lack of conflict and the absence of war between democracies during the last half-century. It is a robust relationship, showing substantial strength even after alternative explanations are taken into account. Both normative and institutional restraints make a difference; they affect the political process in different ways, and can complement each other. Nor are they always either analytically or empirically distinguishable. But the evidence here brings together pieces of the puzzle in a coherent way, and serves as necessary background for the more intensive analyses of other historical eras and social contexts in the rest of the book.

We conduct some systematic tests of propositions about the democratic peace in the modern era. To do so we use multivariate statistical analysis, accounting for patterns of dispute involvement by using indicators of most of the potential causes of involvement mentioned in chapter 2. We can see to what extent each of the various influences accounts for conflict, controlling for the others, and giving special attention to political system type. We will also sort out the relative impact of structural/institutional constraints and normative/cultural ones, with the help of a critical test that competitively and simultaneously examines the relative power of the normative and structural models. This is the first systematic aggregate analysis conducted on the two models as distinguished from democracy per se.[1] It will require careful attention to problems of data and statistical analysis. But the rest of the book, written in a somewhat more discursive style, demands that the evidence for this detective story be convincing by technical standards. Readers who do not require convincing can skip some parts and concentrate on "whodunit."

We will be testing the following hypotheses:

1. The more democratic are both members of a pair of states (dyad), the less likely it is that a militarized dispute will break out between them, and the less likely it is that any disputes that do break out will escalate. This effect

will operate independently of other attributes such as the wealth, economic growth, contiguity, alliance, or capability ratio of the countries.

2. The more deeply rooted are democratic norms in the political processes operating in the two states, the lower the likelihood that disputes will break out or escalate. (Normative/cultural model.)

3. The higher the institutional constraints on the two states, the lower the likelihood that disputes will break out or escalate. (Structural/institutional model.)

WHO AND WHEN

For this purpose we look intensively at the behavior of all pairs of independent states in the world during the period 1946–86—in essence, the Cold War era. (Some important data have not yet been systematically compiled and checked for 1987 and later.) Despite the evidence that even before World War II democracies rarely fought or engaged in militarized disputes with each other, the post–World War II era is more appropriate for systematic testing, for three good reasons.

1. Although a score or more of democracies existed in much of the first half of the twentieth century, the number of pairs of democratic states was three times as large in the later era. With a small number of democratic dyads, the impact of possible confounding influences would be harder to distinguish.

2. Many influences put forward as confounding and contributing to the phenomenon of peace between democratic states were much more prominent after World War II than before. The post–1945 period brought unprecedented wealth and growth on a global scale, and the alliance system that incorporated democracies (and others) against the perceived communist threat was far wider and more durable than any that preceded it. Data on economic levels and growth rates are markedly more reliable and widespread for the past half-century than before. Thus a more complex test, designed to display the power of competing hypotheses, becomes possible.

3. As a generalization partly dependent upon specific historical conditions, the role of democracy in restraining violence between democratic dyads may have been stronger in the past half-century than before. The norms of democracy have become more deeply entrenched, as many democratic states have been democracies for longer periods and such principles as truly universal adult suffrage (for women, or for ethnic minorities) have been put generally into practice. Similarly, many countries' democratic institutions have grown stronger over time. Continuity of democracy in a country encourages its partners in foreign affairs to perceive it as

stably democratic. Finally, the experience of three worldwide conflicts (World War I, World War II, and the Cold War)—each of which was both in rhetoric and to some extent in reality a conflict of democracies against authoritarian states—helped build normative principles that democracies ought not to be fighting among themselves.

Our unit of analysis will be pairs of countries per year, or the dyad-year. That is, we will look at each pair of countries in each year to see whether they engaged in any kind of militarized dispute. Over the period 1946 to 1986 the international system grew from about 50 states to about 160. With an average of just over 110 countries per year, that gives us almost 265,000 dyad-years to study—a very formidable task. Fortunately, the job is more manageable since the vast majority of those dyads are nearly irrelevant. The countries comprising them were too far apart and too weak militarily, and had too few serious interests potentially in conflict, plausibly to engage in any militarized diplomatic dispute. Contiguity and major power involvement are the two most important static factors accounting for the likelihood of war between any pair of states (Bremer 1992a). Thus if we limit the analysis to pairs of states that are directly or indirectly contiguous, or in which one member of the pair is a major power ("contiguity" and "major power" are defined below) we have a total of 36,162 dyad-years. Disputes occurred in 714 of these according to one of the data sets used here, and in 448 according to the other—these sets, and the reasons for using two of them, will be discussed shortly.

Some disputes do of course arise between "implausible" pairs. They include some involving minor European powers (e.g., Belgium, the Netherlands) and former colonies, and some states taking part in distant collective security actions such as those in Korea and Vietnam. In spite of dropping all but about 12 percent of total dyad-years, the list of plausible pairs retains 74 percent of the disputes in the first data set, and 80 percent in the other one. In the more comprehensive data (714 disputes) it picks up 78 percent of all the disputes democracies engaged in with anyone, and all but one of the total fifteen disputes between democracies. Thus we certainly have not biased our case selection in favor of the hypothesis, and the refined "universe" of politically relevant dyads is both theoretically appropriate and manageable.

Disputes. We want to explain patterns of conflict. The conflict data are drawn from two different and recently completed data sets, compiled for somewhat different analytical purposes using somewhat different definitions. The use of both sets allows us to establish whether the conclusions we draw about the causes of conflict are robust; that is, whether they remain consistent even when some changes in the measures of conflict and war are introduced. The more robust the results are to changes—in measures of the influencing factors as well as those of conflict—the more confidence we can have in the generalization.

One of these data sets—already employed in the simple table 1.2 appearing in the first chapter—is the Militarized Interstate Disputes (MID) data from the Correlates of War (COW) project.[2] A militarized interstate dispute is defined as "a set of interactions between or among states involving threats to use military force, displays of military force, or actual uses of force. To be included, these acts must be explicit, overt, nonaccidental, and government sanctioned" (Gochman and Maoz 1984, 586). The MID data list the starting and ending date for each dispute, the states that participated on each side, and the highest level of hostility each state reached in the course of the dispute. We include all the dyads involved in any dispute; thus a dispute with three states on one side and four on the other makes twelve dispute dyads.

We use the dispute data in two forms. First, we identify each dyad-year in either-or terms, as having some kind of dispute or none. In doing so we include both disputes begun in this year and ongoing disputes that continued into this year from a previous one. This variable is called *dispute involvement*. Second, we record for each dyad the highest level of hostility reached by either member of the dyad in that particular year, using a five-level scale of hostility.[3] This becomes *dispute escalation*.

The other set of conflict data was collected by the International Crisis Behavior (ICB) project (Brecher, Wilkenfeld, and Moser 1988; Brecher and Wilkenfeld 1989). Its compilers identify an international crisis by "an increase in the intensity of disruptive interaction between two or more adversaries, with a high probability of military hostilities. . . . The higher-than-normal conflictual interactions destabilize the existing relationships of the adversaries and pose a challenge to the existing structure of an international system—global, dominant, and/or subsystem" (Brecher and Wilkenfeld 1989, 5). Levels of hostility for international crises are the same as for disputes in the MID data, and are used the same way. The ICB data are fully described in the sources just given.

The two data sets are not, however, strongly related. Due to different definitions and criteria, among politically relevant dyads there are 959 MID conflicts begun or underway (multiyear disputes counted more than once); only 260 (27 percent) of these are identified by the ICB data set. This is not surprising, given the latter's concern with "a high probability of military hostilities" and the likelihood that many MIDs did not carry (and, being often symbolic acts in a bargaining process, were in many cases not intended to carry) any great likelihood of escalating to actual violence and fatalities. It is also true, however, that out of the 359 politically relevant crisis dyads identified by the ICB listing, only 260 (72 percent) were to be found in the MID data. This does not mean that either set is inaccurate; rather, they vary enough in how they identify cases for us to use the two data sets as a check on how robust our results are.

WHAT INFLUENCES CONFLICT?

Democracy.   With conflict as the dependent variable to be explained, our foremost independent variable as a potential influence on conflict is of course form of government, or regime. Our primary source here is the Polity II data by Gurr, Jaggers, and Moore (1989). It updates and extends data collected earlier by Gurr (1974, 1978) based on the regime classification of Eckstein and Gurr (1975). We defined the type of regime using a three-step procedure:

First, following Gurr et al. (1989), we defined political systems in terms of a combination of (a) competitiveness of political participation, (b) regulation of participation, (c) competitiveness of executive recruitment, (d) openness of executive recruitment, and (e) constraints on the chief executive. Combining these dimensions produced one 11-point scale for the level of democracy (*DEM*) and another for autocracy (*AUT*).

Second, because the Eckstein-Gurr conception of regime type is not linear, a state can have mixed characteristics. Some features may be typically democratic and, at the same time, others can be highly autocratic. We therefore created a *continuous* index that takes into account both democratic and authoritarian features and also the level of power concentration, which reflects the extent to which the state authorities exercise effective control over their constituents. (This measure of power monopolization by the authorities is also an 11-point scale from 0 to 10 [Gurr et al., 1989, pp. 39–40].) The regime index (*REG*) then is defined as *PCON* (*DEM* − *AUT*), with a possible range from −100 (most autocratic) to +100 (most democratic). Toward the extremes these judgments are not problematic, but around zero the regime characteristics are not clearly defined. Either democratic and authoritarian features cancel each other out (for example, if a state scores fairly high on both scales), or the power concentration score is so low that neither the predominantly democratic nor the predominantly autocratic characteristics of a regime can effectively express themselves. This situation is common in highly unstable political systems or in systems undergoing rapid change. Though more recent than these codings, conditions in the Soviet Union/Russia in 1990–92 offer a good example.

Since our analysis requires a dyadic characterization of regime type, we needed to convert the individual scores into a joint democratization one. The joint measure (*JOINREG*) must reflect two things simultaneously:

How democratic or undemocratic are the members of the dyad, and how different or similar in their regime types are the two states? Our measure is calculated as:

$$\frac{REG_h + REG_l}{REG_h - REG_l + 1}$$

where REG_h is the regime score of the member with the higher score and REG_l that of the lower-scoring member.[4]

Our continuous variable improves on most previous research on the relationship between democracy and international conflict, which usually dealt with a simple democracy or nondemocracy dichotomy. Nevertheless, we also need to derive a *discrete* (dichotomous) measure from the continuous regime score. Whereas our hypothesis, like that of Rummel (1983, 1985), says that the more democratic both members of the pair are they less likely they are to become embroiled in a militarized dispute, other hypotheses simply posit a difference in conflict behavior between different regime categories. Moreover, our continuous index is generated by an arithmetic operation performed on ordinal variables. Since the ordinal variables (*DEM, AUT, CON*) are not linear within categories, the overall regime index may be only crudely reliable—across certain ranges but not for specific values as, say, between states scoring 35 and 50.

We use a threshold of +30 as the lower limit for democratic states, and categorize all states with scores of −25 or lower as authoritarian. States scoring between these two limits, with a mixture of democratic and autocratic characteristics or a low concentration of power, are termed anocratic (Gurr 1974; Maoz and Abdolali 1989). We made these cuts after comparing a random sample of states, characterized intuitively as democracies, with the computed scores, and identified the most reasonable cutoff point. India, which until 1975 had a democracy score of 30, provided a litmus test. In 1975 Indira Gandhi declared emergency measures that caused India's score to drop to 27, rising back to 30 only in 1980 when the emergency measures were lifted. This seems valid on its face, since most observers regard India as generally democratic (if imperfectly so), but not during the period of emergency rule. With the simple categorization of each regime as democratic or not (combining authoritarian and anocratic), we use just a dichotomous variable of democratic-democratic and all other pairs.[5] Save for a few anomalies, most of the cutoffs look reasonable; the appendix shows our universe of states, with their regime categories.

As a further check we created an alternative scheme of regime categories from data of Arthur Banks (1986), reprinted in the Polity II data set. We identified democratic states as those in which both the executive and the legislature were selected in a competitive election, and in which the legislature was at least partially effective. This simpler categorization, compiled earlier than that of Gurr et al. and less fully documented, is probably less discriminating. A cross-tabulation of the Gurr-derived measure with the Banks-derived one showed a moderate relationship. This suggests, as with the two conflict data sets, that each measures a similar concept, but with enough difference to provide a good test as to whether our findings are robust.[6] We performed most analyses with both data sets, but since the results were not markedly different, in the tables to follow we will show only those with the preferred Gurr data.

To begin with, table 4.1 offers a little more nuance to the presentation in table 1.2. Table 4.1 is merely an expansion, providing more detail, of the earlier table, using our categories for level of hostility and type of political system, and based on the MID dispute data. It shows with greater specificity how likely democracies were to have disputes with various other kinds of states, expanding the second column in table 1.2 into five columns. It does so by comparing the actual frequency of different kinds of disputes with the frequency to be expected if disputes were distributed simply according to the number of dyads in each category.

As in the earlier presentation, column 1 shows the frequency of various disputes between democracies. Disputes become rarer—relative to what would be expected by a chance distribution of disputes—as one moves down the table to greater levels of violence. Note that there is little difference between the actual and expected incidence of disputes between non-democracies (column 4) except for the large number in the least violent category—threats. Democracies, by contrast, are less likely than expected to engage in disputes with nondemocracies stopping at the level of merely threats, but somewhat more likely to engage in higher levels of dispute—with the greatest positive discrepancy for wars with autocracies. *The less democratic a democracy's adversary is, the greater the likelihood of a high-level militarized dispute.* Overall, there is little to support the proposition that democracies' international relations are especially peaceful, but only that their relations with each other are relatively very peaceful.

Already—in the rarity of even the lower-level disputes characterized by the symbolic signaling typical of bargaining behavior in the structural model—we have evidence of *normative* restraints on disputes between democracies. We also have some evidence of the importance of perceptions of the character of other regimes. The anocratic states are those near the middle of the scale from democracy to autocracy. They are frequently unstable regimes in transition; an adversary has incomplete information about what kind of regime it is facing. As predicted by the theory, disputes between democracies and nondemocracies are more common than expected. But, reflecting the uncertainty about what kind of regime one is

TABLE 4.1
Expected and Observed Frequencies of Dispute for Different Types of Politically
Relevant Dyads, 1946–1986

		Dem- Dem	Dem- Anoc	Dem- Aut	Anoc- Anoc	Anoc- Aut	Aut- Aut
Threats	Actual	2	3	4	7	8	17
	Expected	5.6	6.9	11.4	1.7	7.5	7.9
Display	Actual	4	27	38	6	24	21
	Expected	12.5	23.1	34.9	4.0	21.8	23.7
Use of	Actual	8	90	138	47	151	87
Force	Expected	23.3	85.9	129.3	49.0	135.7	97.9
War	Actual	0	5	14	0	7	6
	Expected	4.3	5.5	8.9	1.3	5.9	6.1
TOTALS	Actual	14	125	194	60	190	131
	Expected	45.7	121.4	184.5	56	170.9	135.6

dealing with, actual disputes also occur more often, relative to the expected frequency, between autocracies and anocracies, and between pairs
of anocracies.

Degree of Institutional Constraint. To create the variables needed to
distinguish between the two theoretical models for explaining the rarity
of conflict between democracies we used several key attributes identified
by Eckstein and Gurr (1975) and Gurr et al. (1989). We constructed a
multifaceted measure composed of four related but distinguishable elements, in which an executive is subject to the least restraint under conditions when it can operate by one-person rule, without institutionalized
constraint on the executive, in a centralized political system, and in which
the government exerts wide control over economic and social life.

Degree of concentration of power is on a five-point ordinal scale from
states where one-person rule prevails to "those in which some kind of
assent is required, . . . by especially prestigious minorities" on to those
requiring the assent of "numerical majorities, or virtually all" of the citizens (Eckstein and Gurr 1975, 375).

Degree of executive constraint represents, on a seven-point ordinal
scale, the extent to which the executive must abide by clear and distinguishable rules—institutionalized constraints—while making policy decisions, whether the chief executive be an individual or a collectivity.

Centralization distinguishes between unitary and federal political systems on a three-point ordinal scale. As Gurr et al. (1989, 21) point out,
"federal polities have greater complexity of Conformation than do cen-

tralized polities. Opportunities for participation also tend to be higher in federal systems, and regional units of government potentially are more responsive to local inputs than are centralized governments." Federalism probably is a greater constraint on domestic policy, but even on foreign policy it somewhat restricts the ability to mobilize economic and political resources rapidly in the event of a serious international dispute. It also provides an institutional base from which regional political leaders can challenge government policy.

Scope of government actions concerns the state's ability to mobilize resources. It "refers to the extent to which all levels of government combined—national, regional, and local—attempt to regulate and organize the economic and social life of the citizens and subjects of the state." Its seven-point scale ranges from totalitarian ("governments that directly organize and control almost all aspects of social and political life") to minimal ("governments whose operations are largely or wholly limited to such core functions as maintenance of internal security and administration of justice"; Gurr et al. 1989, 21–22).

These four measures added together produce an overall scale of institutional constraints ranging from 4 (a totalitarian political system lacking any form of constraint) to 22 (a highly constrained political system in which the government must go through a long, complex, and highly uncertain political process to invoke national action). As with regime type, we divided the scale into three levels (4–10, 11–15, and 16–25), and for a dichotomized variable defined high constraint as 16 and above. This measure is related to, but substantially diverges from, the measure of democracy, suggesting that we can validly use it as an independent measure to test the structural explanation.[7] Democracies exhibiting low constraint include the French Fifth Republic under Charles de Gaulle and Georges Pompidou, Venezuela after the 1958 overthrow of the military dictatorship, and Argentina under the elected government of Juan and Eva Perón in 1973–75. Nondemocratic governments operating under rather high constraint include Pakistan shortly after independence, Indonesia into 1956, and several Middle Eastern states (King Hussein's Jordan is the clearest example) in the 1950s.

Democratic Norms.   The extent to which the norms of democratic behavior have become accepted in a political regime may not be closely related to states' political structures. For example, a system may lack a democratic institutional structure, yet be widely regarded by its citizens as politically legitimate; such a regime would require little overt suppression of opposition in ways obviously violating democratic norms. On the other hand, a democratic government undergoing violent insurgency and a fundamental crisis of legitmacy might resort to political and military suppression in the name of maintaining public order, and indeed of maintaining democratic institutions.

We employ two related but distinct ways of measuring the extent to which democratic or other kinds of norms operate in a society. The first is through the concept of political stability. It takes time for norms to develop. A society that undergoes fundamental change requires a considerable period of time to develop new norms of political conduct, and for the citizens to internalize those norms and become accustomed to them. Thus, the longer a given political system or regime exists without fundamental change, the more likely norms of political conduct—be they democratic or nondemocratic norms—are to form and to influence the foreign policy codes of conduct of the regime.

We then can measure the extent of normative influence on conflict behavior as the persistence of its political regime in years (Gurr 1974). By this conception, democracies that are highly stable—i.e., have kept their fundamental political structure for a relatively long time—are more influenced by democratic norms than are democracies that have existed only a short while. Conflicts between stable democracies should therefore be far less common than are conflicts between democracies in which one, or especially both, are unstable. Note that our stability measure is not fully distinct from structures. It can represent an institutional constraint in the limited sense that an unstable democracy is subject to overthrow that would release the structural restraints on leaders. Also, we are measuring the duration of political institutions more directly than the norms that support them. Nevertheless, this index still is separable from the indices we introduced above to measure the strength and breadth of institutions.

An alternative measure of democratic norms is perhaps more direct: the level of violent internal social and political conflict. All states experience some degree of social conflict. The difference between states where democratic norms prevail and those where they do not, however, is twofold. First, in democracies these conflicts are predominantly nonviolent; both challengers and defenders of the status quo usually find peaceful avenues for expressing their differences. But in nondemocratic systems, conflicts are likely to become violent because most forms of peaceful protest are forbidden. Second, in a democracy the government rarely needs to use force to resolve conflicts; order can be maintained without violent suppression. In nondemocratic states, however, overt state violence is often used to maintain order. Democratic norms are tested in times of political unrest and instability.

Therefore we measure the extent to which democratic norms are influential by looking at the extent of domestic political and social unrest, and at the ways the regime treats unrest. Specifically, we look at the amount of political violence within a state, using two different measures to test for robustness. First, from Taylor and Jodice (1983) we use two related indicators: the annual number of violent political deaths indicates the general level of internal violence in a state, and the number of political executions indicates the degree of regime-initiated violence. The measure of democratic norms is the number of deaths from internal political violence (or of political executions) over the last five years per state, averaged over the dyad. For a dichotomized variable the scale is divided at the mean.[8]

An alternative source, producing the measure referred to as political conflict in the tables, is the Conflict and Peace Data Bank (COPDAB) data on domestic political events (Azar 1980). On a 14-point scale, scores 1–7 represent high to low cooperation, 8 is for neutral actions, and 9–14 represent ascending levels of conflict. Since the unit of analysis in these data is an event, we first had to aggregate conflictual and cooperative events. We added the scale values for each of the conflictual events and for each of the cooperative ones separately over the entire year, and produced a five-year average like that from deaths and executions.[9] When used in dichotomous form the scale is divided at the mean.

We also need measures for the variables specified in the alternative theories that say the effect of democracy is spurious.

Wealth. Average levels of income were rising over the period, so we needed a measure of relative rather than absolute wealth. Since the standard economic data are delineated in U.S. dollars, we simply used the U.S. per capita gross domestic product, determined by a careful cross-national comparison (Summers and Heston 1988), as a baseline for each year. The income data produced a continuous dyadic measure computed in the same way as that for pairs of regimes.

Economic Growth. Economic growth is measured as the percentage rate of change in a state's GDP (in constant prices) from one year to the next, using the average growth rate over the preceding three years.[10]

Alliance. Alliance data were compiled as part of the COW project (Singer and Small 1968), to which we added a category for indirect alliance with the United States. We reason, with Weede (1983), that this kind of alliance, perhaps because of restraints imposed by the leading power, may moderate disputes between indirectly linked states. An indirect alliance arises where two states that have no direct alliance with each other are each individually allied with the United States. Examples are the United Kingdom and Argentina, and Egypt and Israel after 1983.[11] The dichotomous break is between any direct or indirect alliance and none.

Contiguity. Here too we used a revised version of a COW data set listing several degrees of contiguity, to which we added colonial contiguity for cases where one state borders another's colony or trusteeship.[12] Conceptually, contiguity is meant to identify states with the capability and possible reason for fighting each other, so for this purpose we added all dyads including a major power with the ability to exert military force beyond contiguous states. We identified the United States, United Kingdom, France, and the Soviet Union as major powers, and (perhaps more arguably) followed the COW designation of China as a major power from 1950 onward. This procedure is close to that employed by Weede (1983) in testing for conflict only among "strategically interdependent" dyads. The major difference is our inclusion of France and Britain to pick up their many postcolonial conflicts. We make a dichotomous break between noncontiguous dyads involving a great power and all types of true geographic contiguity.

Military Capability Ratio. Are two states with similar power bases more, or less, likely to dispute with each other than are states whose inherent economic and military capabilities are very disparate? This question has been vigorously debated, without a clear resolution. Theories of hegemonic stability or "power transition" (Gilpin 1981, Organski 1968) urge that great power disparity, by making it clear who will likely win if push comes to shove, generally discourages war. Others in the "balance of power" tradition (e.g., Claude 1962) argue that uncertainty about the probable outcome of war between evenly matched states will promote restraint. The situation is complex in many instances, depending for example on whether decisionmakers are risk-prone or risk-averse. It is also likely that the effect is different for lower-level militarized disputes than for actual war. For example, weak states may be willing to threaten or display military force to test the resolve of strong ones, but ready to back down before using force in a clash that inflicts casualties. Bremer (1992a) and Geller and Jones (1991) have recently found that power disparity is associated with a lower probability of war than is near-equality of power.

While it is hard to sort the motivations out convincingly at the theoretical level, they may confound and confuse an analysis. Power disparity thus represents one final variable that must be included as a control. We use a widely employed military capability index (Singer, Bremer, and Stuckey 1972) that weights about equally (two separate indices for each) military forces in being, economic strength, and demography, suggesting both capacity to win a short war with existing military forces and long-term capacity to win a war of attrition. This measure only imperfectly reflects the perception or reality of military power (Russett and Starr 1992, 145–46), but is adequate as an interval measure of the ratio of the capability score of the stronger state to the weaker, and dichotomously with a break where the composite score of the stronger state is more than one-and-a-half that of the weaker.

DEMOCRACY MATTERS

We now move to some statistical analyses to test competing hypotheses. We will be looking both at the relative incidence of disputes (at all levels of dispute) between various pairs of nation states, and at the likelihood of war or escalation to war. We begin with an analysis of the various factors that might produce a spurious relationship between democratic pairs and peaceful pairs. The form of analysis employed, logistic regression, is suitable for identifying the independent effect of each potential explanatory variable while holding all the others constant. Logistic regression is similar to the more familiar multiple regression analysis, but, unlike the latter, is suited to a dependent variable that is dichotomous (war/no war; dispute/no dispute) rather than continuous.[13] The independent or explanatory variables may be dichotomous, categorical (with three or more categories), or continuous. The tables will usually present the results with most independent variables in either continuous or categorical form, representing the least loss of information. Most analysis was also done by analyzing all the independent variables as dichotomized. Unless otherwise indicated, it confirmed the essential findings in the tables.

We then proceed to an effort to examine jointly the structural/institutional and cultural/normative models of democratic peace, so as to find out whether one is supported consistently while the other is rejected consistently.[14] If this were the case, we could make a clearer judgment about just how the causal mechanism of peace between democracies operates. But since those results turn out to be only suggestive and not clearcut, with some support for each model, we then move to a third analysis with a critical test.

Table 4.2 and table 4.3 provide the first test, addressing the hypothesis 1 above. Each table shows the effect of the independent variables, measured in continuous terms except for alliance and contiguity, on the dependent variables. Tests with dichotomized measures of democracy give essentially the same results and need not be shown. Several variables that might confound the relationship between democracy and participation in militarized disputes are controlled for. As a check on whether the results are stable and robust, these tables also use measures of the dependent variable from both the MID and the ICB data sets. In table 4.2 the dependent variable is the presence or absence of a dispute (crisis) between a pair of states in a given year. In table 4.3, the dependent variable is the five-point ordinal scale from 0 representing no dispute (crisis) to 4 for full-scale war. Each cell shows the coefficient for the effect of a one-unit change in each independent variable. Since the measurement units for different variables differ greatly, to compare the relative impact of each

TABLE 4.2
Effects of Joint Democracy and Potentially Confounding Factors on Conflict
Involvement

Independent Variable	Militarized Disputes	International Crises
Democracy	−0.004 (.002)**	−0.005 (.003)**
Wealth	−0.022 (.007)**	−0.040 (.016)*
Growth	−0.107 (.021)**	−0.132 (.032)**
Alliance	−0.517 (.105)**	−0.339 (.165)*
Contiguity	1.419 (.108)**	1.964 (.190)**
Capability Ratio	−0.007 (.001)**	−0.002 (.001)**
N = 19,020 Gamma =	0.54	0.59

Note: Entries are parameter estimates; standard errors are in parentheses. Gamma is a statistical measure of the difference between the observed and expected values throughout the analysis, analogous to R^2 in multiple regression (Hildebrand et al. 1977).
  * $p < 0.05$. ** $p < 0.01$.

TABLE 4.3
Effects of Joint Democracy and Potentially Confounding Factors on Conflict
Escalation

Independent Variable	Militarized Disputes	International Crises
Democracy	−0.004 (.002)*	−0.007 (.003)*
Wealth	−0.022 (.007)**	−0.040 (.016)*
Growth	−0.111 (.021)**	−0.139 (.031)**
Alliance	0.258 (.053)**	−0.336 (.163)*
Contiguity	0.710 (.054)**	1.962 (.190)**
Capability Ratio	−0.007 (.001)**	−0.002 (.001)*
N = 19,020 Gamma =	0.54	0.59

Note: Entries are parameter estimates; standard errors are in parentheses.
  * $p > 0.05$. ** $p > 0.01$.

independent variable on the outcome we look at the ratio between the coefficient and its standard error (in parentheses).[15]

The evidence in table 4.2 clearly supports the hypothesis as it postulated the effect of democracy on dispute or crisis involvement. A strong, independent, and robust role for democracy is evident, even after the potentially confounding variables also show a significant effect. The importance of democracy is apparent in both conflict data sets.

Table 4.3 shows similarly strong support for the hypothesis as it relates to dispute or crisis escalation. Democracy significantly affects escalation, even when we control for the significant effects of all the potentially confounding variables. Democracies are far less likely to escalate disputes against other democracies than are states that have other types of political systems. Analyses performed on the same dependent variables using the Banks measure of democracy yielded consistently similar results.

Taken together, these findings confirm a simpler bivariate analysis published earlier (Maoz and Russett 1992). All the potentially confounding variables are related to both the occurrence and the escalation of conflict. Not surprisingly, power relationships matter a lot. Great disparities in power sharply discourage the expression of diplomatic disputes in any militarized form. As Thucydides' Athenians put it in the Melian dialogue, "the strong do what they have the power to do, and the weak accept what they have to accept" (1954/1972, 5.89). Contiguity also is important, with its power-related emphasis on capability as well as on the possibility of incentive for dispute. Other variables also usually make a significant difference. Thus competing theories find solid support. Rich, rapidly growing, and noncontiguous states are less likely to fight one another, and the analysis corroborates Bremer's (1992a) findings regarding the effect of alliance on dispute involvement and dispute escalation. Whereas the bivariate relationship between alliance and conflict between states is positive (Maoz and Russett 1992), when other relevant variables are controlled for, allied parties are less likely to fight than chance alone would predict.

Yet even after all these confounding variables are taken into account, when both states are democratic that has a significant effect on dispute occurrence and escalation. Its effect is independent; statistical tests not shown here indicate that it does not have to work in interaction with such influences as wealth and growth.[16] *And in the tables the effect is continuous, in that the more democratic each member of a dyad is, the less likely is conflict between them.* That is important, because it picks up the effect of the moderate democratization common among Third World states that in the categorical terms are labeled anocracies. Partial democratization of these "non-Western" states therefore significantly reduces their likelihood of conflict with other partially or substantially democratic states. The effect of democratic peace is widespread, and it is not spurious.

NORMS AND INSTITUTIONAL CONSTRAINTS

We can now compare support for the two competing models for explaining the democratic peace. Table 4.4 shows the effects of democratic norms and institutional constraints on the occurrence of conflicts. Equations for escalation produced very similar results and need not be shown. Norms are measured once through political stability (regime duration) and once through the frequency of political executions. The table reports only a summary of the equations we computed for this analysis. Other tests used alternative indicators of democratic norms (i.e., deaths from political violence, and level of domestic conflict from COPDAB).[17]

TABLE 4.4
Effects of Joint Democracy and Potentially Confounding Factors on Conflict
Involvement

Independent Variable	Militarized Disputes	International Crises
Political Stability	−0.051 (.013)**	−0.112 (.032)**
Institutional Constraints	−0.012 (.004)**	−0.020 (.007)**
Democracy	−1.783 (.270)**	−1.404 (.447)**
Wealth	0.001 (.006)	−0.013 (.014)
Capability Ratio	−0.009 (.001)**	0.002 (.001)*
Alliance	−0.532 (.111)**	−0.289 (.177)
Contiguity	1.166 (.106)**	1.809 (.190)**
N = 18,762 Gamma =	0.58	0.63
Political Executions	0.236 (0.45)**	0.146 (.067)*
Institutional Constraints	−0.007 (.004)*	−0.225 (.008)**
Democracy	−2.007 (.313)**	−1.256 (.457)**
Wealth	0.007 (.007)	−0.006 (.013)
Capability Ratio	−0.009 (.001)**	−0.002 (.001)**
Alliance	−0.627 (.117)**	−0.405 (.184)**
Contiguity	1.115 (.111)**	1.718 (.195)**
N = 17,317 Gamma =	0.58	0.61

Note: Entries are parameter estimates; standard errors are in parentheses
* $p < 0.05$. ** $p < 0.01$.

The results support both models: in virtually every equation, both democratic norms (however measured) and institutional constraints reduce involvement in disputes and the likelihood that disputes will escalate. Again the result is highly robust. It holds across conflict data sets, and is not sensitive to different measures of the independent variables. The measures of norms and institutions are significant even when the measure of democracy itself is included, and when we control for the potentially confounding factors that have been mentioned by other theories as nonregime causes of democratic peace. When the institutional and normative measures are dichotomized, however (low and high, not shown in the table), the constraints indicator is no longer statistically significant with either dispute involvement or escalation.

This initial piece of evidence suggests that institutional constraints may not offer as good an explanation as democratic norms for the lack of conflict between democracies, since they are not as robust predictors of conflict behavior. But this is not sufficient evidence for choosing between the models. We must move to the critical test.

To do so we focus on the two categories of dyads in which the two models give opposite predictions:

Dyad's Characteristics

Political Stability	Political Constraints	Prediction of Normative Model	Prediction of Structural Model
Low	Low	Conflict	Conflict
Low	High	Conflict	Low Conflict
High	Low	Low Conflict	Conflict
High	High	Low Conflict	Low Conflict

Obviously the cases in the two middle rows, with conflicting predictions, are those that require a critical test. We also control for democracy here. Both models imply that the relationship between political constraints or democratic norms and conflict behavior is independent of whether or not the states are democracies. If this does not hold, and the introduction of democracy significantly alters the relationship between the independent and dependent variables, then the relationship of the critical variable derived from a specific model may be spurious.

The critical test examines the differences in the probabilities of conflict in the cases denoted by the second row above (low level of norms, high political constraints) and the third (high norms, low constraints). If the probability of conflict among the cases in row 2 is significantly lower than the probability of conflict among cases in row 3, then the structural/institutional model is superior to the cultural/normative one. If, however, the probability of conflict in row 2 cases is significantly higher than in row 3, the normative model provides a better account of the data. Should the difference between them not be statistically significant, then the critical test would be inconclusive.

To provide a focused analysis of which model offers a better account we conducted a set of log-linear analyses of the dichotomized versions of the independent variables, using multiple indicators of democratic norms (stability, executions, and the COPDAB domestic conflict data). We performed the analyses first only with measures of norms and of institutional constraints as independent variables; then we also controlled for democracy to see if it made a separate contribution.

Table 4.5 shows the summary statistics of these analyses. The normative model is significantly related to the (logged) likelihood of conflict and war in virtually all the comparisons, whatever measure of norms we use.[18] In the table as a whole, normative constraints are significant in all but one of the twenty-four cells, whereas institutional ones are significant only in eleven. Also, introducing democracy into the second half of table 4.5 eliminates many of the previously significant parameter estimates for constraints.

Normative restaints help prevent both the occurrence of conflict and the occurrence of war. But the relationship of the structural model to

TABLE 4.5
The Effects of Democratic Norms, Institutional Constraints, and Regime Type on
Conflict Involvement and War Involvement

Independent Variable	N	Militarized Disputes	International Crises
		Effects on Conflict Involvement	
Stability	26,129	−0.401 (.058)**	−0.525 (.110)**
Constraint		−0.211 (.051)**	−0.223 (.089)**
Executions	22,870	0.416 (.041)**	0.391 (.068)**
Constraint		−0.890 (.056)	−0.108 (.095)
Domestic Conflict	16,254	0.178 (.045)**	0.191 (.079)**
Constraint		−0.100 (.058)	−0.129 (.105)
		Effects on War Involvement	
Stability	26,129	−1.528 (.503)**	−0.709 (.231)**
Constraint		−0.977 (.293)**	−0.739 (.231)**
Executions	22,870	0.715 (.127)**	0.426 (.118)**
Constraint		−0.795 (.298)**	−0.591 (.236)**
Domestic Conflict	16,254	0.511 (.156)**	0.245 (.129)*
Constraint		−0.674 (.299)*	−0.667 (.300)*
		Effects on Conflict Involvement	
Stability	26,129	−0.306 (.058)**	−0.437 (.110)**
Constraint		0.013 (.052)	−0.025 (.091)
Democracy		−0.985 (.128)**	−0.900 (.215)**
Executions	22,870	0.339 (.041)**	0.322 (.068)**
Constraint		0.124 (.057)	−0.087 (.097)
Democracy		−1.031 (.146)**	−0.864 (.218)**
Domestic Conflict	16,254	0.131 (.044)**	0.146 (.072)*
Constraint		0.109 (.059)	−0.077 (.107)
Democracy		−1.037 (.157)**	−1.010 (.300)**
		Effects on War Involvement	
Stability	26,129	−1.504 (.503)**	−0.665 (.230)**
Constraint		−0.790 (.293)**	−0.508 (.230)**
Democracy		−4.750 (—)**ᵃ	−4.927 (—)**ᵃ
Executions	22,870	0.657 (.126)**	0.364 (.116)**
Constraint		−0.585 (.295)*	−0.335 (.233)
Democracy		−4.716 (—)**ᵃ	−4.991 (—)**ᵃ
Domestic Conflict	16,262	1.054 (.155)	1.314 (.149)*
Constraint		−0.468 (.297)	−0.429 (.299)
Democracy		−4.926 (—)**ᵃ	−4.968 (—)**ᵃ

Note: Entries are parameter estimates; standard errors are in parentheses.
[a] Standard error cannot be estimated due to zero value in one category of the dependent variable. Chi-square statistics are infinite.
* $p < 0.05$. ** $p < 0.01$.

conflict occurrence is not nearly as robust. Institutional constraints prevent escalation to war, but they do not by themselves prevent states from becoming involved in lower-level conflicts. The structural model's implications for encouraging signals of toughness and commitment in bargaining, as laid out in the previous chapter, explain why. Constraining institutions alone do not prevent that kind of bargaining behavior; they may in fact encourage it so long as each side knows that its adversary will be tightly constrained from escalating the dispute all the way up to war. Insofar as democracies only rarely engage in conflicts at all, normative restraints seem to deserve the greater credit.

Table 4.6 uses information from the table 4.5 analyses in the critical test format, to give us a sense of how the models perform. The lower half of the table also shows what happens when the joint regime type of each dyad is controlled for in the analysis. In each half of the table we first explain the occurrence of conflicts, and then the occurrence of war. For simplicity we omit the individual cells and show just the standarized estimates of effects.

TABLE 4.6
Critical Test of the Effects of Democratic Norms, Institutional Constraints, and Regime Type on Conflict Involvement and War Involvement

	Probability of Disputes	Probability of Crises
Effects on Conflict Involvement		
Stability		
Low Norms/High Constraint	2.89%	0.95%
High Norms/Low Constraint	2.11%	0.56%
N = 26,129	Z-Score = −2.07**	Z-Score = −1.87**
Executions		
Low Norms/High Constraint	5.71%	1.95%
High Norms/Low Constraint	2.27%	0.82%
N = 22,870	Z-Score = −3.76**	Z-Score = −2.08**
Domestic Conflict		
Low Norms/High Constraint	3.96%	1.20%
High Norms/Low Constraint	1.97%	0.38%
N = 16,262	Z-Score = −5.37**	Z-Score = −4.51**
Effects on War Involvement		
Stability		
Low Norms/High Constraint	0.08%	0.14%
High Norms/Low Constraint	0.03%	0.15%
N = 26,129	Z-Score = −0.96	Z-Score = 0.09
Executions		
Low Norms/High Constraint	0.15%	0.20%
High Norms/Low Constraint	0.20%	0.30%
N = 22,870	Z-Score = 0.35	Z-Score = 0.58
Domestic Conflict		
Low Norms/High Constraint	0.56%	0.42%
High Norms/Low Constraint	0.00%	0.00%
N = 16,262	Z-Score = −6.18**	Z-Score = −5.30**

TABLE 4.6 (*cont.*)

	Probability of Disputes	Probability of Crises
Controlling for Regime Type		
Effects on Conflict Involvement		
Not Both Democracies: Stability		
Low Norms/High Constraint	3.82%	1.29%
High Norms/Low Constraint	2.16%	0.58%
	Z-Score = −3.56**	Z-Score = −2.68**
Among Democracies: Stability		
Low Norms/High Constraint	0.95%	0.03%
High Norms/Low Constraint	0.00%	0.00%
	Z-Score = −3.32**	Z-Score = −1.73**
Not Both Democracies: Executions		
Low Norms/High Constraint	5.91%	2.12%
High Norms/Low Constraint	2.48%	0.89%
	Z-Score = −3.58**	Z-Score = −2.08**
Among Democracies: Executions		
Low Norms/High Constraint	0.25%	0.00%
High Norms/Low Constraint	0.00%	0.00%
	Z-Score = −1.01**	No Z-Score
Not Both Democracies: Domestic Conflict		
Low Norms/High Constraint	3.31%	0.64%
High Norms/Low Constraint	4.10%	1.24%
	Z-Score = 1.34	Z-Score = 2.16**
Among Democracies: Domestic Conflict		
Low Norms/High Constraint	0.85%	0.15%
High Norms/Low Constraint	0.00%	0.00%
	Z-Score = −3.33**	Z-Score = −1.42
Effects on War Involvement		
Not Both Democracies: Stability		
Low Norms/High Constraint	0.12%	0.21%
High Norms/Low Constraint	0.03%	0.15%
	Z-Score = −1.21	Z-Score = −0.49
Not Both Democracies: Executions		
Low Norms/High Constraint	0.16%	0.00%
High Norms/Low Constraint	0.22%	0.00%
	Z-Score = 0.38	No Z-Score
Not Both Democracies: Domestic Conflict		
Low Norms/High Constraint	0.58%	0.09%
High Norms/Low Constraint	0.00%	0.00%
	Z-Score = −6.18**	Z-Score = −2.45**

Notes: Z-Scores represent a difference of proportions test. Negative scores imply that the normative model provides a better explanation than does the structural model; positive scores imply that the structural model provides the superior explanation.

There are no entries for effects on war involvement between democracies because there were no such wars.

* $p < 0.05$. ** $p < 0.01$.

The table shows the differences in the probabilities of conflict in the critical cases. It compares the frequency of conflict and war involvement (both dispute and crisis data) by pairs of states with the combination of low normative constraints and high institutional ones versus that of high normative constraints and low institutional ones. It strengthens our previous impression that the normative explanation is superior. In seventeen of the thirty separate tests, the probability of involvement when democratic norms are high and constraints are low is significantly below the probability of involvement when democratic norms are low and constraints are high (with only one test significantly the other way). As before—and as expected—the difference almost always appears for conflict involvement in general, and much less often for war involvement. The second part of the table, controlling for regime type, shows clearly that the three different measures of democratic political norms usually reduce significantly the odds of conflict between pairs of states—even when the institutional constraints on the regimes are low and even when at least one member of the pair is not democratic.

Overall, the results give strong support to hypothesis 1 about the effect of democracy in general and to hypothesis 2 about the effect of democratic norms, and weaker support to hypothesis 3 about institutional constraints. Whatever measures are used, almost always the cultural/normative model shows a consistent effect on conflict occurrence and war. The structural/institutional model sometimes provides a significant relationship but often does not. Moreover, in the critical situations—when one model suggests high conflict and the other low—the predictions of the cultural/normative model are more consistently borne out. Institutional constraints appear more important in preventing war than in preventing involvement in lower-level crises and disputes.

Even so, some pairs of states in both of which the executive is highly constrained did experience wars; for example, between Israel and Egypt in 1949, and the "Soccer War" between El Salvador and Honduras in 1969. The democracies in each of these pairs (Israel and El Salvador) were not yet stable; Israel, for instance, was newly independent. Moreover, their anocratic adversaries could not be characterized as stable either. No warring dyads, of course, were composed of two democratic states.

Statistical analysis of many cases rarely can provide a fully satisfying explanation of underlying political processes, and it would be a mistake to emphasize too strongly the subtlety or persuasiveness of the distinctions between cultural/normative and structural/institutional variables used here. Yet these results do suggest that the spread of democracy in international politics—currently far wider than in the period we just analyzed—can reduce the frequency of violent conflicts among nations. The realist top-down, outside-in view—that characteristics of the international system have far more influence on states' decisions for war and peace than do characteristics of the states themselves—misses a great deal. But to improve the prospects for peace, the norms of peaceful conflict resolution that can restrain new democracies must themselves be consolidated. To the degree that new democracies are stable over time, minimizing the resort to violence to settle their internal disputes, the better the chances for avoiding violence between them.

APPENDIX
STATES AND THEIR POLITICAL REGIMES, 1946–1986

Codings were derived by Zeev Maoz from Gurr et al. 1989. A few codings are doubtful, chiefly categorization as anocratic when the numeric score is just below the cutoff for democracy. But since the analysis proved very robust to differences in measures we chose not to recode Gurr's material on an ad hoc basis that might seem self-serving.

Afghanistan	1946–72	AUT	Brazil	1946–64	ANOC
	1973–79	ANOC		1965–73	AUT
	1980–86	AUT		1974–86	ANOC
Albania	1946–86	AUT	Bulgaria	1946	ANOC
Algeria	1963–86	AUT		1947–86	AUT
Angola	1975–86	ANOC	Burma	1948–51	ANOC
				1952–57	DEM
Argentina	1946–47	ANOC		1958–61	ANOC
	1948–54	AUT		1962–86	AUT
	1955–65	ANOC	Burundi	1962–65	ANOC
	1966–72	AUT		1966–86	AUT
	1973–75	DEM	Cambodia	1953–54	ANOC
	1976–81	AUT		1955–69	AUT
	1982	ANOC		1970–75	ANOC
	1983–86	DEM		1976–78	AUT
Australia	1946–86	DEM		1979–86	ANOC
Austria	1955–86	DEM	Cameroun	1961–72	ANOC
Bangladesh	1973–74	ANOC		1973–86	AUT
	1975	AUT	Canada	1946–86	DEM
	1976–86	ANOC	Central African Republic	1962–86	AUT
Belgium	1956–86	DEM			
Benin	1960–68	AUT	Chad	1962–74	AUT
	1969–73	ANOC		1975–86	ANOC
	1974–76	AUT	Chile	1946–73	ANOC
	1977–79	ANOC		1974–86	AUT
	1980–86	AUT	China	1946–86	AUT
Bhutan	1971–86	AUT	Colombia	1946–47	DEM
Bolivia	1946–86	ANOC		1948–56	AUT
Botswana	1966–86	DEM		1957–86	DEM

Congo (Brazzaville)	1961–86	ANOC		Germany, East	1955–86	AUT
				Germany, West	1955–86	DEM
Costa Rica	1946–86	DEM		Ghana	1960–68	AUT
Cuba	1946–54	ANOC			1969–71	ANOC
	1955–58	AUT			1972–75	AUT
	1959–60	ANOC			1976–80	ANOC
	1961–86	AUT			1981–86	AUT
Cyprus	1960–74	ANOC		Greece	1946–66	ANOC
	1975–86	DEM			1967–73	AUT
Czechoslovakia	1946	DEM			1974	ANOC
	1947	ANOC			1975–86	DEM
	1948–67	AUT		Guatemala	1946–49	DEM
	1968	ANOC			1950–53	ANOC
	1969–86	AUT			1954–56	AUT
Dahomey	1960–64	ANOC			1957–81	ANOC
	1965–69	AUT			1982	AUT
	1970–71	ANOC			1983–86	ANOC
	1972–86	AUT		Guinea	1959–83	AUT
Denmark	1946–86	DEM			1984–86	ANOC
Dominican Republic	1946–60	AUT		Guyana	1966–79	ANOC
	1961–86	ANOC			1980–86	AUT
Ecuador	1946–86	ANOC		Haiti	1946–49	ANOC
El Salvador	1946–46	AUT			1950–84	AUT
	1947–63	ANOC			1985–88	ANOC
	1964–71	DEM		Honduras	1946–86	ANOC
	1972–83	ANOC		Hungary	1946–47	ANOC
	1984–86	DEM			1948–55	AUT
Egypt	1946–52	ANOC			1956	ANOC
	1953–77	AUT			1957–86	AUT
	1978–86	ANOC		Iceland	1946–86	DEM
Ethiopia	1946–73	AUT		India	1950–74	DEM
	1974–86	ANOC			1955–79	ANOC
Finland	1946–86	DEM			1980–83	DEM
France	1946–80	DEM			1984–86	ANOC
	1981–86	ANOC		Indonesia	1949–65	ANOC
Gabon	1961–86	AUT			1966–86	AUT

Iran	1946–54	ANOC		Luxembourg	1946–86	DEM
	1955–86	AUT		Malawi	1966–86	AUT
Iraq	1946–69	ANOC		Malagasy	1966–74	AUT
	1970–86	AUT			1975–86	ANOC
Ireland	1950–51	ANOC		Malaysia	1957–86	DEM
	1952–86	DEM				
Israel	1949–86	DEM		Mali	1960–86	AUT
Italy	1946–47	ANOC		Mauritania	1961–62	ANOC
	1948–86	DEM			1963–77	AUT
					1978	ANOC
Ivory Coast	1960–86	AUT			1979–86	AUT
Jamaica	1962–86	DEM		Mauritius	1968–86	DEM
Japan	1951–86	DEM		Mexico	1946–86	ANOC
Jordan	1946–50	AUT		Mongolia	1946–86	AUT
	1951–56	ANOC		Morocco	1956–64	ANOC
	1957–86	AUT			1965–86	AUT
Kenya	1965–73	ANOC		Mozambique	1976–86	AUT
	1974–86	AUT				
Korea, North	1948–86	AUT		Nepal	1946–50	ANOC
					1951–57	AUT
Korea, South	1949–59	AUT			1958–59	ANOC
	1960	DEM			1960–79	AUT
	1961–62	AUT			1980–86	ANOC
	1963–71	DEM				
	1972–86	ANOC		Netherlands	1946–86	DEM
Kuwait	1963–86	AUT		New Zealand	1946–86	DEM
Laos	1954–57	ANOC		Nicaragua	1946–78	AUT
	1958	DEM			1979–86	ANOC
	1959–74	ANOC		Niger	1960–86	AUT
	1975–86	AUT		Nigeria	1960–65	ANOC
Lebanon	1946–86	ANOC			1966–77	AUT
					1978–83	ANOC
Lesotho	1966–69	DEM			1984–86	AUT
	1970–86	ANOC				
Liberia	1946–86	AUT		Norway	1946–86	DEM
Libya	1953–63	ANOC		Oman	1971–86	ANOC
	1964–86	AUT		Pakistan	1947–57	ANOC

	1958–61	AUT	Sri Lanka	1948–86	ANOC
	1962–86	ANOC	Sudan	1956–57	ANOC
Panama	1946–68	ANOC		1958–63	AUT
	1969–86	AUT		1964–70	ANOC
Papua	1976–86	DEM		1971–84	AUT
New Guinea				1985–86	ANOC
Paraguay	1946–86	AUT	Sweden	1946–86	DEM
Peru	1946–67	ANOC	Switzerland	1946–86	DEM
	1968–77	AUT	Syria	1946–48	ANOC
	1978–79	ANOC		1949	AUT
	1980–86	DEM		1950–51	ANOC
Philippines	1946–71	ANOC		1952–53	AUT
	1971–85	AUT		1954–86	ANOC
	1986	ANOC	Taiwan	1949–86	AUT
Poland	1946–47	ANOC	Tanzania	1963–86	AUT
	1948–86	AUT	Thailand	1946–57	ANOC
Portugal	1946–73	AUT		1958–67	AUT
	1974–75	ANOC		1968–70	ANOC
	1976–86	DEM		1971–72	AUT
Rumania	1946–47	ANOC		1973–75	ANOC
	1948–86	AUT		1976	AUT
				1977–86	ANOC
Rwanda	1962–86	AUT	Togo	1961–86	AUT
Saudi Arabia	1946–86	AUT	Trinidad/	1962–86	ANOC
Senegal	1960–63	ANOC	Tobago		
	1964–77	AUT	Tunisia	1959–80	AUT
	1978–86	ANOC		1981–86	ANOC
Sierra Leone	1961–86	ANOC	Turkey	1946–52	DEM
Singapore	1965–86	ANOC		1953–60	ANOC
				1961–70	DEM
Somalia	1961–68	ANOC		1971–72	ANOC
	1969–86	AUT		1973–79	DEM
South Africa	1946–86	ANOC		1980–86	ANOC
Spain	1946–74	AUT	Uganda	1962–66	ANOC
	1975–77	ANOC		1967–86	AUT
	1978–86	DEM	USSR	1946–86	AUT

United Kingdom	1946–86	DEM		Yemen	1946–47	ANOC
United States	1946–86	DEM			1948–61	AUT
					1962–86	ANOC
Uruguay	1946–51	ANOC		Yemen, South	1967–86	ANOC
	1952–71	DEM				
	1972	ANOC		Yugoslavia	1946–50	AUT
	1973–84	AUT			1951–86	ANOC
	1985–86	DEM		Zaire	1960–66	ANOC
Venezuela	1946–57	ANOC			1967–86	AUT
	1958–86	DEM		Zambia	1964–71	ANOC
Vietnam, North	1954–86	AUT			1972–86	AUT
Vietnam, South	1955–74	ANOC		Zimbabwe	1966–86	ANOC

CHAPTER 5

The Democratic Peace in Nonindustrial Societies

With Carol R. Ember and Melvin Ember

A VERY DIFFERENT empirical domain is that of ethnographically described societies which usually are not politically unified, the nonindustrial societies traditionally studied by anthropologists. As Segall puts it, cross-cultural research "is an unparalleled research strategy for discovering what goes with what on the broadest possible canvass" (1983, 7). As will be apparent, however, the domain really is so different from that in which the hypothesis first was generated that serious conceptual problems confront any such effort. The test of that hypothesis in this domain will therefore be, like that in chapter 3, a demanding one with reasonable expectations tilted against finding any significant relationships of the sort we are seeking. But the results will be, in fact, to find that democratically organized political units are less likely to fight each other than are nondemocratic ones.

In order to test the hypothesis on information from the ethnographic record, we must rephrase it to fit that record. Cross-cultural research differs from cross-national research in a number of ways. First, the unit of analysis is different. Cross-national research compares countries, each of which is politically unified at least in some formal respects. Cross-cultural research compares societies, each of which is a population that more or less contiguously inhabits a geographical area and speaks a language (or lingua franca) not normally understood by people in neighboring societies. Thus in the modern world many countries or states contain more than one society in the anthropological sense. Nigeria is one such country, with scores of territorially based societies or language groups (e.g., Hausa, Ibo, Yoruba).

A second difference between cross-cultural and cross-national research is implied by the first. A cross-cultural comparison, particularly one of worldwide scope, involves many types of society that vary in degree of political development, much more than do nation states. One aspect of that variation is that about 50 percent (calculated from Murdock 1967) of the societies known to anthropology (as of the times they were first described) had no political organization beyond the local community. In cross-cultural research, societies or cultural units may contain many smaller political units (Otterbein 1970).

Finding an adequate isomorphism between wars involving these societies and wars, external and internal, involving modern states is problematic. Among ethnographic units, at one extreme, deadly violence within autonomous local political units like villages is clearly internal, corresponding to civil violence within a state. At the other extreme, a war between the ethnographic unit (society) as a whole and another society is clearly external, perhaps corresponding to modern interstate war. Between these extremes is warfare between the various and often very independent local or small political units (e.g., bands, villages, districts, with numbers of people measured at most in the hundreds or thousands) within the larger societal or ethnolinguistic unit. For societies not politically unified, or at best tenuously so, even "internal" war among the different autonomous political units can also be considered analogous to interstate warfare, or to warfare among the city-states of medieval and Renaissance Italy or ancient Greece. This seems an appropriate context for testing the basic hypothesis about what kinds of political units will fight each other, and is what we shall examine here. Good ethnographic data for each of several neighboring societies, which would be required for a test at the full external end of the spectrum, are rarely available.

Finally, the terminology of "democratic" versus "nondemocratic" is even more problematic when used to describe the political process in the ethnographic record than when applied to modern or ancient states. We therefore rephrased our general hypothesis in terms of degree of political participation, largely using the framework and coding scales of Ross (1983).

WARFARE AND PARTICIPATION

The revised hypothesis, then, is that political units with wider political participation show less warfare with one another than do less participatory political units, even when appropriate controls are introduced into the analysis. Usually, in the ethnographic record, the political units that fight each other within a society are similar with respect to degree of political participation, since they speak the same language and share the same culture.[1]

If we are correct that political units with widespread political participation are unlikely to fight each other, we should find that warfare in the society is rare, whereas if the political units within a society have little political participation, we would expect warfare to be common among the units within the society. We test our hypothesis in three ways: (1) across all societies no matter what their level of political unification; (2)

in societies with only local political organization (i.e., the communities are politically autonomous); and (3) only in societies with multilocal political organization such as autonomous districts or chiefdoms. We assume that people in one political unit will know that people in other units are similarly organized. The perception of similarity across the society is generated by contacts among groups that occur, for example, because of marriages, feasts, and trade.

Our data base began with the Murdock and White (1969) sample of mostly preindustrial societies. We decided to use this sample because Ember and Ember (1992a, b) had previously coded Murdock and White's 186 societies on overall frequency of war as well as on the separate frequencies of internal warfare and external warfare. We used modified versions of Ross's (1983) codes on local political participation and Tuden and Marshall's (1980) codes on multilocal political organization for the societies in the Murdock and White sample. We also added to these cases 51 not previously coded that were randomly selected (using a table of random numbers) from Murdock (1967), for which we did our own coding on warfare and political participation.[2]

By "warfare" we mean socially organized armed combat between members of different territorial units (communities or aggregates of communities). This was the operational definition used in the Ember and Ember (1992a, b) research on warfare in the ethnographic record. It is a much more expansive definition of war than that commonly used in the social-scientific international relations literature, but is more appropriate here for much smaller and far less institutionalized units than nation states, armed at a much simpler level of lethal technology. Moreover, it is important to use a definition that picks up lower levels of violence than is characteristic of modern war, since our basic hypothesis is merely that participatory political units will be less likely to fight one another than do nonparticipatory units—not, as in the strong proposition sometimes asserted for modern nation states, that there will be no war between democracies. Actually, in the past, warfare in such societies was often *proportionately* more lethal than modern warfare (Meggitt 1977).

All the warfare variables were rated by at least two coders who worked independently.[3] Warfare was rated for a twenty-five-year period around the ethnographic present pinpointed by Murdock or Murdock and White (from fifteen years before to ten years after the time referred to in the ethnography). We exclude any cases that were pacified by an external society or had frequencies of warfare clearly diminished by external pacification attempts.

We are concerned primarily with the levels and forms of participation at the local or face-to-face level: isolated small bands, neighborhoods of dispersed households, villages, or precincts of towns or cities. We chose to examine participation in decision-making at the local level because such immediate, personal experience should be most relevant to individuals' perceptions of their own and other groups' political decision-making procedures.

For measures of local political participation we adapt the variables coded by Ross (1981) that in a multivariate analysis clustered together most strongly on a factor he labels "concentration of political power." These include: (1) checks on leaders' power (Ross's variable 6); (2) ease of removing leaders from power (variable 7); (3) degree to which leaders must consult or persuade (variable 8); and (4) importance of decision-making bodies versus an individual leader (variable 9). (The definitions of these variables appear in the appendix.) In addition, Ross provided some clarifications of his coding rules and suggested in a personal communication that we use extensiveness of adult political involvement (his variable 11); it loads less highly in his factor analysis but includes another dimension about how extensively adults participate in decisions. In a recent analysis Ross (1988) used just variable 11 (involvement) as his measure of political participation and variable 10 as his measure of range of decision-making. If we identify modern democracy with a wide voting franchise, contested elections, a responsible executive, and protection of civil liberties, Ross's variables can be seen as appropriate to conditions in pre-industrial societies in which formal elections rarely occur and in which full-time political officials are usually nonexistent.[4]

The substantive meaning of our codings in the context of these societies will be clearer when we discuss cases below. Institutional constraints at the local level of such systems are not likely to be very strong, but variables 6 (checks on power), 8 (need for consultation), and 9 (formal decision-making bodies) should tap what is there. Variables 7 (removal, especially toward the end of the scale where formal leaders may be ignored) and 11 (extent of participation) may be better suited to test the effect of norms for informal control and widespread involvement in decision-making. Variable 11 approximates the modern requirement for a wide franchise. Variables 6 and 8 are related to the requirement for a responsible executive, and variables 7 and 9 to that for contested elections. As with the theoretical arguments in the international literature that generated them, assignment of one of our measures to one requirement rather than another is nonetheless somewhat arbitrary.[5] Our effort to measure the explanatory power of participation in general, therefore, will be more satisfactory than any attempt to distinguish the relative explanatory power of institutions versus norms or perceptions.

The criteria for participation may seem stringent by criteria appropriate to modern states, at least at the most participatory end of each scale. But remember that the majority of these political units are small, without the institutions of a modern state. If there is to be participation in any recognizable form it has to be in continuing involvement in decision-making, not simply as delegation to representatives elected every few years. Again a relevant analogy is to Greek city-state democracy, with its assembly of the citizenry approving all broad policy initiatives in free debate.

Because Ross did not code all the cases in the Murdock and White sample and we wanted to expand the sample substantially, we trained two assistants in his coding procedures by recoding 10 percent of his sample cases. When we were reasonably sure that we understood his coding procedures, we coded all the remaining nonpacified cases that had been rated reliably on internal warfare frequency in the Embers' previous research on warfare, and then the sample from Murdock (1967).[6]

In the course of reading the ethnographic materials we realized that two more factors coded by Ross were relevant to our theory and needed to be incorporated explicitly. They were: number of decisions that are made at the local level (Ross's variable 10), and absence of fission as a result of conflicts (variable 30). One of the cases that helped us understand the importance of these two variables was that of the Yanomamo Indians ("the fierce people") on the Brazil-Venezuela border. As most anthropologists know, the Yanomamo—at least the subgroup described by Chagnon (1966, 1968), the place and time focus in the Murdock and White sample—have a great deal of warfare between villages, and fights within villages often erupt. Yet their decision-making process seems quite participatory. The functions of leaders are described as ill-defined and few. Leaders lose power when support diminishes, so there are checks on their powers. Many people (except perhaps women, who have little status) are involved in decisions. A leader does not present decisions as commands to the community, and cannot force anyone to do anything. Rather, he must rely on the force of example and persuasion; often decisions are made by the community at large, and the leader initiates activities that the entire group has already decided to undertake. So, the Yanomamo look like a strong exception to our hypothesis.

We realized, however, that the Yanomamo villages frequently split apart when there is a dispute. If people flee or are forced out of a local group following a "political" dispute, members of such a culture cannot be said to "agree to disagree." Agreement to disagree, tolerance of continuing dissent by a loyal opposition, is a major feature of democracy. Conflict in a democratic system is settled less by avoidance or aggression than by accepting, not necessarily approving of, the different points of view. (Voice or loyalty rather than exit; Hirschman 1970)[7] This is reminiscent of the argument that the fabled democracy of the New England town meeting was limited because it often resulted in the physical departure of losing factions (Handlin and Handlin 1986, chap. 2). Thus, we adapted

Ross's "fission" variable (variable 30): imprisonment (rare in these systems), or punishment or voluntary exile (more common) following political disputes are counted as fission.

We also realized that the Yanomamo make relatively few collective decisions aside from war. If people participate in decision-making when it occurs, but it hardly ever occurs, they can hardly learn to generalize from the experience of peaceful conflict resolution. That is, the other political participation variables would probably not have the expected effect if a local group makes minimal collective decisions. (The Yanomamo turn out not to be as minimal in decision-making as do some other peoples.) Thus we used Ross's variable of range of decision-making (variable 10) to eliminate as "nonparticipatory" those societies in which there was minimal collective decision-making (coded 4) that affected people's lives. In terms of the theories about democracy discussed earlier, the last two also perhaps apply better to "normative" than to "institutional" explanations. (The definitions for these two additional variables also appear in the appendix.)

In relations among modern states, individuals (whether among the general public or in leadership roles) must continually make inferences about the preferences and motivations of the leaders making decisions for other states. Poor information, barriers of secrecy, cultural and linguistic differences make it hard to discern those preferences directly. Rather, individuals in large part adduce those preferences from the better-known preferences of people physically and socially closer, with whom they are more immediately interdependent.

Individuals may attribute to distant actors preferences derived from social and political relations in diminishing degree from concentric circles beginning with family, through neighborhood, workplace, city, and nation. If relations at closer range manifest substantial degrees of participation and peaceful conflict resolution, one may impute similar behavior and motivations to the more distant others. By contrast, if proximate relations are nasty, brutish, or anarchic, one is likely to expect others, from more distant social or political units, to be similar. Arguments that aggressiveness is rooted in certain child-rearing practices are of course common. (In anthropology see Whiting 1969.) At the extreme, images of a divinity are seen through a glass very darkly, if at all. Hence those images would seem to derive from immediate relationships. Where socialization in the first years of life is strict and punitive, such behavior is typically imputed to the supernatural. (Spiro and D'Andrade 1958; Lambert, Triandis, and Wolf 1959). Similarly, images of political jurisdiction in the supernatural world tend to parallel those in political jurisdictions above the family (Swanson 1969).

If attributions of preferences and motivation to distant actors are in large part socially learned from more proximate relationships, then our measurement of political behavior in the smallest political unit (band, neighborhood, village) is the most relevant. Some of these societies indeed have no higher level of political organization. Others do, and about half of them manifest "multilocal" political organization for the entire society. Since this organization encompasses the cultural and linguistic unit, patterns of behavior at this level may also influence the preference attributions individuals make to members of other local political units within the society with which war "internal" to the society may take place. But the influence should be weaker than that from patterns of behavior closer to home. Consequently we need also to measure participation within the wider institutions, while hypothesizing a weaker effect on the frequency of war among the smaller component units.

Decision-making at the multilocal level is usually more delegated, indirect, and specialized than in small local units. Thus a different set of coding rules is required. We constructed an ordinal scale using three different "structural" variables from Tuden and Marshall (1980)—concerning the executive, the selection of the executive, and deliberative and consultative bodies. When we started to code cases, however, we and our assistants were often unable to replicate all of Tuden and Marshall's distinctions. Accordingly, we developed a simplified coding scheme, combining many categories into an ordinal scale (see appendix). The condensed coding made unnecessary the most problematic categorical distinctions, and yet was adequate to our theoretical purposes which emphasize structural constraints in the presence or absence of checks and balances and division of powers. At the most participatory end of the scale are systems with an authoritative deliberative body and/or wide-franchise elections.

In analyzing the effect of decision-making procedures on war frequency, we are concerned only with peacetime decision-making at the local level, except for our final analysis of those societies where a multilocal level of authority is present. We restrict ourselves to peacetime decision-making because most societies become more hierarchical in wartime—and some societies, such as the Yanomamo, make few decisions as a group except to initiate or conduct a war.

PARTICIPATION MATTERS

In testing this hypothesis we need to control for two influences known to be related to the frequency of war within societies. One is societal size, since warfare is predominantly external in small populations (C. Ember 1974). One reason, of course, may be their relative vulnerability to external aggression. Another, according to Olson (1965, 1991), is that the great gains to be had from peaceful order rather than anarchy motivate voluntary agreements to maintain order in the unit. The benefits from peace are readily seen, as are the costs to an individual from failing to contribute to that peace. Similar motivations might apply to establishing and maintaining a participatory political order in such a society. Informal ties among individuals, denser in small societies, contribute. Thus it is especially important to control for size. We transformed population to a logarithmic scale for the analysis, expecting a declining marginal effect at the high end of the population scale.

Second, certain physical conditions, notably location on an isolated island or islands with no other language groups, make external war very unlikely—and thus may increase the likelihood of intrasocietal warfare in the absence of external enemies against whom to divert aggression (C. Ember, 1974; see Levy 1989 on externalization in modern states). We therefore constructed a dummy variable for societies located on an island or series of islands with no other society within fifty miles. Use of these controls allows us to focus on the independent contribution of the political variables.

We did not use variable 10 (range of decision-making) directly in the multivariate analysis below, but rather used it to remove from the analysis those societies in which very few collective decisions were made (coded 4 originally). Since there was no linear bivariate relationship between war and variable 9 (decision-making bodies), we dropped it from the multivariate analysis.

Missing data became a serious problem; it simply was not possible to code many of the variables from the fragmentary ethnographic materials available. Because different variables were missing for different societies, the result sharply reduced the sample available for multivariate analysis. More seriously, the available ethnographic material is often incomplete, using different vocabularies, and gathered for purposes very different from ours and certainly not with our analytical categories in mind. It is information produced by professional anthropologists or other ethnographic observers, typically compiled decades and occasionally even centuries ago, often of societies now no longer existing as they did when observed. The imprecision of this material invites coding ambiguities, and introduces error into our data set. Insofar as that error is essentially random—as we believe it is—it reduces the likelihood that we will find strong empirical relationships in the data. That we do find strong relationships is thus all the more surprising.[8]

Although many of our measures are ordinal, we employ them as interval measures in our analysis. Treating them as interval measures allows us to use more powerful and versatile analytical techniques (Labovitz

1970). Multiple regression analysis works like the multivariate analysis used earlier. It not only allows us to evaluate how much of the variance in warfare frequency we are explaining, but also to evaluate whether each explanatory variable is an independent and significant predictor when we control for the effect of all other explanatory variables.

Table 5.1 shows, in column 1, the basic analysis for all thirty-seven cases on which we have complete data. All but one of the variables (6, checks on leaders' power) are highly significant predictors of warfare, using a one-tailed level of significance (except for variable 8, consultation; see below). Measures of democratic participation are generally associated with a reduction in warfare between small political units. Although the sample size is considerably smaller than our original sample, because of missing, unreliable, or inapplicable data, the regression coefficients nevertheless are generally strong and highly significant. (The R^2 is .60, indicating that these variables account for three-fifths of the variance in warfare).

As expected, the controls for total population and island are important, in the expected direction.[9] But so too are three of the five political variables that we retained, exerting a strong effect independent of the controls. The coefficients for the three political variables that are significant as hypothesized (variables 7, 11, 30) have a combined weight of −1.577, accounting for more variance than the controls do. (The two controls have a combined weight of 1.014.)

The distinctions between our "perceptual" and "institutional" variables are not sharp enough to provide a strong test of the two competing explanations, but there is nevertheless some basis for comparison. All three significant variables are normative or perceptual ones as characterized above: ease of removal of leaders (7), extensivity of participation (11), and political fission (30). The institutional variables do much less well. One (6, checks on power) has close to a zero coefficient, and one (consultation) is statistically significant but in the opposite direction from what we expected (which is why we apply the two-tailed statistical test to it).

Careful examination of the residuals showed that one case was a statistical outlier; standard procedure is to show both equations, with and without outliers. (Lewis-Beck 1980, 40). So, to be sure the outlier was not unduly responsible for the explanatory power of the political variables we reestimated the equation without it. Column 2 shows those results. The earlier pattern is essentially unchanged save that an even larger proportion of the variance is explained and most of the previously significant variables become even more significant.

Column 3 repeats the analysis for those societies that have only local-level political organization. By doing so we eliminate the possibility that a multilocal organization might take a markedly more or less participatory form than at the local level, and so send confusing "signals" about degree of participation. It is also quite possible that multilocal authority serves in part to pacify local warmaking proclivities. What we see in these relatively "pure" cases is that most of the previous results are basically repeated with even more variance accounted for (though generally lower significance levels due to the small sample size). Removal of leaders and absence of fission remain strong, and checks on power (6) becomes stronger, in the expected direction. Overall, the results are very robust.

TABLE 5.1
Explaining Frequency of Warfare between Political Units within Societies

	All Societies			
	All with Data (1)		Omitting Outlier (2)	
	Std. coef.	P =	Std. coef.	P =
Constant	.000	.354	.000	.379
Population	.522	.000	.634	.000
Island	.492	.001	.513	.000
Checks on Power (6)	.023	.458	−.018	.464
Removal of Leaders (7)	−.482	.002	−.470	.001
Consultation (8)[a]	.553	.012	.552	.003
Extent of Part. (11)	−.476	.006	−.366	.015
Absence of Fission (30)	−.619	.000	−.643	.000

$$R^2 = .60 \qquad R^2 = .68$$
$$n = 37 \qquad n = 36$$
$$p = .000 \qquad p = .000$$

	Local Level Polities Only	
	(3)	
	Std. coef.	P =
Constant	.000	.448
Population	.656	.001
Island	.396	.019
Checks on Power (6)	−.310	.124
Removal of Leaders (7)	−.367	.048
Consultation (8)[a]	.664	.071
Extent of Part. (11)	−.184	.284
Absence of Fission (30)	−.590	.005

$$R^2 = .74$$
$$n = 20$$
$$p = .009$$

TABLE 5.1 (cont.)

| | Polities with Multilocal Authority[b] | | | |
| | All with Data (4) | | Omitting Outlier (5) | |
	Std. coef.	P =	Std. coef.	P =
Constant	.000	.247	.000	.452
Population	.541	.036	.767	.006
Island	.620	.028	.805	.006
Checks on Power (6)	−.116	.384	−.007	.491
Removal of Leaders (7)	−.533	.029	−.622	.009
Consultation (8)[a]	.400	.209	.474	.095
Extent of Part. (11)	−.395	.169	−.534	.066
Absence of Fission (30)	−.663	.008	−.778	.002
Multilocal Part.	−.359	.094	−.163	.213
	$R^2 = .78$		$R^2 = .87$	
	$n = 16$		$n = 15$	
	$p = .080$		$p = .033$	

[a] p value with two-tailed test; all other coefficients with one-tailed tests.
[b] One polity was not codable on the multilocal scale.

Finally, columns 4 and 5 show the effect of multilocal political participation. Political organization exists at the multilocal level for fewer than half of our cases. The total variance accounted for is again high. The signs for the coefficients are the same as in column 3. Variables 7 (removal of leaders) and 30 (fission) remain highly significant. The multilocal participation scale, which crudely identifies the existence of political institutions to check leaders' power, is significant in column 5 at the 10 percent level. This is not an unreasonable level when working with such a small sample; remember too that we hypothesized that the influence of experience at the (higher) multilocal level would be weaker than at the local level. By our measure, at least, participatory institutions at higher levels of political organization may make some contribution to reducing the frequency of warfare, but—especially without the outlier (column 5)—that effect is weak.

The unexpected reversal of direction for variable 8 (consultation) demands attention. At first we thought high correlations (multicollinearity) among the variables might be responsible, since several are related conceptually, and 6, 7, and 8 all clustered together in Ross's (1981) analysis. Multicollinearity might also account for the failure of variable 6 to be significant earlier. Accordingly, we repeated the initial analysis three times, each time dropping one of the possibly collinear variables. The effect was not substantial. It failed to produce a consistent relationship between variable 6 and war, and it made no material difference in columns 4 or 5 for the other two variables. Multicollinearity does not explain why variable 8 always has a reversed effect.[10]

In bivariate correlations all three are related to war frequency—but rather weakly—in the anticipated direction. This is true even of variable 8 (but far from significantly). Yet if one considers the coding of variable 8, a low score does not mean that the leader was chosen "undemocratically"; it means only that he does not consult widely when making decisions. In a multivariate analysis, once the effect of the other political variables is partialed out, what seems to be left is how much authority the leader has to make decisions. Category 3 for that variable (use persuasion instead of exercising authority), which we originally interpreted as the most "democratic," may instead reflect a lack of legitimacy for the leader, or the lack of stable authority in the political system. If so, the process of vying for leadership in an unstable system may not lead to peaceful resolution of conflict at the local level. It may even make aggression against other low-level units in the society more likely. This is consistent with our earlier hypothesis and evidence that stable democratic states are more likely to be peaceable toward other democracies than are unstable ones.

This interpretation makes sense in the context of the Yanomamo case. Leadership, in the form of village "big men," is determined by "personal courage, fierceness, the ability to be outraged by even the slightest insult, marksmanship, diplomacy in trading . . . and the defense of group members who get into difficulties with other village members" (Chagnon 1966, 44). The leader lacks any stable authority. He must keep the backing of the villagers; without it, even if not formally removed, he will lose influence. There is no agreement to disagree, as villages often split following disputes. Furthermore, leadership positions are achieved and bolstered in large part by violence (this is not coded by our variables). It is hard to imagine how people could learn to resolve conflicts peacefully within the community, much less between communities, in this set of circumstances.

Some might think that the negative relation of participation to warfare between political units within a society might be an indirect consequence of favorable external circumstances. That is, the absence of external warfare might permit these societies to be less hierarchical (more participatory) and thus more peaceful internally. This is the obverse of Tilly's well-known formulation that "the state makes war, and war makes the state," but without implying that the war-induced state necessarily suppresses internal warfare (Tilly 1990; for an anthropological discussion see Cohen 1984). To check this we used information (Ember and Ember 1992a) on these polities' frequency of engaging in external warfare (with different cultures). We redid the analysis in column 1, adding frequency of external warfare as an additional predictor. Even though the sample is smaller ($n = 27$) because some cases are not rated reliably on external warfare frequency, three indicators of political participation—removal of leaders (7), participation (11), and absence of fission (30)—remain significant. Moreover, external war is not a significant predictor of internal war. Thus any causal link from absence of external warfare to participation (and hence to low internal warfare) is unlikely in these societies.[11]

SOME EXAMPLES

Discussion of four cases in some depth will help to clarify how the practices of participation operated. One is the Marshallese, approximately ten thousand people living on more than thirty rather widely scattered coral islands in the Pacific. Our coders recorded participation and warfare in the period around 1875—ten years before Germany established a protectorate and pacified the islands.

Marshallese society was divided into a clear status hierarchy. The paramount chief came from the senior lineage of the *iroij* (royalty); succession to that title descended in the maternal line. He was not elected or tested, nor were there any grounds for exclusion from the position. Lesser chiefs came from the remaining *iroij* lineages. The Marshall islands as a whole were not united under one paramount chief; some islands had their own paramount chief, while in other areas groups of islands were united together under one paramount. Below the *iroij* were the *bwirik* (nobility), and then the commoners. The chiefs (along with the nobles) controlled the land and its products, and provided "dogmatic" leadership. Both paramount chiefs and the lesser chiefs were described as having autocratic powers and the power of life and death. They were supposed to command the best information on political affairs (Spoehr 1949; Senfft 1903/1942; Erdland 1914/1942/1961; Wedgewood 1942).

Thus the Marshallese provide an example of a highly autocratic society, at every level from the paramount chiefdom to descent groups. Not only was the ability to lead constrained by heredity, but there appear to have been virtually no checks on the power of political leaders, no way to remove leaders, and no decision-making bodies. And they fought a great deal internally. The island chiefs were described as continuously warring among themselves prior to pacification (Spoehr 1949, 32).

The Turkic-speaking Kazakhs of Central Asia—the principal ethnic group in the present-day independent state and former Soviet republic of Kazakhstan—are of some interest. They also were a rather hierarchically organized and quite warlike people. Ethnographers report their political organization in the late nineteenth century, after formal Russian conquest but when Russian authority was only loose and the Kazakhs certainly were not "pacified." The *aul*, sometimes characterized as village but basically a set of related family groups living and migrating together, constituted the smallest political organization. Although it was nominally subject to the multilocal leader (khan) of the roughly four million Kazakhs, in practice it was autonomous. The khan's "chief activity was to collect taxes," but he commanded no centralized system or standing army. He might convene a council to settle questions of general policy, but the system was "not democratic;" the council was composed of chiefs, rich elders, and great warriors, and took no binding decisions. The death of a khan normally induced civil war among local leaders (Hudson 1936, 64–65).

The aul's leader, known as the *bij* or *aqsaqal*, was usually the largest herd-owner. His position was often hereditary, but he, or his son, typically lost office if he was unable to retain it by merit. A successor would be chosen from among themselves by one of the five or six wealthiest heads of family lines in the *aul*. The leader had substantial power; sometimes a local council might be called, but it might well "break up in a wrangle" (Hudson 1936, 62; also Krader 1953; Krader and Wayne 1955). All the political codings for this level fall from about the middle to low participatory end of their scales: 2 on the four-point scale for checks on leaders' power (leaders not necessarily removed from office but can lose influence); a middling score for consultation (most decisions made by the leader himself); only moderately extensive involvement in decision-making by the community; and expulsion from the community sometimes practiced for offenses. The range of community control over decision-making was also moderately high (2, with 1 highest on the four-point scale). The Kazakhs fought among themselves often, in local wars of reprisals and hereditary feuds (scored 4 on the five-point scale, corresponding to usually every year). Our equation hit this one almost on the nose, predicting a score of 3.9.

By contrast, the Cuna Indians, residing on the Atlantic coast and islands of Panama, had a highly participatory system and virtually no internal war. As of 1927 (the date for our codings) the more than twenty-two thousand Cuna were still independent politically, despite repeated attempts by the Spanish, Colombian, and finally Panamanian authorities to subjugate them.

They had village chiefs and a high chief (called *nele*) for a confederacy of villages. The *nele* also represented one of two political parties (which tended to be territorial in base); he was elected by the chiefs of all the villages affiliated with his party. The *nele* might act as his own village chief, but there was always another village chief; in the *nele*'s village the second chief acted as village chief when the *nele* was away. Village chiefs were in principle elected for life by all the men in the village, but could at any time be impeached. None of the chiefs were paid. Few men wanted to be chief, since it was difficult to perform the obligations and also support oneself and family. Chiefs thus tended to be older men with help from sons-in-law. The *nele* gave advice to other villages by sending committees to their councils but could not force the chief of another village to carry out his order. In the *nele*'s village a great "Congress House" seated about one hundred representatives from the confederacy; women were sometimes present. The *nele* presided at the center table with his counselors and visiting chiefs immediately around him. When he addressed the council he neither domineered nor pleaded, but tried to convince them with reasons and facts (Nordenskiold 1938; McKim 1936; Stout 1947).

Although elections of the chiefs might not be contested, they seem to have been consistent with the will of the people. Since they could be impeached, there was an institutionalized way to remove them. (Moreover, since they tended to be old at the inception of office there was some limit to their term.) They appear to have taken account of popular opinion by consultation in councils, and did not appear to have the power to force a particular decision. Participation in decision-making was widespread, in the form of people (including women) attending council meetings. The Cuna had virtually no internal war.

The Mapuche of the temperate rain forest of Chile constitute a partial exception to our generalization. Prior to pacification at the end of the nineteenth century, warfare among them was common; even when nominally at peace they often carried on raids. Yet in some ways their system appears fairly participatory. Peacetime political organization was strictly local, with no overall tribal authority. The headman (*lonko*) was usually one of the oldest men; at his death the office descended to his son, brother, or nephew, with the choice somewhat open. He could be deposed. Neighboring headmen came in to supervise the choice of his replacement. They decided who seemed to have the best qualifications and greatest support in the unit (Titiev 1951, 53–56; also Latcham 1909, 355).

The *lonko*'s advice was always sought, but his authority was strictly limited. He chiefly served as the unit's spokesman, and was expected to hold frequent assemblies of all his adult male followers. The *lonkos*' powers were "exclusively or almost exclusively consultative and persuasive, with little or no coercive power. They had no recognized right to inflict punishment, to claim tribute or personal service, or to demand obedience from their kinsfolk or 'subjects.' The latter paid no attention to them and did as they pleased if the leaders showed themselves arrogant or domineering" (Cooper 1946, 724).

In terms of our codings, this political system presents a mixed picture. It had moderate input from the community, and strong checks on power. Governance was by consultation and persuasion. Power was usually in some way hereditary, but institutionalized means to remove a leader were invoked occasionally, with other groups' leaders choosing the new *lonko*. It reminds us that the correlations between measures of participation and lack of war are not perfect, without exceptions. Moreover, the nonpolitical predictors are also important. Mapuche society was relatively large (110,000 people), which may have favored frequent internal warfare despite a somewhat participatory system. A further reason may be, as with the Yanomamo, that the leader had very little authority to enforce decisions. Here is another case in which a lack of authority is coded as "high consultation" (variable 8), where that denotes a political system with little control over its membership even when decisions reflect substantial participation. But the instability seems not so severe as among the Yanomamo, and the ethnographic information on this culture—now pacified—is too incomplete to tell us enough of what we need to know.

Despite such partial exceptions, the statistical results are strong and robust, even with the relatively small sample and the difficulties in measuring the variables to minimize random error. Detailed study of the ethnographic reports helps in interpreting the quantitative analysis. Participatory institutions contribute to reducing the frequency of warfare between units within the society, but in many of these cases the institutions as such are weak or virtually nonexistent. Yet warfare between such political units remains relatively rare. This contrasts to our results with the Greek city-states, where the institutional constraints were weak, the normative restraints only developing, and the consequent limitations on warfare between polities presented mixed results.

In the anthropological material, it seems important to have a culture wherein people can develop perceptions of themselves and others as having an opportunity to participate widely in political decision-making. We believe we can, allowing for the very different circumstances, characterize these practices and cultures as in a meaningful way "democratic." If so, we have one more piece of evidence that democratically governed peoples are less likely to fight one another than are autocratically governed peoples.

We have taken our hypothesis from the cross-national literature and supported it in a very different domain. In doing so we have a finding that is not widely anticipated in anthropology[12] but which, by extension, strengthens similar theory and empirical research on international relations. We reinforce something that we have found in other political contexts: When people learn to agree to disagree and have some control over the political process, they may learn that conflicts with other people who share similar ideas about political process can also be resolved in peaceful ways.

APPENDIX
CODES FOR POLITICAL DECISION-MAKING

The codes for local decision-making are adapted from Ross (1981, 176–77); those for multilocal decision-making are adapted from Tuden and Marshall (1980, 120–21).

Local Decision-making

VARIABLE 6. CHECKS ON LEADERS' POWER

1 There are few checks on political power in the society, or those that exist do not seem to be invoked very often
2 There are checks on leaders' power that seem to make them sensitive to popular pressures
3 Political leaders in the society are careful to act only after securing substantial support for particular actions
4 There are no leaders who act independently, lest they lose their backing in the community
9 Not codable

VARIABLE 7. REMOVAL OF LEADERS

1 There appears to be virtually no way in which incompetent or disliked leaders can be removed except for rebellion or popular uprisings
2 There are institutionalized means for removing leaders that are invoked from time to time, possibly by other elites in the community
3 Leaders are not necessarily removed from office in a formal manner, but they may be ignored and come to lose their influence in the community
4 Leadership is not formalized, so individuals lose power when support disappears or diminishes
9 Not codable

VARIABLE 8. LEADERS' NEED FOR CONSULTATION

1 Leaders frequently act independently and make authoritative decisions that are then presented to the community
2 Leaders seem to make relatively few decisions on their own without consultation with members of the community
3 Leaders or influential individuals use persuasion (personal skills as opposed to exercise of authority) to help organize and structure group action
9 Not codable

VARIABLE 9. DECISION-MAKING BODIES

1 Most decisions seem to be made by an individual or individuals, perhaps with advice from a few advisers
2 Most decisions seem to be made by individual(s) working with an elite
 council
3 Most decisions seem to be made by individual(s) working with a
 broad-based council
4 Most decisions seem to be made by a broad-based community council
5 While few explicit decisions are made, those that are seem to be made
 by the community at large, sometimes meeting together
9 Not codable

VARIABLE 10. POLITICAL PARTICIPATION: RANGE OF DECISION-MAKING

 Range of participation refers to the number of different areas of life in
which community decision-making occurs. This variable assesses the extent to which community control is exercised over different areas of life
through collective decision-making, whether of a formal or informal
nature.
1 The community makes collective decisions (formally or informally)
 that impinge on many aspects of people's lives
2 The community makes collective decisions that impinge on a moderate number of areas of people's lives
3 The community makes collective decisions that impinge on relatively
 few aspects of people's lives
4 There seem to be minimal collective decisions made that impinge on
 people's lives (Used to eliminate from the analysis polities with minimal collective decision-making)
9 Not codable

VARIABLE 11. POLITICAL PARTICIPATION: EXTENSIVITY OF INVOLVEMENT

 A second dimension of participation concerns patterns of involvement
in those areas where collective decision-making is present. How widespread or restrictive is adult political participation in a community?
Within those areas where community decision-making occurs, adult involvement in decision-making is best characterized as:
1 Low or nonexistent: leaders make most decisions and involvement of
 the average person is highly limited or absent
2 Moderate: some consultation is present and there is some input from
 the community but on the average it is not high
3 High for some: substantial political involvement for certain persons
 or groups, but others are excluded on the basis of gender, age, or
 kinship status

4 Widespread: decision-making forums (formal or informal) are open to all adults and involvement seems relatively great. (Societies with widespread participation for men but not women are scored 3)
9 Not codable

VARIABLE 30. LOCAL POLITICAL FISSION

This includes imprisonment or internal banishment for crimes against the "state" as well as external banishment for such crimes; it does not include imprisonment or banishment for "civil" crimes such as incest or theft.

1 Dissatisfied persons often move to another community following disputes
2 Dissatisfied persons sometimes move to another community following disputes
3 Dissatisfied persons rarely or never move to another community following disputes
9 Not codable

Multilocal Decision-Making

VARIABLE 1. EXECUTIVE AND LEGISLATIVE AUTHORITY

2 Supreme decision-making authority is vested in a council, assembly, or other deliberative body, or it is shared more or less equally by such a body and a single or plural executive (king, president, or prime minister). Tuden and Marshall codes C or S
1 Supreme decision-making authority is concentrated in a single or plural executive (e.g., committee, dual, triumvirate; influence of advisers is irrelevant). Tuden and Marshall codes P or L
8 There is no effective sovereignty above the local community
9 Not codable

VARIABLE 2. SELECTION OF EXECUTIVE

3 Succession is nonhereditary and by a formal electoral procedure in which a substantial portion of the free citizenry participates. Tuden and Marshall code e
2 Executive is selected or otherwise chosen (perhaps by consensus) by a council or other deliberative body, or there is no executive other than a presiding officer of the council. Tuden and Marshall code c
1 Executive is chosen by heredity, divination, or a body of limited size (ruling clique, party, or small body of electors), and any wider elections are merely a stereotyped confirmation of the decision of a limited power group, or by an alien society. Tuden and Marshall codes p, q, m, n, f, l, a, s

7 There is no executive, even though multilocal level exists
8 There is no effective sovereignty above the local community
9 Not codable

VARIABLE 3. DELIBERATIVE AND CONSULTATIVE BODIES

If there are two deliberative bodies, we coded the one that gave a code 2 for executive authority if applicable, or, if that was not applicable, which gave a code 2 for selection of executive. If still not identified, we coded the one chosen by the broader franchise.

3 An elective legislature or parliament is chosen independently by the franchise of a substantial proportion of the free citizenry. Tuden and Marshall code E
2 There is a deliberative body representative of most or all of the major social, class, or ethnic components. Tuden and Marshall code R
1 There is no deliberative body, or only an aristocratic body whose membership is hereditary or confined to ascribed statuses, e.g., a council of nobles, or one whose members are appointed by the chief executive or a ruling clique or party. Tuden and Marshall codes O, C, A
8 There is no effective sovereignty above the local community
9 Not codable

The codes for multilocal decision-making were subsequently reduced as follows:

5 Previous 1 = 2, 2 = 2, 3, or 7, 3 = 3
4 Previous 1 = 2, 2 = 2 or 7 and 3 = 2, or 2 = 1 and 3 = anything (1 = 2, 3 = 1 is a null set)
3 Previous 1 = 1, 2 = 3, 3 = anything
2 Previous 1 = 1, 2 = 2, 3 = 3
1 Previous 1 = 1, 2 = 2 and 3 = 1 or 2, or 2 = 1 and 3 = anything

CHAPTER 6

The Future of the Democratic Peace

COMPARED WITH their actions toward other kinds of states, democracies in the modern world are unlikely to engage in militarized disputes with each other. When they do get into disputes with each other, they are less likely to let the disputes escalate. They rarely fight each other even at low levels of lethal violence, and never (or almost never) go to war against each other. They are not in any of these respects markedly more peaceful toward authoritarian states than authoritarian states are toward each other. But democracies' relatively peaceful relations toward each other are well established, and are not spuriously caused by some other influence such as sharing high levels of wealth or rapid economic growth or ties of alliance. Peace among democracies was not maintained simply by pressure from a common adversary in the Cold War, and it is outlasting that threat. The more democratic each state is, the more peaceful their relations are likely to be.

The phenomenon of democratic peace can be explained by the pervasiveness of normative restraints on conflict between democracies. That explanation extends to the international arena the cultural norms of live-and-let-live and peaceful conflict resolution that operate within democracies. The phenomenon of democratic peace can also be explained by the role of structural restraints on democracies' decisions to go to war. Those restraints ensure that in a conflict of interest with a democracy another state can expect ample time for conflict-resolution processes to be effective, and virtually no risk of incurring surprise attack.

Evidence supports both of these explanatory models. The debate between their proponents is not settled, nor should it be seen entirely as a debate. They are not fully separable in theory or in practice. Both make a contribution, and the two kinds of influences reinforce each other to produce the phenomenon of democratic peace.

Nevertheless, some evidence suggests that the normative model is the more powerful. Norms, as measured by the absence of violence in domestic politics and the duration of democratic regimes, were somewhat more strongly associated with peace between democracies than was our measure of structural/institutional constraints. When democracies do have serious diplomatic disputes, they are unlikely to escalate them—as a normative explanation would predict, contrary to common structural models. They are more likely to reciprocate each other's behavior, to accept third party mediation or good offices in settling disputes, and to settle disputes peacefully. The spread of democratic norms and practices in the world, if consolidated, should reduce the frequency of violent conflict and war. Where normative restraints are insufficient, institutionalized restraints on foreign policy decision-making may be a second-best influence. Yet in democracies with institutional constraints but weak normative ones (due to recency of democracy, or violence or instability), charismatic or adventurous leaders may override the institutional limits.

In the world of ancient Greece the institutions that could be expected to restrain the resort to force by democracies were almost entirely lacking, and the norms that democracies should not fight each other were nascent and weak. But there was some evidence of restraint attributable to norms. In most of the wars that did occur between democracies, perception of political instability in the adversary state, and misperception of its democratic nature, played an important role in instigating the war.

Nonindustrial societies, as studied by anthropologists, also provide an opportunity to look for restraints on warfare among democratically organized polities that typically lack the institutional constraints of a modern state. Yet despite that absence, democratically organized units evince significantly less warfare with each other than do nondemocratically organized units. Moreover, political stability (or its absence) again proves an important influence on the resort to violence by those democratically organized units. These findings, more than those about ancient Greece, support the proposition that democracies are in general relatively peaceful toward each other. Though the relationship is not quite so strong and consistent as that which emerges in the modern international system, to find it at all in nonindustrial societies shows that the phenomenon of democratic peace is not limited to contemporary Western democracies.

Several loose ends to this analysis remain. Some comments on limitations on the fact and expectation of democratic peace are in order, specifically on the problem of covert action by democracies against democracies. The contemporary discourse about aggressive dictators and peaceful democracies needs to be examined. So too does the character of public images of international relations. Finally we must consider how a policy of facilitating the democratic peace might work: the interaction of democracy with nationalism, the problem of democratic stability, and the prospects for changing fundamental patterns of international behavior.

COVERT ACTION AGAINST OTHER DEMOCRACIES

In the twentieth century the pattern of restraint is clear, as is evidence for normative restraints. Yet an important anomaly exists in the form of covert action by democracies against democracies. If democracies rarely use force against each other overtly, what about the circumstances of acts, sometimes called "state terrorism" (Stohl 1984; George 1991), in which the United States assisted or organized covert forcible actions against elected governments of less-developed countries? This has happened more often than is consistent with "rarely." A recent article (Forsythe 1992) lists and analyzes six such acts since 1950: against the governments of Iran (1953), Guatemala (1954), Indonesia (1957), Brazil (from 1961), Chile (1973), and Nicaragua (from 1981). It also discusses a variety of nonviolent threats or actions against other states, and some cases that have not been clearly substantiated. Unsubstantiated cases, and ones not actually involving the threat or use of military force, need not deeply concern us here. But the six listed actions must.

All of these happened during the Cold War era. They were undertaken against governments that were politically leftist and thought, by many Americans, to be too sympathetic to communism. The Guatemalan, Indonesian, and Nicaraguan regimes had accepted arms from communist states. In each of the six cases (least probably Brazil, most probably Nicaragua) some American officials feared that at some point the leftist regime might become formally allied with the contending superpower, the Soviet Union. By the American ideology of the day, once democracy were truly lost its return from totalitarianism could not be expected. Whereas some of the targeted chiefs of state were certainly not communists (Mossadegh in Iran, Sukarno in Indonesia, Goulart in Brazil), others were openly Marxist in their ideology: Allende in Chile and Arbenz in Guatemala, for example; and Ortega in Nicaragua could with reasonable confidence and accuracy be labeled a Leninist. American officials might believe they were defending at least the chances for democracy.

American fears were often excessive—certainly as regards the possibility of a military security threat to the United States emerging—and masked deep aversion to governments openly advocating socialist principles and ready to expropriate assets of Western investors. Unopposed success in such endeavors would surely have undermined economic interests that the United States was trying to defend globally. Yet all of these leaders had been installed by some form of electoral process, a process that in several instances was clearly democratic. Arguments over the exact ideological proclivities of particular leaders, or the potential for Cold War security threats, may help explain the reasoning behind American actions, but they cannot obscure the democratic elections that put these leaders into power. What then, do these events imply for our propositions about democratic governments behaving peacefully toward each other?

Two responses are relevant. First, these governments were not fully democratic according to the criteria that have been applied here for late twentieth-century regimes; rather, all were anocracies. Mossadegh, while chosen by an elected parliament, shared formal executive authority and control of the army with the shah—who was far more sympathetic to Western interests. When Mossadegh's coalition began to collapse, he demanded and received authoritarian powers to rule by decree, bypassing parliament and seizing command of the army from the shah. The country's economic situation became desperate. Democracy in Iran was tenuous at best (Bill 1988; Saikal 1980; Reisman and Baker 1992, 49). Ortega and the Sandinistas, who took power in a popular revolution against the Somoza dictatorship, disdained Western-style institutions and elections. After seizing power in 1979 and initially promising elections, in 1980 they announced that elections would be postponed until 1985 (Pastor 1987). When the Reagan administration first moved to organize violent military actions against them, the Sandinistas may have been popular, but they were not democratic. Elections were in fact held in 1984, with an open if restricted opposition, in which the opposition gained about 38 percent of the vote. But some oppositionists boycotted the election, protesting it was not truly free. The Nicaraguan situation is not clearly democratic.

By Guatemalan standards, the election installing Arbenz in 1950 was free, although illiterate men had to vote in public rather than by secret ballot, and illiterate women could not vote at all. Arbenz was probably truly preferred by the majority (Gleijeses 1991). His regime turned from anocratic to authoritarian in 1954, but this was in large part a response to the growing security pressures he knew he faced from the United States. Sukarno also came to power after Indonesia's first election, a reasonably free and competitive one in 1955. But the parliamentary system was messy and unstable, with eight different governments in as many years since independence. In February 1957 Sukarno returned from a tour of communist countries to deliver a speech prescribing "guided democracy" for Indonesia: parties were to be disbanded and he would rule with an advisory council that he himself would appoint (Prados 1986, 134). Although he did not formally institute "guided democracy" until several years later, he did quickly proclaim a state of war and seige, restricting civil liberties and leaning more on the military for support. While Guatemalan and Indonesian practices were freer than those of many other Third World states of the time, few of the standard lists of regime types call either of these governments democratic.

In Brazil, Goulart's government certainly came to power by normal democratic processes, though severe economic difficulties, aggravated by the growing scope of his proposed reforms, undermined its political stability. Various efforts to rule by decree and plebiscite, bypassing Congress, weakened democratic institutions and fed fears that they would not long survive. As for Chile, the Allende regime harassed the opposition in minor ways, but the country is widely regarded as a democracy until the Pinochet coup in 1973. Had war erupted between the United States and Chile we would have had to reexamine any generalization that democracies do not make war on each other.

Where the governments were overthrown (Iran, Guatemala, Brazil, Chile) their replacements were less democratic than their predecessors (though that was not necessarily the U.S. intention). Nevertheless, in every case the targeted governments could plausibly be seen as unstably democratic, with a leader either unwilling or unable to resist radical pressures for reform employing authoritarian methods. Hence we find support in these cases for the hypothesis from chapter 2 that when a democracy does use or threaten to use force against another, it will be at a target that is perceived to be unstably democratic.

Furthermore, these were not wars, openly fought by military units of the United States. They were low-cost operations designed to minimize public attention. They were covert actions in which involvement was denied or publicly minimized by the U.S. government. Although the CIA provided money, weapons, and advice to the Brazilian military, the U.S. role in the seizure of power was marginal—awareness, sympathy, little immediate support, but perhaps active assistance had it been needed (Skidmore 1967; Stepan 1971; Black 1977). The seizure itself was bloodless. The others, as in Chile, were not. Whereas Treverton (1987) contends that the U.S. role in the Pinochet coup has been exaggerated, the CIA and the U.S. military were not distant. Prados (1986, 320–21) says that U.S. military advisers were in the field with Chilean units, and reports the presence of various U.S communication and military units. U.S. advisers and operatives took an active part in the coup against Mossadegh and the failed effort against Sukarno. The United States fully armed and directed the invasion of Guatemala from Honduras by units of the Guatemalan army. And of course the United States maintained and supplied the contras in a nine-year civil war that could never have been sustained—nor probably even begun—without deep U.S. involvement. The United States even mined Nicaraguan ports—a formal act of war by the standards of international law (Moynihan 1990). Even that act, however, was covert and denied at the time.

Whatever legal and moral responsibility the United States government bears for these acts must not obscure the fact that American military units did not fight in an organized fashion in any of these cases. They were covert, and American participation could be denied, with varying degrees of plausibility. The Nicaraguan operation—the most protracted, expensive, and bloody of all—illustrates the point most clearly. These operations were covert, and denied, because as overt actions support for them in the U.S. political system would have been dubious at best. Whereas there was widespread support for the contras in American public opinion, and the executive branch made no bones about its hope of bringing the Sandinistas down, opposition to the Reagan administration's acts was equally widespread. In 1983 Congress explicitly forbade the administration to support military activities, and cut off funding for any actions designed to overthrow the government of Nicaragua—a prohibition that preceded the next year's election in Nicaragua. The administration's unwillingness to abide by constitutional restraints drove its operations deeper underground into a network of international arms and financing deals that led ultimately to the Iran-Contra scandals and legal prosecutions.

In a very important sense, the U.S. democratic political system worked to limit intervention. To the degree the constraints succeeded, they sprang from wariness about the prudence of being drawn into another Vietnam, combined with normative barriers to subverting the Sandinista revolution which was widely regarded as in some way legitimate. The normative restraints of democracy were sufficient to drive the operations underground amid circumstances when the administration otherwise might well have undertaken an overt intervention. Normative/cultural and structural/institutional restraints were strong enough to forestall open military action, but not strong enough to prevent a secret operation or to stop it except belatedly. The constraints could and did prevent an interstate war, but could not preserve the United States from deep culpability in initiating and sustaining one side in a formally "civil" war.

THE DISCOURSE AT THE END OF THE COLD WAR

Looking intensively at the discourse of conflict can illuminate the fundamental norms underlying decisions, and the importance of the norms by which an adversary is perceived to govern. Decisions must be seen to conform to those norms if they are to be publicly acceptable. The evolution of President Bush's statements about the Iraqi invasion of Kuwait, and about the need for the United States to counter it, pointedly illustrates the impact that Bush expected his characterization of the Iraqi regime to make. Preparing the entire military and diplomatic effort required a great deal of time. The delay was partly caused by the time needed to put the vast Desert Storm military machine into place. But surmounting the structural constraints initially posed by Congress and public opinion, and the need to bring together a great international coalition in the rather democratic forum of the United Nations, also slowed the juggernaut. The Bush administration's rhetoric had to establish, beyond any doubt, that normative restraints did not apply against Iraq; indeed that proper norms of international conduct "required" military action against it.

As reported in *Public Papers of the Presidents of the United States*, Bush's speeches and responses to reporters' questions early in August 1990 referred almost exclusively to Iraq and its government rather than to Saddam Hussein personally—by a ratio of more than four to one. But his August 15 remarks to Department of Defense employees brought a marked shift. He referred less than half as often to Iraq as an actor than to Iraq's "leader." He described "Saddam" as having "lied to his Arab neighbors," as "the man who has used poison gas against the men, women, and children of his own country," and drew a clear distinction: "It is the Iraqi people who suffer today because of the raw territorial ambition of Saddam Hussein." Bush also carefully separated Saddam Hussein from Arabs in general, asserting that "the vast majority of the Arab people are with us."

His August 20 speech reiterated, still implicitly but clearly enough, the analogy that would soon be explicit and endlessly repeated. After referring to the experience of World War II, he declared: "The world is now called upon to confront another aggressor, another threat made by a person who has no values when it comes to respecting international law, a man of evil standing against human life itself." The next day his comparison of Saddam Hussein with "the base characteristics of Hitler" was overt, and on August 30 he again made the distinction between him and his nation: "The Iraqi regime stands in opposition to the entire world and to the interest of the Iraqi people. . . . We have no argument with the people of Iraq." Even so, in this period when there was some hope for a peaceful resolution of the crisis Bush typically referred twice as often to Iraq as specifically to its leader.

By late October, however, expectations of offensive military action against Iraq grew. After increasingly leaning that way for several weeks, on October 30 the president authorized the doubling of U.S. forces in the Persian Gulf area, to permit an offensive. To build political support, his references to Saddam Hussein grew more frequent and more vitriolic: a vicious dictator, a tyrant, and a bully. Bush regularly drew the distinction between his "outrageous aggression," violating "every standard of civilized behavior," and the Iraqi people for whom "we have only friendship." The Iraqi leader used "chemical weapons against his own people," who had seen him "take his own country, one that should be wealthy and prosperous, and turn it into a poor country all because of insatiable appetite for military equipment and conquest." By late November Bush was referring to Saddam Hussein more than three times as often as to Iraq, and many of the latter references were there simply to make the distinction. The analogy to Hitler became part of the regular litany. (Also see O'Neill forthcoming, chap. 5.) On January 5 he proclaimed, "Each day that passes increases Saddam's worldwide threat to democracy."

In building popular support for Desert Storm, George Bush evidently thought it essential to make unmistakable the antidemocratic nature of Saddam's rule as a threat to the "freedom of friendly countries around the world" (conveniently ignoring the character of some of the regimes allied with the U.S). Mention of the danger posed by Iraq to U.S. access to oil supplies nearly vanished after Bush's early pronouncements, and such a reference in his January 5 address was prefaced by: "The struggling new-born democracies of Eastern Europe and Latin America already face a staggering challenge in making the transition to a free market. But the added weight of higher oil prices is a crushing burden they cannot afford." Other realist themes such as the defense of the territorial integrity and sovereignty of small states, and the threat of Iraqi chemical and potential nuclear weapons, were certainly represented aplenty. But these strategic dangers were regularly and increasingly coupled with Bush's view of the odious nature of Saddam Hussein and his regime.[1] It surely would have been harder to build consent to military action against a less readily diabolized political system.

Consider also the end of the Cold War. The Cold War was of course a conflict about power and security, well characterized by realist models of the insecurity of states in an anarchic system. But it was also, in ideology and rhetoric, a conflict about political/economic systems and a struggle between democratic and totalitarian ones. So long as power realities pitted two great alliances against each other, and the differences between the political systems of most members of each bloc were (warts and all) evident, theory about whether the conflict would remain even if both sides were democratic was little more than idle speculation. But when all the basic parameters of Cold War politics changed at the beginning of the 1990s, theory became immediately relevant to policy. Academics still theorized, but policymakers had to make decisions, and to justify them in the realm of public discourse. Not surprisingly, they chose to use both theories.

Andrei Kozyrev (1988, 3), who under Boris Yeltsin became Russia's foreign minister, stated what is instantly recognizable in Western discourse as an argument about the linkage between domestic political systems and international relations:

> Nor can there be any trust in dictatorial, antipopular regimes which are all but inevitably spreading methods of violence beyond their national borders as well. . . And why were our partners frightened by Stalinism? There are many reasons, but one is perfectly clear; i.e., it is difficult to have confidence in a

society which is mired in all-out suspicion, it is hard to trust a regime that has no faith in its own people.

And in his state visit of May 1988 Ronald Reagan twice in the same day expressed a similar belief—both more tentatively and yet more poetically.

> We believe that the greater the freedoms in other countries the more secure both our own freedoms and peace.
>
> In this Moscow spring, this May 1988, we may be allowed to hope that freedom . . . will blossom forth at last in the rich soil of your people and culture. We may be allowed to hope that the marvelous sound of a new openness will keep rising through, ringing through, leading to a new world of reconciliation, friendship, and peace.

Reagan was among the first Western leaders to articulate this hope. Mikhail Gorbachev responded in an address to the United Nations in December, "Our ideal is a world community of states with political systems and foreign policies based on law." An immediate question, however, was whether the hope could become reality. Despite further liberalization in the Soviet Union, members of the new Bush administration were wary. In May 1989 Secretary of State James Baker praised the release of political prisoners and emigration reforms, and declared that "the Soviets now talk of enforcing the rule of law and other guarantees of individual rights. . . . Limited elections have taken place. . . ." But, he added, "We must all, I think, face the fact that the Soviets continue to pose a sigificant military threat. . . . For all the talk of 'defensive defense,' Soviet military exercises still continue to show a marked inclination for taking the offensive. For all the talk of openness, the Soviets have yet to publish a real defense budget. . . ." And in the same month, President Bush, after repeatedly expressing "hope" of fundamental domestic change, warned, "But the national security of America and our allies is not predicated on hope. It must be based on deeds. We look for enduring, ingrained economic and political changes." He went on to list a long series of changes in diplomatic behavior and military capabilities that were needed if the Soviet government's professions of new ideals were to be persuasive.

Both men stayed cautious throughout 1989. On October 16 Baker elaborated on the realist risks (continued or even reinvigorated Soviet power), the distance yet to go, and the *possibility* of a fundamental linkage between democracy at home and peaceful international behavior.

> We must not succumb to a false optimism that *perestroika* in Soviet foreign policy has gone far enough that we can rely on new thinking to take account of our interests. It would be an equally great blunder to ignore the possibility that

perestroika might go much further and to retreat instead into a suspicious stance of disengagement that would never put *perestroika* to the test. . . .

We want *perestroika* to succed at home and abroad because we believe that it will bring about a less aggressive Soviet Union, restrained in the use of force, and less hostile to democracy. A *perestroika* that resulted simply in a more efficient and capable Soviet State would, instead, be a more formidable and dangerous competitor.

But I do not believe that *perestroika* can succeed without . . . a more democratic society, more respectful of human rights and legal norms which could provide a lasting foundation for more constructive, less dangerous Soviet behavior abroad . . . a society where citizens have a say in what their government does at home and abroad.

In Moscow the next February, after the destruction of the Berlin Wall, Baker was less skeptical about internal change: "Universal, democratic values are taking root here. . . . In just 5 short years, your peoples are enjoying freedom and liberty in a way that—at least to a foreign observer—seems unparalleled in Soviet history." But in May, on receiving the Hans J. Morgenthau Memorial Award from the National Committee on American Foreign Policy, he remained very much the realist about politics among nations, expressing continued concern about Soviet military capabilities: "Even if all Soviet armed forces return to the USSR and conventional arms control moves forward, the Soviet military will retain forces many times larger than those possessed by any other single state. . . . Deterrence must be maintained by an appropriate and reliable mix of conventional and nuclear forces."

Despite the reunification of Germany in October 1990 and the collapse of communism throughout Eastern Europe, President Bush stayed cautious. Kremlin repression in Lithuania in 1991 did not help. "Change in the Soviet Union has helped to create a basis for unprecedented cooperation and partnership between the United States and the Soviet Union. . . . The events that we're witnessing now are completely inconsistent with that course. . . . Events like those now taking place in the Baltic States threaten to set back or perhaps even reverse the process of reform which is so important in the world and the development of the new international order."

But by 1992, after the failed coup and the breakup of the Soviet Union, both Bush and Baker proclaimed that things had indeed changed. In doing so, they accepted the principle of democratic peace—and explicitly discarded the principle that power relationships alone matter, or even matter most.

Baker on February 5: "The Cold War has ended, and we now have a chance to forge a democratic peace, an enduring peace built on shared values—democracy and political and economic freedom. The strength of these values in Russia and the other new independent states will be the surest foundation for peace—and the strongest guarantee of our national security—for decades to come." And on April 21: "Shared democratic values can ensure an enduring and stable peace in a way the balance of terror never could. Real democracies do not go to war with each other." As for Bush, on April 1, he sought economic support: "A victory for democracy and freedom in the former USSR creates the possibility of a new world of peace for our children and grandchildren, but if this democratic revolution is defeated, it could plunge us into a world more dangerous in some respects than the dark years of the Cold War. . . . This effort will require new resources from the industrial democracies, but nothing like the price we would pay if democracy and reform failed. . . ." And on April 9: "A democratic Russia is the best guarantee against a renewed danger of competition and the threat of nuclear rivalry." The potential of power in the old Soviet Union had not gone away, but the chance to nullify it with the peaceful intentions of democracy was at hand. A very unrealist position.

FROM THE INSIDE OUT

The image of a world of peaceful relations among democracies represents an extension of democratic politics within states generally, and of immediate interpersonal relations. In democracies, ordinary people's images of other countries' behavior are heavily conditioned by perceptions of their politics and culture, and especially whether the politics and culture is like their own (Nincic and Russett 1979). Surveys in Japan and the United States in late 1989 asked people, "What countries do you think can be trusted?" For Americans, the twelve most trusted countries all were democracies (including Japan); in Japan, the top ten were democracies (including America; number 11 was China, which had fallen dramatically after the Tienanmen Square repression). (See Hastings and Hastings, eds., 1991, 684–85.)

A *Euro-baromètre* (no. 25, June 1986, 35–43) survey asked citizens of each country in the European Community whether the people of every other country in the community, and citizens of six other states (China, Japan, the Soviet Union, Switzerland, Turkey, and the United States), were "in general very trustworthy, fairly trustworthy, not particularly trustworthy, or not at all trustworthy." At the time, all twelve members of the EC were democracies, as were three of the others (not China or the Soviet Union, and Turkey's democratic processes had been largely suspended under military rule). In six of the twelve EC countries, Russians, Chinese, and Turks—in different orders—rated as the three least trustworthy nations, after all fourteen democracies. Either the Russians or the Turks were last on everyone's list, and eight of the twelve listed the Chinese on the untrustworthy side of the balance. Some country quirks are evident, but it is not just a matter, for example, of trusting their fellow EC partners. (Italians rated nine nations as on the untrustworthy side, and were not rated terribly high by others either). Only two countries considered the Japanese to be on balance untrustworthy. Whatever the quirks, political system type is a very strong correlate of trust, and it was generally the democratic nations that were trusted. Here is further evidence, consistent with the theoretical argument of this book, that even an ordinary citizen makes clear distinctions between international partners and adversaries based their political systems.

It is time to take seriously the proposition that the policies of states in international relations, and their peoples' support for those policies, derive in large part from their fundamental values and images.[2] That people's views on domestic politics are associated with their views on foreign policy is old news (Russett and Hanson 1975; Holsti and Rosenau 1988; Wittkopf 1990). Yet it is worth emphasizing that particular kinds of beliefs about political responsibility and political order at home and abroad are related.

Among American leaders ("elites"), attitudes on a congeries of domestic political issues (civil rights, civil liberties, the death penalty, redistribution of income) are strong predictors of attitudes toward aid to poor countries, strengthening the United Nations, and other forms of international cooperation (Murray 1993). New work on the political basis of support for economic assistance to poor countries (Lumsdaine 1992; 1993, chap. 5) shows at great length how, in industrial democracies in general, support for foreign aid paralleled personal values and positions on domestic politics. Among both elites and masses (public opinion data), people who favored aid were more often politically left on domestic politics, religious, supporters of equality and social spending to alleviate poverty, and private contributors to voluntary organizations concerned with overseas development. Supporters of realist policies (strengthening defense, colonialism) were less likely to support this kind of foreign aid. Among nation states, those devoting the highest proportions of their GNP to foreign aid were also those with very high levels of domestic social spending.

There is more here than just the fact that liberals on domestic policy tend to be cooperative internationalists, or accomodationists, or idealists, on foreign policy. Personal moral beliefs, values in domestic politics, and views on international relations are all related. And there is less here than a demonstrated causal relationship from one to the other. Yet many policy attitudes—on foreign and domestic issues—may be the result of a deeper causal structure rooted in core values (Rokeach 1973). Attitudes toward the Soviet Union, for example, were deeply resistant to change. Finlay, Holsti, and Fagen's (1967) classic study showed how, with the application of an "inherent bad faith" model, a political "enemy's" behavior, however conciliatory, could always be interpreted as manifesting hostile intent. Changes do sometimes occur, however, even in images of the "enemy," in response to changes in other states' attributes and behavior. To understand their effects a complex analytical framework may be required.

Hurwitz and Peffley (1990) and Peffley and Hurwitz (1992) studied the foreign policy belief systems of Americans. They developed a layered set of direct and indirect influences operating from core values (patriotism, moral traditionalism, religious fundamentalism), to images of the Soviet Union (trust, threat), to general foreign policy postures (militarism, containment), and ultimately to specific foreign policy attitudes. Using a panel study with repeated interviews of the same people, once in June 1987 and again in June 1988, Peffley and Hurwitz (1992) related images of the Soviet Union to general attitudes on foreign policy. Moreover, they looked at both current and previous (a year earlier) images to see how they affected changes in foreign policy attitudes. Items on the Soviet Union included whether the Soviet government was "deceitful" and "dishonest," why Gorbachev proposed loosening censorship, and why he was holding elections—whether he was sincere in wanting to give citizens more freedom, or just trying to create that impression. In other words, had the Soviet political system changed significantly at home and in its behavior abroad?

They found that changes in responses to these questions about images produced changed policy preferences on nuclear armaments, defense spending, aid to the Nicaraguan contras, and military policy in Central America more generally. Images of other countries' political systems, though partially rooted in core values, often do change in response to changes in the countries themselves. Moreover, changes in those images causally (directly and indirectly) affect how people wish to behave toward other countries.[3]

STRENGTHENING DEMOCRACY AND ITS NORMS

The Bush-Baker rhetoric about the need to strengthen democracy in the former Soviet Union was, in terms of this book's findings, on target. But it may have raised excessive expectations about the ability of the United States (and perhaps its allies) effectively to do so. It is an old American foreign policy error to exaggerate the effect the United States can have on others. It is an even greater mistake in an era when the United States lacks the economic resources it could muster in earlier decades, and especially at the end of World War II. More to the point, the United States has lacked the will to employ the resources it does have. As of early 1992 its total contribution to economic recovery in the former Soviet Union amounted to a miserly one-ninth of Germany's (Light 1992, 73–74). There will be no repetition of the Marshall Plan to consolidate today's emerging democracies. But amid all the helpful internal conditions for aspiring democracies, external influences can make a contribution—often modest, sometimes critical.

The literature on the "prerequisites" of democracy is vast, and much of it is deeply flawed—ethnocentric and too enamoured of economic pre-conditions. Yet some things have been learned, and stated with some modesty, in recent analyses. Among several good efforts (Dahl 1989; O'Donnell, Schmitter, and Whitehead 1986; Diamond, Linz, and Lipset, eds., 1989; DiPalma 1990; Rueschmeyer, Stephens, and Stephens 1992; also the review in Allison and Beschel 1992), the most prominent may be Samuel Huntington's new book (1991, 45–46). Since it reviews most of the earlier literature a summary of its conclusions should suffice. Nor do its conclusions depart markedly from those of most other recent analyses. Huntington begins by identifying five changes in the world that played significant parts in *producing* the latest wave of recent transitions to de-mocracy: (1) deepening legitimacy problems of authoritarian govern-ments unable to cope with military defeat and economic failure; (2) eco-nomic growth that has raised living standards, educational levels, and urbanization—raising expectations and the ability to express them; (3) changes in religious institutions that made them less defenders of the status quo than opponents of governmental authoritarianism; (4) changes in the policies of other states and international organizations, to promote human rights and democracy; (5) "snowballing" or demonstra-tion effects, enhanced by international communication, as transitions to democracy in some states served as models for their neighbors.

Later in the book (1991, 270–79), Huntington lists conditions that have favored or are favoring the *consolidation* of new democracies: (1) experience of a previous effort at democratization, even if it failed; (2) a high level of economic development; (3) a favorable international politi-cal environment, with outside assistance; (4) early timing of the transition to democracy, relative to a worldwide "wave," indicating that the drive to democracy derived primarily from indigenous rather than exogenous influences; (5) experience of a relatively peaceful rather than violent tran-sition; (6) the number and severity of the problems confronted.

Such lists do not lead to simple diagnosis or prescription, with "neces-sary" or "sufficient" conditions, but they do offer a helpful focus for discussion. Most importantly, they single out both internal and external influences on the process of democratization. Internal influences are certainly prominent, especially in the consolidation list. It is hard to imagine a successful consolidation of democracy without many or most of them. But the list of international conditions is impressive also. Favorable international conditions may not be essential (either alone or in combination) in every case, but they can make a difference, and sometimes a crucial one when the internal influences are mixed. The United States and its allies have made a difference—for the defeated Axis powers after World War II, and sometimes in other cases since that time.

Currently, with economic conditions so bad in much of the Third World, Eastern Europe, and the former Soviet Union, and the consequent dangers to the legitimacy of new democratic governments, external assistance—technical and financial—is especially important. Rather small amounts—but more than have been forthcoming to date—could make a difference. As a stick, aid can surely be denied to governments that regularly violate human rights, for example of ethnic minorities. Clear antidemocratic acts, such as a military coup or an aborted election, can be punished by suspending aid. As to the carrot of extending aid on a conditional basis, broader goals of developing democratic institutions require creation of a civil society, and are less easily made conditional. Recipients may see multilateral aid, with conditions of democratic reform attached, as a less blatant invasion of their sovereignty than aid from a single country (Nelson 1992). Without exaggerating the prospects for success, it would be a terrible loss if the United States and other rich democracies did not make serious efforts. It would be a loss, as the Bush-Baker rhetoric claims, to themselves as well as to the peoples of the struggling democracies.

A special complication, one hardly unique to the current era but felt acutely now, is nationalism in the quilt of ethnicities left behind from the former Soviet Empire. Nationalism, with its combination of inclusion and exclusion, readily conflicts with the quasi-universalistic ethos of "democracies don't fight each other." Hatreds, long suppressed, emerge to bedevil any effort to build stable, legitimate government. They bring border conflicts to liberate or incorporate "oppressed" minorities, and civil wars. Civil wars often are contests between ethnic groups for exclusive control of the central coercive institutions of the state. The conflict then becomes one over the right of some minority ethnic groups to secede from the control of those institutions, and in doing so frequently to take with them other ethnic groups who may in turn consider themselves oppressed by their new government. Neither the institutions nor the experience of "live and let live" may exist.

An irony is that the initial creation of democratic institutions may contribute to the explosion of ethnic conflicts, by providing the means of free expression, including expression of hatred and feelings of oppression. That does not mean, however, that the solution lies in less democracy. Rather, it likely lies in devising institutions, and nurturing norms and practices, of democratic government with respect for minority rights. It may also require allowing the secession of groups who are not satisfied that their rights and interests can be sufficiently respected under a single government. A consolation may be that nationalism in a democratic era probably dooms any substantial effort of imperialism that would incorporate into a larger political unit different ethnic groups against their will. The will of acquired peoples to separation can be repressed only at great cost and risk. Nationalism need not be inconsistent with respect for human rights (Tamir 1993). The creation of institutions, norms, and practices to protect minorities has never been easy. But it presents the fundamental challenge of world political development in this era.

Again recall the requirement, for a democratic peace, of stability of democracy and perceptions of stability. For the near future, at least, that condition is likely to be in short supply in much of the world. If one's neighbor has vast unsolved economic problems, is it politically stable? Has it experienced democracy long enough, with some success in managing its problems, to be stable? If it is "democratic" for some, even a majority, of its citizens, but forcibly represses its minorities, is it "stable?" Many of the new states of the old Soviet Union fail these and other tests. Some have not yet had a real democratic transition.

Georgia, for example, did elect, by reasonably democratic procedures, Zviad Gamsakhurdia as president when it was still a republic in the Soviet Union. But on independence, he seized dictatorial powers. In January 1992 he was finally overthrown in bitter fighting, and replaced (but not by election) by Eduard Shevardnadze, who fought off a subsequent coup attempt. Meanwhile, severe ethnic violence continued in the secessionist region of Abkhazia. Elections to confirm Shevardnadze's status as democratic leader were not held until October. Georgia in 1992 may have been an aspiring democracy or a nascent democracy, but it was not yet a stable democracy nor, by any reasonable international standard, even just a "democracy." Until its democracy is established, it should surprise no one if Georgia or states like it get into war with their neighbors. Nor would such a war invalidate a "democracies don't go to war with each other" generalization.

Another threat to the theory and the reality of "democracies don't go to war with each other" lurks in the Middle East. Save for Turkey much of the time, and Lebanon for a while, Israel has been the only stable democracy in that part of the world. Israel's democracy is surely flawed by the treatment of its Arab subjects, but in most respects it has well earned the label of democracy. If an Arab state should achieve an equivalent degree of democracy, and then go to war with Israel, we would have a blatant exception to the proposition.

Unless one categorically rules that "Arab democracy" is an oxymoron—and I do not—such an event is imaginable. A Muslim fundamentalist movement might achieve power in the name of democracy. We will never know what might have been in Algeria had the military not seized power after the elections of 1991. But, conceivably, such a regime could have been both stable and somewhat democratic; i.e., while promoting Islamic values of a majority it might have respected minority rights and tolerated the expression of secular opposition under domestic and international pressures. Such a government probably would not be seen as a major security threat to nonfundamentalist neighboring regimes. Would such a fundamentalist government fight Israel if the military situation seemed propitious? Perhaps, as part of an alliance with other Islamic states. Certainly the normative restraints on democracies not fighting each other would be sorely stressed by the entrenched normative roots of Arab-Israeli hostility. But such a state might be less likely itself to initiate a war, thanks to structural as well as possible normative constraints.

CAN A WIDER DEMOCRATIC PEACE BE BUILT?

Understanding that democracies rarely fight each other, and why, has great consequence for policy in the contemporary world, as well as for theoretical debates of "realists" vs. "idealists" or "liberal transnationalists." It should affect the kinds of military preparations believed to be necessary, and the costs one would be willing to pay to make them. It should encourage peaceful efforts to assist the emergence and consolidation of democracy. But a misunderstanding of it could encourage warmaking against authoritarian regimes, and efforts to overturn them—with all the costly implications of preventive or hegemonic military activity such a policy might imply. Not all authoritarian states are necessarily aggressive. In fact, at any particular time, the great majority are not.

Recollection of the post-1945 success with defeated adversaries can be both instructive and misleading. It is instructive in showing that democracy could supplant a thoroughly discredited totalitarian regime, at a time when authoritarianism in general was not held in high esteem globally. It can be misleading if one forgets how expensive it was (Marshall Plan aid, and important economic concessions to Japan), and especially if one misinterprets the political conditions of military defeat. The United States and its allies utterly defeated the old regimes. To solidify democratic government the allies conducted vast (if incomplete) efforts to remove the former elites from positions of authority. But they had something to build on, in the form of individuals and institutions from previous experiences with democracy. The model of "fight them, beat them, and then make them democratic" is irrevocably flawed as a basis for contemporary action. It probably would not work anyway, and no one is prepared to make the kind of effort that would be required. A crusade for democracy is not in order.

External military intervention, even against the most odious dictators, is a dangerous way to try to produce a "democratic world order." Sometimes, with a cautious cost-benefit analysis and with the certainty of substantial and legitimate internal support, it may be worthwhile—that is, under conditions when rapid military success is likely *and* the will of the people at issue is clear. Even so, any time an outside power supplants any existing government the problem of legitimacy is paramount. The very democratic norms to be instilled may be compromised. At the least, intervention should not be unilateral. It must be approved, publicly and willingly, by some substantial international body like the UN or the OAS. Under most circumstances, even such international bodies are better used as vehicles to promote democratic processes at times when the relevant domestic parties are ready. Peacekeeping operations to help provide the conditions for free elections, monitor those elections, and advice on the building of democratic institutions are usually far more promising than is military intervention. The UN, newly strengthened with the end of the Cold War, has emerged as a major facilitator of peaceful transitions and democratic elections in such places as Cambodia, Namibia, El Salvador, and Nicaragua.[4]

Perhaps most important, understanding the sources of democratic peace can have the effect of a self-fulfilling prophecy. Social scientists sometimes create reality as well as analyze it. Insofar as norms do guide behavior, repeating those norms helps to make them effective. Repeating the norms as descriptive principles can help to make them true. Repeating the proposition that democracies should not fight each other helps reinforce the probability that democracies will not fight each other. It is an empirical fact that democracies rarely fight each other. They do not need to fight each other because they can employ alternative methods of conflict resolution, and at less cost than through violent conflict. A norm that democracies should not fight each other thus is prudentially reinforced, and in turn strengthens the empirical fact about infrequent violent conflict.

Norms may be violated and break down. Nevertheless, norms do constrain behavior, both by affecting what one wants to do and what one may be able to persuade others to do or not to do. The discourse of ethics, and of politics, is for instrumental as well as moral reasons largely a normative one. For example, the wrenching abortion debate is overwhelmingly a normative conflict ("respect life" versus "respect choice") for the control of public policy. In a world where democracy has become wide-spread, understanding the fact of the "democratic peace" proposition will help to make it true. So too will wider acceptance of the norm.

In turn, a stable and less menacing international system can permit the emergence and consolidation of democratic governments. Harold Lass-well's (1941) dire warnings of "a world of garrison states" may have been extreme, and some of the charges about a "military-industrial complex" a quarter of a century ago were shrill and exaggerated. Nevertheless, it is hard to refute the argument (Gurr 1988) that international threats—real or only perceived—strengthen the forces of secrecy and authoritarianism in the domestic politics of states involved in "protracted conflict." Relax-ation of international threats to peace and security reduces both the need, and the excuse, for repression of democratic dissent. Democracy and the expectation of international peace can feed on each other to mitigate both the real and the perceived dangers of a still anarchic international system. An evolutionary process may even be at work. Because of the visible na-ture and public costs of breaking commitments, democratic leaders may be better able to persuade leaders of other states that they will keep the agreements they enter into (Fearon 1992; Gaubatz 1992). Democracies more often win their wars than do authoritarian states (Lake 1992), whether because they are more effective in marshaling their resources or are more accurate and efficient information processors (Deutsch 1963). And the government of the loser of a war is much more likely to be over-thrown subsequently (Stein and Russett 1980; Bueno de Mesquita, Siver-son, and Woller 1992), and may be replaced by a democratic regime.

Perhaps major features of the international system can be socially con-structed from the bottom up; that is, norms and rules of behavior interna-tionally can become extensions of the norms and rules of domestic politi-cal behavior. The modern international system is commonly traced to the Treaty of Westphalia and the principles of sovereignty and noninterfer-ence in internal affairs affirmed by it. In doing so it affirmed the anarchy of the system, without a superior authority to ensure order. It also was a treaty among princes who ruled as autocrats. Our understanding of the modern anarchic state system risks conflating the effects of anarchy with those stemming from the political organization of its component units. When most states are ruled autocratically—as in 1648 and throughout virtually all of history since—then playing by the rules of autocracy may be the only way for any state, democracy or not, to survive in Hobbesian anarchy. Alexis de Tocqueville's doubts (1945, esp. part I, chap. 13) about democracies' ability to pursue stable and enlightened foreign poli-cies are well known. But Tocqueville was writing in 1835, mindful of a realist anarchic system in which the vast majority of states were still au-tocracies. A democracy which tried to operate by democratic norms was at a great disadvantage, and might well shift policy unstably in trying to adjust to the risks.

The emergence of new democracies with the end of the Cold War presents an opening for change in the international system more fundamental even than at the end of other big wars—World Wars I and II and the Napoleonic Wars. For the first time ever, in 1992 a virtual majority of states (91 of 183; McColm et al., 1992, 47) approximated the standards we have employed for democracy. Another 35 were in some form of transition to democracy. Democracy in many of these states may not prove stable. This global democratic wave may crest and fall back, as earlier ones have done. But if the chance for wide democratization can be grasped and consolidated, international politics might be transformed.

A system composed substantially of democratic states might reflect very different behavior than did the previous one composed predominantly of autocracies. If, after winning the Cold War at immense cost, the alliance of industrial democracies should now let slip a chance to solidify basic change in the principles of international order at much lower cost, our children will wonder. If history is imagined to be the history of wars and conquest, then a democratic world might in that sense represent "the end of history." Some autocratically governed states will surely remain in the system. But if enough states become stably democratic in the 1990s, then there emerges a chance to reconstruct the norms and rules of the international order to reflect those of democracies in a majority of interactions. A system created by autocracies centuries ago might now be recreated by a critical mass of democratic states.

Notes

CHAPTER 1
THE FACT OF DEMOCRATIC PEACE

1. This finding is sometimes attributed to Doyle (1983a, b; 1986). The first empirical reports were Babst 1964, 1972; Wallensteen 1973; and Small and Singer 1976. Early theoretical contributions, later empirical reports, and reviews include Rummel 1976, 1979, 1981, 1983, 1987; Russett and Starr 1981, chap. 15; Chan 1984; Weede 1984; Gantzel 1987; Domke 1988; Duroselle 1988; Maoz and Abdolali 1989; Fukuyama 1989; Russett 1990, chap. 5; Bremer 1992a; Bueno de Mesquita and Lalman 1982; and Maoz and Russett 1992. Ray 1990, 240, concurs with Levy 1988 that this constitutes "as close as anything we have to an empirical law in international relations"; also see Gleditsch 1992. For a general statement on the importance of studying international relations at the level of pairs of states, rather than at the state or system level, see Most and Starr 1989.

2. The Baker and Bush statements are quoted in chapter 6; Clinton's emerged prominently in his speech to the Los Angeles World Affairs Council, August 13, 1992 (*New York Times*, August 14, 1992, A15).

3. Virtually all the authors cited in note 1 agree that democracies are not in general markedly less likely to go to war than are other states. The principal dissenter is Rummel 1983, 1985. But his empirical analysis (1983) is limited to 1976–80—a period that omits, among others, the Vietnam War and most post-colonial wars—and his literature review (1985) has been overtaken and corrected by subsequent empirical analyses. Other work (Bremer 1992a,b) suggests a mixed and still muddy picture; i.e., democracies are less likely to originate wars with all kinds of states, but more likely to join ongoing wars being fought by other states.

4. With some variations in the mix and in the precise empirical applications, these elements are common in the cross-national literature. By the middle to late twentieth century the requirement for a responsible executive becomes largely redundant to the other conditions (Vanhanen 1990), but it certainly is not for the nineteenth century. A good measurement discussion is Merritt and Zinnes 1991.

5. Rotberg 1980, 30, further reports that voters had to be "approved by the elders of the Dutch Reformed Church," but the constitutional provision requiring a voter to be a member of the church was repealed immediately after its passage in 1858 (Eybers 1918, 368–69).

6. The formula for calculating the number of possible pairs is $N(N-1)/2$. Systematic statistical analyses, however, belong in subsequent chapters. The data here and for table 1.2 are from the compilation of Militarized International Disputes discussed in chapter 4.

CHAPTER 2
WHY DEMOCRATIC PEACE?

1. The trend to democratic government has been documented worldwide up to 1988 by Gastil 1989 and later by Freedom House (McColm et al. 1992), and traced back to the eighteenth century by Modelski 1989 and Gurr et al. 1991; also see Starr 1991 and Huntington 1991.

2. Weart (forthcoming) suggests that certain types of oligarchies rarely have fought each other in various historical eras, but Bremer 1992a finds no evidence for this in the modern world. Previous analyses of very broad measures of social and cultural similarity have produced mixed results (Richardson 1961; Wilkinson 1980, chap. 9; Russett 1967, chap. 11; Rummel 1979, chap. 16).

3. Russett 1967, chap. 12, finds that, if anything, states sharing membership in international organizations are more likely to be involved in violent conflict with each other.

4. See, for example, Deutsch et al. 1957 and Destler et al. 1976, esp. chap. 5. A milestone in the transnational relations literature is Keohane and Nye 1977, with institutions defined less as formal organizations than as "recognized patterns of practice around which expectations converge" (Young 1980, 337) and as facilitators of communication. An important new look at transnational relations is Risse-Kappen, forthcoming.

5. First established by Richardson 1961, corroborated in reviews by Wilkinson 1980, chap. 5; Singer 1981; and Diehl 1991, and confirmed as an independent influence by Bremer 1992a.

6. Huntington 1989 expressed great skepticism about democratic peace on this ground, and even Small and Singer 1976 strongly implied that their pioneering results on the absence of war between democracies were only an effect of distance.

7. Siverson and Emmons 1991 confirm a generalization, stronger since World War II than before it, that democracies are more likely to ally with each other than with nondemocracies. Bueno de Mesquita and Lalman 1992, chap. 5, do not confirm that over the long period they analyze.

8. Weede 1983 attributed peace among states of the Western alliance system to the U.S. hegemonic role. Recently (1992), however, he has acknowledged that mutual democracy provides a better explanation.

9. Also see Bremer 1992a, 1993 for the effect of democracy even with other controls for relative power, great power status, hegemony, and militarization.

10. Bueno de Mesquita and Lalman 1992, 155, find that by their measure the mean domestic costs to democracies of using force are greater than for nondemocracies, but the difference is small. Bremer 1992a, 1993 suggests a mixed picture; i.e., democracies are less likely to originate wars with all kinds of states, but more likely to join ongoing wars being fought by other states.

11. Most of the authors cited in chapter 1, note 2, write predominantly from this perspective.

12. I owe this argument to Zeev Maoz.

13. As we shall see in chapter 5, in fact "preindustrial" peoples often had participatory forms of government that shared many democratic attributes.

14. They are not, however, more likely just before elections to engage in the full-scale use of military force known as war; if anything they are more likely to go to war during the year just after the election has passed (Gaubatz 1991).

15. Lake 1992 (also Brawley 1992) makes a structural argument that democracies with broad franchises are inherently less imperialistic than are autocratic states, and while democracies may fight to resist autocracies, the conjuncture of two democracies with low imperialist drive makes them unlikely to fight each other. His empirical test is indirect, however, of a derived proposition that democracies will win wars in which they engage more often than will autocracies. The latter can alternatively be attributed to democracies' greater ability to motivate their citizens and to superior information-processing capability (Russett 1990, 150).

16. Ben Hunt has suggested, in a personal communication, that the degree of elites' control by public opinion may be the key variable, and that, while it is highly correlated with democracy, the correlation is not perfect—some democracies' elites may be less constrained than are others by public opinion, and some autocracies more so than others.

17. Bueno de Mesquita and Lalman 1992, chap. 5, present this hypothesis and some confirming evidence. (Similar reasoning goes back at least to Wright 1942, 842–45, and Starr 1992a,b extends the insight that forms of government signal a state's likely international behavior.) They reject (pp. 152–55) the argument that "the political culture of democracies leads to an abhorence of violence" in general, and build their theory on the assumption that democratic leaders "face a greater political cost for using force." In context they treat this as an institutional constraint, though in a personal communication Bueno de Mesquita suggested that democratic norms may similarly raise the costs.

18. Fearon (1992) argues from the structural tradition that escalation represents a costly signal especially for democratic leaders, who risk being forced to back down in front of their powerful domestic audience. If so, disputes between democracies should indeed show less escalation, but the initiation of disputes between democracies would not necessarily be less frequent.

CHAPTER 3
THE IMPERFECT DEMOCRATIC PEACE OF ANCIENT GREECE

1. The closest is Weart, forthcoming, chaps. 1 and 2. Weart is inclined to dismiss on "insufficient evidence" some ambiguous cases we count as wars between democracies.

2. All citations of Thucydides (1954/1972) are from the Warner translation; all citations of classical authors are in parentheses with book and paragraph numbers and the modern publication date. (In the bibliography, only the modern dates are given since the original writing dates are often approximate.) We also consulted translations of Thucydides by Richard Crawley (New York: Modern Library, 1982 [1st ed., 1876]) and Thomas Hobbes (New Brunswick, N.J.: Rutgers University Press, 1975 [1st ed., 1635]) for clarification. Other sources of information were Aristotle 1984; Diodorus Siculus 1962; Xenophon 1964/1979; Kagan 1969, 1971, 1981, 1987); Bury et al. 1927; Davies 1978; Farrar 1989; Finley

1971, 1973; Larson 1955, 1968; McGregor 1956; Manicas 1989. Other relevant volumes are cited at appropriate points below. Our complete listing of states and wars, with full documentation of sources as prepared chiefly by William Antholis, is available from Bruce Russett, Political Science Department, Box 3532 Yale Station, New Haven, Conn., 06520.

3. Lake's (1992) contention that democracies with wide franchises are inherently less imperialistic than are more autocratic states, and that the conjunction of two democracies with low imperialist drive makes them less likely to fight each other, would apply with less force to limited-franchise Greek democracies. Meiggs 1972, however, argues that disfranchised slaves were not so numerous as has been imagined.

4. Some scholars claim that Greek thought lacked the modern distinction between public and private spheres, with individual liberty based on personal rights. See Sartori 1987, chap. 10; Mansfield 1983. But Manicas 1989, 47, asserts: "Recent scholarship has convincingly demonstrated that the view, so frequently put forward by modern and contemporary defenders of the liberal state, that there were no constitutional restraints in the democracy of Athens cannot be sustained. . . . There was a long tradition according to which citizens had 'rights' which must be protected."

5. This is the Warner translation. Crawley reads, "What was nominally a democracy became in [Pericles'] hands government by the first citizen; and Hobbes, "It was in name, a state democratical; but in fact, a government of the principal man." Ste. Croix 1972, 28, retranslates it as "in name a democracy, but in fact on the way to becoming rule by the first citizen," stressing that Thucydides had in mind an incomplete process, not an accomplished fact.

6. Comparing Thucydides with Pseudo-Xenophon, Aristotle, and Plato, whose critiques of democracy and of Pericles were more direct and consistent, Kagan 1969, 135–36, describes Thucydides as a moderate democrat, sympathetic to Pericles and his policy of enlarging the state's scope in providing for all citizens so that they could participate in politics. Also, Finley 1942 sees Thucydides' view evolving from a democratic one in his youth to an oligarchic one in his old age.

7. Finley 1973, 72. Also, as Ostwald 1986 notes, *any* Athenian citizen had the right to lodge a complaint, through the *euthyna* procedure, against an outgoing official at the end of his annual term. See the defense by Kagan 1969, 70, citing McGregor 1956, 93, of Periclean democracy in terms of institutions: "If democracy means and is government by the citizens, if the *ekklēsia* decided policy by vote, if free elections persisted at their constitutional intervals, if Pericles was at all times responsible to the sovereign *dēmos*, and if unoppressed political opposition survived, as it surely did—if all this is so, then Athens was as democratic, not only in theory but in day-to-day practice, as government can conceivably be." Athenian conditions bear a notable resemblance to Dahl's (1971) criteria for modern democracy: wide voting franchise, contested elections, and an executive either popularly elected or responsible to an elected legislature.

8. Thucydides uses several words to refer to popular or democratic factions, including *dēmos, polloi, pleones*, or *plōthos*; the oligarchs are referred to as *oligoi, dynatoi, dynatotatoi*, or *gnōrimoi*. See Ste. Croix 1954–55.

9. Diodorus Siculus (1962, 8. 48. 4) notes: "The peoples who were struggling for leadership in Greece were devoted to opposing principles: the Lacedaemoni-

ans, for example, made it their policy to put control of the government in the hands of the leading citizens of their allied states, whereas the Athenians regularly established democracies in their cities." Yet there were certainly exceptions on both sides, and to attribute regime type solely on the basis of alliance would turn our hypothesis into a virtual tautology.

10. Alternatively, to treat them as "missing data" would throw away much information we do have on their war-fighting behavior. Meritt, Wade-Gary, and McGregor (1950, 149–54) conclude that most but far from all of the cities of the Athenian empire probably had democratic constitutions. Miscoding in the form of treating all the unknowns as nondemocratic even if some were democratic would, by the hypothesis, produce a lower observed frequency of war for democracies with unknowns than with those known to be nondemocratic—which is what we do find.

11. In principle it would be desirable to control for the number of years a given regime existed, or a state was autonomous, but the information is too often unavailable.

12. We thus treat federations of cities—Boeotia, Arcadia, Ozolian Locris, Rhodes, and at times Lesbos—as constituting one state. Their decisions seem to have been made as collectivities, not as an alliance of independent states.

13. Graham 1983 analyses many of these cases well with archaeological evidence; for other other views on the empire-autonomy distinction see Ste. Croix 1954–55, 1981.

14. During the Peloponnesian War, even more than in the modern state system, states' decisions often were not politically independent. Thus it would be more inappropriate to treat each decision as a statistically independent event. Because of that, and especially the likely sampling bias discussed above, we do not apply formal statistical tests here. The independence-of-observation problem nonetheless remains insofar as we compare gross counts of warring pairs in different cells of the table. There is no fully satisfactory solution. All cell comparisons should be read with the problem in mind, and the need remains for contextual analysis of these decisions.

15. On the phenomenon of motivated misperception, see Janis and Mann 1977. Weart, forthcoming, chap. 1, notes the difficulties of reliable communication.

16. Of such states Kagan 1969, 21–22, says, "When Sparta was strong she could and did command obedience from them. When she was weak or distracted they could go their own ways, attack their neighbors, who might also be allied to Sparta, adopt democratic constitutions, and even make alliances with another state unfriendly to Sparta. Such independence, however, was always temporary and sometimes costly." Thucydides' declares that after the Peace of Nicias the Mantineans feared Sparta's strength once it "had the time to deal with other matters."

17. Kagan 1987, 43, 60, calls Chios a mixed oligarchy. Wishing conservatively to code ambiguous cases against our hypothesis, we label Chios an "other" democracy.

18. See Finley 1973; Ste. Croix 1972, 47–48, 394; Morrison and Williams 1968. Forde (1986) gives a different argument linking Athens's democracy to its imperialism. William Antholis found a visit to modern Poros, to see a recon-

structed trireme, highly informative. To operate a trireme required highly developed technical skill in the coordination of 170 oars—a coordination demanding exceptional teamwork and decentralized action. Sparta discovered this the hard way when it attempted to build ships quickly and challenge an outnumbered Athenian fleet at Rhium (Thucydides 1954/1972, 2.83–5). The Athenian fleet never once lost to an entirely nondemocratic fleet.

19. Here our argument runs close to that of Grene 1950, 36–37: "Athenian democracy remained, as Pericles said, a model for outside imitation; but the Athenians did not feel constrained to do anything about spreading it, except as an instrument of political usefulness abroad." We disagree, however, with Grene's assertion (37) that "there were no Athenian armies kept on the spot to back the local government."

20. O'Connell 1989, 58, contends that these marvelously analytical people, while of course concerned with particular wars, paid little attention to war as a general phenomenon. "In the main the Greeks seem to have viewed war as a natural part of life not subject to internal reform." If so, to find any evidence for the notion of restraint between democracies may be especially significant.

21. See Lintott 1982, 97: "Was the *demos* in an allied city prepared to back secession from Athens, if it meant loss of democratic government? On the evidence, as we shall see in detail, the answer to this is 'no,' even when the *demos* was leaderless."

22. For example, Waltz 1979, 66; Keohane 1983, 506–8; Nye, 235. Dissenters include Alker 1988, Garst 1989, and Donnelly 1991, with a mixed judgment rendered by Doyle 1991.

CHAPTER 4
THE DEMOCRATIC PEACE SINCE WORLD WAR II

1. Morgan and Schwebach 1992 construct a measure of institutional constraints by which a few democracies are not highly constrained, and some nondemocracies are so constrained. This allows a preliminary test of institutional versus normative constraints, but only if one assumes the latter are found in all democracies and only in demcracies. Collinearity between the two variables, however, makes their results inconclusive.

2. These data were originally derived from a set developed at the COW project by Gochman and Maoz (1984) covering the period 1816 to 1976. They were updated to 1986 by Zeev Maoz, and compared (with a nearly perfect match) to a list produced by Daniel M. Jones of the University of Michigan.

3. These levels are: (1) no military confrontation, (2) verbal threat to use force, (3) display of force, as by mobilization or troop or naval movements, (4) limited use of force, including blockade, seizure of persons or territory, and clashes with some casualties, and (5) interstate war with a minimum of one thousand battle-related fatalities and, for each participant, at least one hundred such fatalities or commitment of at least one thousand troops (Gochman and Maoz 1984). We will not identify the initiator at each level. It might be valuable for some analyses to know whether, when dealing with nondemocracies, democracies are more or less likely to initiate the threat or use of force, but those questions

are not at issue here. Moreover, simple judgments about who was the first to shoot, for example, ignore complex questions about what may have provoked the shooting.

4. Adding 1 prevents division by 0 when the two states have identical scores.

5. Whether in continuous or dichotomized form, we prefer our multidimensional regime index to the Gurr et al. (1989) eleven-point index employed in some other studies. Gurr's democracy index (ignoring his autocracy scale) characterizes many more states as democratic than does ours—often with dubious face validity. For example, Gurr's democracy score for Rhodesia was 7 for 1965–78, as was South Africa's for the entire period; on our scale both received 16, well below the democracy threshold of 30. India had a Gurr score of 9 during emergency rule while ours was at 27, below the 30 threshold.

6. Tau $- b = 0.48$, Gamma $= 0.58$; $p < .001$, N $= 30,049$.

7. Because one of the variables used to produce the institutional constraints index was instrumental in producing the democracy-autocracy index in the original classification (Gurr et al. 1989), we expected some correlation between degree of constraint and degree of democratization. But because other elements also determined both measures the empirical association is only moderate ($r = 0.76$; $p < .001$ for the two continuous measures; Tau $- b = 0.72$; $p < .001$ for the categorical versions). This allows us to use the two measures in the same analysis without serious problems of multicollinearity. We also checked the validity of this measure by correlating it with Banks's measure of regime type and with Morgan and Campbell's (1991) three separate indicators (method of executive selection, decisional constraints, degree of political competition).

8. Data are available only for 1948 to 1982, restricting the number of years that can be analyzed with this measure. This source tends to overreport democracies and other states in the "center" of the world political system, and to underreport violence in nondemocratic and peripheral states (where information may be suppressed, and to which the press gives less attention). Also, highly repressive states can prevent much manifestation of the kinds of violence identified here (see Duvall and Shamir 1980). The correlation between deaths from internal violence and our regime score is only $-.13$ (p $< .001$).

9. Cooperative events were scaled as $Coop = 8 -$ the event type, and conflictual events as $Conflict = -1 (8 -$ event type). This enabled assignment of high cooperative values to the most cooperative events, and high conflict values to highly conflictual events. The correlation between this measure and democracy is $r = -.10$ ($p < .01$)—suggesting, as with the political deaths measure, an overreporting of conflict in democracies. COPDAB data are available only for 1948–78. Machine-readable data are from the Inter-university Consortium for Political and Social Research, Ann Arbor, Michigan.

10. Since our economic data cover only the period 1950–84, the dyad-years available for analysis with this variable (and for levels of wealth) are reduced.

11. Although the revised and updated COW data provided to us by Allan Ned Sabrosky of Rhodes College do not include the latter alliance, we include it as of 1983, with the signing of the Memorandum of Understanding between the United States and Israel. Egypt has had a practical alliance with the United States since the 1979 Carter Doctrine that provided for joint military maneuvers between the

two. We also updated and refined the COW data from the appendix to Oren 1990.

12. Medium and remote contiguity refer to different levels of contiguity across gulfs (e.g., the Gulf of Mexico, the Persian Gulf, the Gulf of Aqaba). Other examples include the contiguity relations between the United States and Russia in remote areas (Alaska and eastern Siberia), and the United States and Cuba (ninety miles). Starr and Most 1976 pay attention to colonial borders. The original COW data set ended in 1986; we cleaned and updated it to 1986, then checked it with a parallel cleaning and updating by Charles S. Gochman of the University of Pittsburgh (whose data, and a similar typology, are used by Bremer 1992a).

13. In the analysis the actual number of cases is often much lower due to missing data for some variables and years.

Use of the dyad-year involves a statistical problem in that a particular dyad's conflict status is not independent from one year to the next. It is complicated by the fact that in this analysis we treat a continuing conflict as present in each year, not just when it began—as of course continuing peace is counted for each year. More generally, the effect of nonindependence is to inflate the apparent number of cases for statistical testing, lowering the threshold for a relationship to be considered significant. In partial compensation for this effect we report two-tailed statistical tests even thouugh all hypotheses are signed.

Sensitivity checks indicate that our treatment of continuing conflicts does not materially change the results. In any case, using the dyad-year is unavoidable. It is the shortest unit for which many data are available, and a longer time span would be unacceptable given that many states' political systems change frequently and at different times. Aggregation of the differences into a single value for the period would be meaningless. Moreover, in realist theory events are inherently interdependent because the structure of the system, rather than preferences of decisionmakers, "dictates" decisions on conflict and war. Consequently, a decision by one state to engage in conflict with another alters the structural constraints on other states, and the other's set of feasible actions is changed. For example, if the United States were fighting two wars, that would alter the probability that it would engage in a third war, thus "liberating" someone else who might have feared U.S. intervention. (Personal communication from Bruce Bueno de Mesquita, expanding on comments in Bueno de Mesquita and Lalman 1992, pp. 281–82.)

The research design is a pooled time-series analysis. Many of the diagnostics appropriate to such analysis using multiple regression are unavailable when the dependent variable is dichotomous or ordinal; the necessary computing power is lacking. There is no easy way to know whether and to what extent results are biased by heteroskedasticity and autocorrelation. The realist variables (notably contiguity and capability ratio) are generally quite stable over time, introducing autocorrelation. One of the indirect ways of estimating the degree of autocorrelation is also problematic because the skewed nature of the dependent variable (i.e., the ratio of conflict to nonconflict years for each dyad is very low) also introduces autocorrelation.

To redress this problem at least partially we conducted a set of tests. First we sorted our data by dyad by year. Second, we computed a lagged dichotomous conflict variable. Third, we ran all of our logistic regressions (tables 4.2–4.4) twice, once including the lagged conflict variable and once without it. In most of equations, as we had suspected, the lagged conflict variable had a significant positive effect on the likelihood of conflict (both in the MID data and in the ICB data). However, the sign, magnitude, and significance level of the parameter estimates of all other variables in the equations did not change significantly in the analysis with the lagged conflict compared to that without lagged conflict. This led us to conclude that autocorrelation, though present, does not seriously bias the results. We thank Christopher Achen for his advice.

14. To the extent that any of the nonregime factors examined in the first stage were found to have a significant effect on the probability of dispute this factor was controlled for at this stage also, insuring that relationships between either of the two models and dispute involvement or escalation were not spurious.

15. Gamma is a statistical measure of the difference between between the observed and expected values throughout the analysis, analogous to R^2 in multiple regression. In none of our analyses is multicollinearity a serious problem.

16. Interaction effects were largely insignificant. This is true of interactions between pairs of potentially confounding variables as well as of interactions between each of them and democracy.

17. The growth variable is not included in this set of analyses because of the large number of missing cases it generates. Using growth and either political deaths or executions reduces the number of available dyads by 65 percent and seriously distorts the distribution of the dependent variable.

18. Another set of analyses was performed using deaths from political violence as the indicator of democratic norms. This set yielded basically the same results as shown in tables 4.5 and 4.6.

CHAPTER 5
THE DEMOCRATIC PEACE IN NONINDUSTRIAL SOCIETIES

1. For analyzing external war, however, we could not make that assumption. The units that fight each other in external warfare are by definition from different cultures, and we cannot assume that the "enemy" has the same degree of political participation.

2. The Murdock/White sample includes one well-described society from most of two hundred regions of the world. Murdock 1967 is a much larger list of 862 mostly preindustrial societies. To facilitate the retrieval and coding of information on our sample cases, we used the Human Relations Area Files (HRAF) archive whenever possible.

3. The scale ranged from 1 to 5, from less often than once in ten years to "constant" or occurring at any time of year. We exclude here any cases where the coders' initial ratings for internal warfare frequency were not close. By close we mean that one of the following situations applied: (1) The initial ratings did not disagree by more than one point on a five-point ordinal scale; (2) The initial ratings disagreed by more than one point but they did not straddle the boundary between low and high frequency of war that was predictive of various things in past studies (Ember and Ember 1971; C. Ember 1975, 1978); i.e., warfare at least

once every two years (high) versus less often (low); (3) One of the first two coders said "don't know" and the third coder's rating was "close" (as defined above) to the other initial coder's numerical rating.

4. Unpublished data by Melvin Ember show that few of these societies have full-time public officials.

5. In this context we mean something less than formal organizations, but probably more than "stable, valued, recurring patterns of behavior" in Huntington's (1968, 12) definition of institutions. March and Olsen 1984, 738, say that to be identified as a political actor an institution must have a claim of "coherence and authority." Variable 9 (decision-making bodies) most clearly fits, with 6 (checks) and 8 (consultation) relevant to our concern for regularized checks and balances. Variable 7 (removal of leaders) explicitly invokes institutions at the level of a 2 code, but higher levels of restraint depend, appropriately, on norms and perceptions.

6. Coding was initially done independently by two trained assistants. Differences in coding exceeding one scale point were discussed by the two coders, typically in conjunction with Bruce Russett (on political participation) or Carol Ember (on warfare). If it was apparent that one coder had missed relevant information, or had misinterpreted the coding rules, that coder changed her/his rating; sometimes the coders reached a compromise. Where the original codings were more than one point apart and the coders could not reconcile the discrepancy, the case was omitted from the analysis; where the discrepancy was one point or less the computations were performed with the midpoint of the two codings. The assistants did not know our hypotheses; the authors did know, but did not know how the societies had been coded on the other variables. We also thank Marc Ross for consulting with us about the coding rules for political participation.

7. In a personal communication Spencer Weart has indicated that fission/ exile is a clear indication of the breakdown of dissent in ostensibly democratic societies that sometimes do fight each other.

8. The complete data set appears in Ember, Russett, and Ember, 1993.

9. An earlier analysis also included a control for patrilocal residence. Ember and Ember 1971 contend that residence is a consequence of war, but others (e.g., Otterbein and Otterbein 1965, Divale 1974) consider it a cause, because it is an indicator of fraternal interest groups, which are presumed to increase the likelihood of internal war. When included with the above variables patrilocal residence proved far from significant, probably because, the data in C. Ember 1974 show, matrilocal societies tend to be significantly smaller than patrilocal ones, and so residence and population are strongly correlated.

10. When either variable 6 or 11 was dropped, variable 8 retained its previous sign and approximate significance level; the same occurred for variable 11 when either 6 or 8 was dropped. Variable 6 was more unstable: weakly significant with a positive sign in the absence of 8; weakly significant with a negative sign in the absence of 11.

11. Among modern nation states the evidence that internal violent conflict and external conflict are systematically related is somewhat ambiguous and the phenomenon is complex (Stohl 1980; Zinnes 1980; Russett 1990, chap. 2).

12. For some fragmentary suggestions see the review in Ferguson 1984.

CHAPTER 6
THE FUTURE OF THE DEMOCRATIC PEACE

1. See Woodward 1991, 344–45. *U.S. News and World Report* 1992, 179, identifies, from Robert Teeter's polling for the administration, Saddam Hussein's nuclear weapon potential as the "hot button" to produce public support.

2. Wendt 1992 argues that beliefs about whether other states will behave according to the principles of realist anarchy are socially constructed. But his argument is primarily that state actors learn from the behavior of other actors in the international system ("outside") rather than from structure and processes that characterize fundamental beliefs or attitudes in their domestic politics ("inside").

3. This brief discussion identifies a major problem for subsequent research: not just what correlates with what, but what processes of affect and cognition underlie attitudes toward international relations?

4. See Russett and Sutterlin 1991 on UN peacekeeping in a broad sense. One possible hybrid form of peacekeeping might be an agreement, by all parties in advance, that the international agency would have the right (but not an obligation) to intervene if a government, elected in a process certified by the agency as fair and democratic, were subsequently overthrown. Halperin and Scheffer 1992 call such agreements "prior consent" to intervention.

References

Albrecht-Carrié, René. 1970. *Britain and France*. Garden City, N.Y.: Doubleday.

Alker, Hayward R., Jr. 1988. "The Dialectical Logic of Thucydides' Melian Dialogue." *American Political Science Review* 82, 3:805–20.

Allen, H. C. 1955. *Great Britain and the United States: A History of Anglo-American Relations (1783–1952)*. New York: St. Martin's Press.

Allison, Graham T., and Robert P. Beschel. 1992. "Can the United States Promote Democracy?" *Political Science Quarterly* 107, 1:81–98.

Aristotle. 1984. *The Politics*. Chicago: University of Chicago Press.

Axelrod, Robert. 1984. *The Evolution of Cooperation*. New York: Basic Books.

———. 1986. "An Evolutionary Theory of Norms." *American Political Science Review* 80, 4:1095–1112.

Azar, Edward. 1980. "The Conflict and Peace Data Bank (COPDAB) Project." *Journal of Conflict Resolution* 24, 1:143–52.

Babst, Dean. 1964. "Elective Governments—A Force for Peace." *The Wisconsin Sociologist* 3, 1:9–14.

———. 1972. "A Force for Peace." *Industrial Research* (April):55–58.

Banks, Arthur S. 1971. *Cross-Polity Time-Series Data*. Cambridge, Mass.: MIT Press.

———. 1986. *Cross-National Time-Series Data File*. Binghamton: State University of New York, Center for Comparative Political Research.

Bates, Darrell. 1984. *The Fashoda Incident of 1898: Encounter on the Nile*. New York: Oxford University Press.

Behr, Roy. 1980. "Nice Guys Finish Last . . . Sometimes." *Journal of Conflict Resolution* 25, 2:289–300.

Berghahn, Volker. 1973. *Germany and the Approach of War in 1914*. New York: St. Martin's Press.

Bill, James A. 1988. *The Eagle and the Lion: The Tragedy of American-Iranian Relations*. New Haven, Conn.: Yale University Press.

Black, Jan Knippers. 1977. *United States Penetration of Brazil*. Philadelphia: University of Pennsylvania Press.

Boulding, Kenneth. 1979. *Stable Peace*. Austin: University of Texas Press.

Bradeen, D. W. 1960. "The Popularity of the Athenian Empire." *Historia* 9:257–69.

Brams, Steven J. 1990. *Negotiation Games: Applying Game Theory to Bargaining and Arbitration*. London: Routledge.

Brams, Steven J., and D. Marc Kilgour. 1988. *Game Theory and National Security*. Oxford: Basil Blackwell.

Brawley, Mark R. 1992. "Regime Types, Markets and War: The Importance of Pervasive Rents in Foreign Policy." Paper presented at the annual meeting of the International Studies Association, Atlanta, April.

Brecher, Michael, Jonathan Wilkenfeld, and Sheila Moser. 1988. *Handbook of International Crises*. New York: Pergamon.

———. 1989. *Crisis in the Twentieth Century*. New York: Pergamon.

Bremer, Stuart A. 1992a. "Dangerous Dyads: Conditions Affecting the Likelihood of Interstate War, 1816–1965." *Journal of Conflict Resolution* 36, 2:309–41.

———. 1992b. "Are Democracies Less Likely to Join Wars?" Paper presented at the annual meeting of the American Political Science Association, Chicago: September.

———. 1993. "Democracy and Militarized Interstate Conflict, 1816–1965." *International Interactions* 18, 3:231–50.

Bueno de Mesquita, Bruce. 1981. *The War Trap*. New Haven, Conn.: Yale University Press.

Bueno de Mesquita, Bruce, and David Lalman. 1992. *War and Reason*. New Haven, Conn.: Yale University Press.

Bueno de Mesquita, Bruce, Randolph Siverson, and Gary Woller. 1992. "War and the Fate of Regimes: A Comparative Analysis." *American Political Science Review* 86, 3:639–46.

Burley, Anne-Marie. 1992. "Law among Liberal States: Liberal Internationalism and the Act of State Doctrine." *Columbia Law Review* 92, 8:1907–96.

Burke, S. M. 1973. *Pakistan's Foreign Policy: An Historical Analysis*. London: Oxford University Press.

Bury, J. A., S. A. Cook, and F. E. Adcock, eds. 1927. *The Cambridge Ancient History*, vol. 5. Cambridge: Cambridge University Press.

Campbell, A. E. 1960. *Great Britain and the United States, 1895–1903*. London: Longmans.

Campbell, Charles S. 1957. *Anglo-American Understanding, 1898–1903*. Baltimore: Johns Hopkins University Press.

———. 1974. *From Revolution to Rapprochement: The United States and Great Britain, 1783–1900*. New York: Wiley.

Carr, Raymond. 1980. *Modern Spain 1875–1980*. Oxford: Oxford University Press.

Chagnon, Napoleon Alphonseau. 1966. "Yanomamo Warfare, Social Organization and Marriage Alliances." Ph.D. dissertation, University of Michigan, Ann Arbor.

———. 1968. *Yanomamo, The Fierce People*. New York: Holt Rinehart.

Chan, Steve 1984. "Mirror, Mirror on the Wall . . . Are the Freer Countries More Pacific?" *Journal of Conflict Resolution* 28, 4:617–48.

Christof, Horst. 1975. "Deutsch-amerikanische Entfremdung: Studien zu den deutsch-amerikanischen Beziehungen von 1913 bis zum Mai 1916." Ph.D. dissertation, Julius-Maximilians-Universitäte, Warzburg.

Claude, Inis R. 1962. *Power and International Relations*. New York: Random House.

Coby, Patrick. 1991. "Enlightened Self-Interest in the Peloponnesian War: Thucydidean Speakers on the Right of the Stronger and Inter-state Peace." *Canadian Journal of Political Science* 24, 1:67–90.

Cogan, Mark. 1981. *The Human Thing: The Speeches and Principles of Thucydides' History*. Chicago: University of Chicago Press.

Cohen, Ronald. 1984. "Warfare and State Formation: Wars Make States and States Make Wars." In *Warfare, Culture, and Environment*, ed. R. Brian Ferguson, pp. 329–58. Orlando, Fla.: Academic Press.

Cooper, John M. 1946. "The Araucanians." In *Handbook of South American Indians*, ed. Julian H. Steward, 2:687–760. Washington, D.C.: U.S. Government Printing Office.

Czempiel, Ernst-Otto. 1992. "Governance and Democratization." In *Governance without Government: Order and Change in World Politics*. ed. Ernst-Otto Czempiel and James N. Rosenau, pp. 250–71. Cambridge: Cambridge University Press.

Dacey, Raymond, and Norman Pendergraft. 1988. "The Optimality of Tit-for-tat." *International Interactions* 15, 1:45–64.

Dahl, Robert A. 1971. *Polyarchy: Participation and Opposition*. New Haven, Conn.: Yale University Press, 1971.

———. 1989. *Democracy and Its Critics*. New Haven, Conn.: Yale University Press.

Davies, J. K. 1978. *Democracy and Classical Greece*. Atlantic Highlands, N.J.: Humanities Press.

Destler, I. M., H. Sato, P. Clapp, and H. Fukui. 1976. *Managing an Alliance: The Politics of U.S.–Japanese Relations*. Washington, D.C.: Brookings Institution.

Deutsch, Karl W. 1963. *The Nerves of Government: Models of Political Communication and Control*. New York: Free Press.

Deutsch, Karl W., et al. 1957. *Political Community and the North Atlantic Area*. Princeton, N.J.: Princeton University Press.

Diamond, Larry, Juan Linz, and Seymour Martin Lipset, eds. 1989. *Democracy in Developing Countries*. Boulder, Colo.: Lynne Rienner.

Diehl, Paul. 1991. "Geography and War: A Review and Assessment of the Empirical Literature." *International Interactions* 17, 1:11–27.

Diehl, Paul F., and Gary Goertz 1992. *Territorial Changes and International Conflict*. London: Routledge.

Diodorus Siculus. 1962. *Diodorus of Sicily*. Cambridge: Loeb Classic Library.

DiPalma, Giuseppe. 1990. *To Craft Democracies: An Essay on Democratic Transitions*. Berkeley: University of California Press.

Divale, William. 1974. "Migration, External Warfare, and Matrilocal Residence." *Behavior Science Research* 9, 1:75–133.

Dixon, William. 1992. "Democracy and the Peaceful Settlement of International Conflict." Paper presented at the annual meeting of the American Political Science Association, Chicago, September.

———. 1993. "Democracy and the Management of International Conflict." *Journal of Conflict Resolution* 37, 1:42–68.

Domke, William. 1988. *War and the Changing Global System*. New Haven, Conn.: Yale University Press.

Donnelly, George. 1991. "Thucydides and Realism." Paper presented to the annual meeting of the International Studies Association, Vancouver, March.

Doyle, Michael. 1983a. "Kant, Liberal Legacies, and Foreign Affairs, part 1."
Philosophy and Public Affairs 12, 3:205–35.
———. 1983b. "Kant, Liberal Legacies, and Foreign Affairs, part 2." *Philosophy
and Public Affairs* 12, 4:323–53.
———. 1986. "Liberalism and World Politics." *American Political Science Review* 80, 4:1151–61.
———. 1991. "Thucydides: A Realist?" In *Hegemonic Rivalry: From Thucydides
to the Nuclear Age*, ed. Richard Ned Lebow and Barry S. Straus. Boulder,
Colo.: Westview Press.
Duroselle, Jean-Baptiste. 1988. "Western Europe and the Impossible War." *Journal of International Affairs* 41, 2:345–61.
Duvall, Raymond, and Michal Shamir. 1980. "Indicators from Errors: Cross-
National, Time-Serial Measures of the Repressive Disposition of Govern-
ments," In *Indicator Systems for Political, Economic, and Social Analysis*, ed.
Charles L. Taylor, pp. 155–82. Cambridge, Mass.: Oelgeschlager, Gunn and
Hain.
Eckstein, Harry S., and Ted Robert Gurr. 1975. *Patterns of Authority: A Struc-
tural Basis for Political Inquiry*. New York: Wiley-Interscience.
Ember, Carol R. 1974. "An Evaluation of Alternative Theories of Matrilocal
Versus Patrilocal Residence." *Behavior Science Research* 9, 2:135–49.
———. 1975. "Residential Variation Among Hunter-Gatherers." *Behavior Sci-
ence Research* 10, 3:199–228.
———. 1978. "Men's Fear of Sex with Women: A Cross-Cultural Study." *Sex
Roles* 4, 5:657–78.
Ember, Carol R., and Melvin Ember. 1992a. "Resource Unpredictability, Mis-
trust, and War: A Cross-Cultural Study." *Journal of Conflict Resolution* 36,
2:242–62.
———. 1992b. "Warfare, Aggression, and Resource Problems: Cross-Cultural
Codes." *Behavior Science Reseach* 26, 1–4:169–226.
Ember, Carol R., Bruce Russett, and Melvin Ember. 1993. "Political Participa-
tion and Peace: Cross-Cultural Codes." *Behavior Science Research* 27, in press.
Ember, Melvin, and Carol R. Ember. 1971. "The Conditions Favoring Matrilocal
Versus Patrilocal Residence." *American Anthropologist* 73, 3:571–594.
Erdland, P. August. 1914. *Die Marshall-Insulaner: Leben und Sitte, Sinn und
Religion eines Südsee-Volkes [The Marshall Islanders: Life and customs,
thought and religion of a South Sea people]*. Münster: Anthropos Bibliothek
Ethnological Monographs. English translation 1942 and 1961 for the Yale
Cross-Cultural Survey and Human Relations Area Files.
Eybers, G. W. 1918. *Select Constitutional Documents Illuminating South African
History, 1795–1910*. London: Routledge.
Farrar, Cynthia. 1989. *The Origins of Democratic Thinking*. Cambridge: Cam-
bridge University Press.
Fearon, James. 1992. "Audience Costs, Learning, and the Escalation of Interna-
tional Disputes." Manuscript, Political Science Department, University of
Chicago.
Ferguson, R. Brian. 1984. "Introduction, Studying War." In *Warfare, Culture,
and Environment*, ed. Brian Ferguson, pp. 1–81. Orlando Fla.: Academic Press.

Finlay, David J., Ole R. Holsti, and Richard R. Fagen. 1967. *Enemies in Politics*. Chicago: Rand McNally.

Finley, J. H. 1942. *Thucydides*. Cambridge, Mass.: Harvard University Press.

Finley, M. I. 1971. *The Use and Abuse of History*. New York: Viking.

———. 1973. *Democracy Ancient and Modern*. New Brunswick, N.J.: Hogarth Press.

Fleiss, Peter J. 1966. *Thucydides and the Politics of Bipolarity*. Baton Rouge: Louisiana State University Press, 1966.

Forde, Steven. 1986. "Thucydides on the Causes of Athenian Imperialism." *American Political Science Review* 80, 2:433–48.

Forsythe, David P. 1992. "Democracy, War, and Covert Action," *Journal of Peace Research* 29, 4:385–95.

Fukuyama, Francis. 1989. "The End of History?" *The National Interest* 16:3–18.

Gantzel, Klaus Jürgen. 1987. "Is Democracy a Guarantor against War-Making Policy?" Working Paper no. 14, University of Hamburg, Institute of Political Science, Center for the Study of Wars, Armaments, and Development.

Garst, Daniel. 1989. "Thucydides and Neorealism." *International Studies Quarterly* 33, 1:3–27.

Gasiorowski, Mark, and Solomon Polachek. 1982. "Conflict and Interdependence: East-West Trade and Linkages in the Era of Detente." *Journal of Conflict Resolution* 26, 4:709–29.

Gastil, Raymond. 1989. *Freedom in the World: Political Rights and Civil Liberties, 1988–1989*. New York: Freedom House.

Gaubatz, Kurt Taylor. 1991. "Election Cycles and War." *Journal of Conflict Resolution* 35, 2:212–44.

———. 1992. "Democratic States and Commitment in International Relations." Paper presented at the annual meeting of the American Political Science Association, Chicago, September.

Geller, Daniel, and Daniel M. Jones. 1991. "The Effect of Dynamic and Static Balances on Conflict Escalation in Rival Dyads." Paper presented to the annual meeting of the American Political Science Association, Washington, D.C., August.

George, Alexander. 1991. "The Discipline of Terrorology." In *Western State Terrorism*, ed. Alexander George, pp. 76–101. Cambridge: Polity Press.

Geva, Nehemia, Karl DeRouen, and Alex Mintz. 1993. "The Political Incentive Explanation of the 'Democratic Peace' Phenomenon: Evidence from Experimental Research," *International Interactions* 18, 3:215–29.

Gillis, David. 1971. "The Revolt at Mytilene." *American Journal of Philology* 92, 2:38–47.

Gilpin, Robert. 1981. *War and Change in World Politics*. New York: Cambridge University Press.

Gleditsch, Nils Petter. 1992. "Democracy and Peace." *Journal of Peace Research* 29, 4:369–76.

Gleijeses, Piero. 1991. *Shattered Hope: The Guatemalan Revolution and the United States, 1944–1954*. Princeton, N.J.: Princeton University Press.

Gochman, Charles, and Zeev Maoz. 1984. "Militarized Interstate Disputes, 1816–1975." *Journal of Conflict Resolution* 29, 4:585–615.

Graham, A. J. 1983. Colony and Mother City in Ancient Greece. 2nd ed. Chicago: Ares.

Greenidge, A. H. J. 1911. A Handbook of Greek Constitutional History. London: Macmillan.

Grene, David 1950. Man and His Pride. Chicago: University of Chicago Press.

Gurr, Ted Robert. 1974. "Persistence and Change in Political Systems." American Political Science Review 68, 4:1482–1504.

———. 1988. "War, Revolution and the Growth of the Coercive State." Comparative Political Studies 21, 1:45–65.

Gurr, Ted Robert, Keith Jaggers, and Will Moore. 1989. Polity II Handbook. Boulder: University of Colorado Press.

———. 1991. "The Transformation of the Western State: The Growth of Democracy, Autocracy, and State Power since 1800." In On Measuring Democracy, ed. Alex Inkeles. New Brunswick, N.J.: Transaction Books.

Habeeb, William Mark. 1988. Power and Tactics in International Negotiations: How Weak Nations Bargain with Strong Nations. Baltimore: Johns Hopkins University Press.

Halperin, Morton H., and David J. Scheffer, with Patricia L. Small. 1992. Self-Determination in the Modern World. Washington, D.C.: Carnegie Endowment for International Peace.

Hammond, N. G. L. 1986. A History of Greece to 322 B.C. 3rd ed. Oxford: Clarendon Press.

Handlin, Oscar, and Lilian Handlin. 1986. Liberty and Power, 1600–1760. New York: Harper and Row.

Hastings, Elizabeth Hann, and Philip K. Hastings, eds. 1991. Index to International Public Opinion 1989–1990. Westport, Conn.: Greenwood Press.

Herman, Gabriel. 1987. Ritualized Friendship and the Greek City. New York: Cambridge University Press.

Hildebrand, David, James Laing, and Howard Rosenthal. 1977. Prediction Analysis for Cross Classifications. New York: Wiley.

Hirschman, Albert O. 1970. Exit, Voice, and Loyalty Cambridge, Mass.: Harvard University Press.

Holsti, Ole, and James N. Rosenau. 1988. "The Domestic and Foreign Policy Beliefs of American Leaders." Journal of Conflict Resolution 32, 2:248–94.

Hudson, Alfred E. 1936. Kazak Social Structure. New Haven, Conn.: Yale University Press.

Huntington, Samuel P. 1968. Political Order in Changing Societies. New Haven, Conn.: Yale University Press.

———. 1989. "No Exit: The Errors of Endism." The National Interest 17, 1:3–11.

———. 1991. The Third Wave: Democratization in the Late Twentieth Century. Norman: University of Oklahoma Press.

Hurwitz, Jon, and Mark Peffley. 1990. "Public Images of the Soviet Union: The Impact on Foreign Policy Attitudes." Journal of Politics 52, 1:3–28.

Huth, Paul, and Bruce Russett. 1993. "General Deterrence between Enduring Rivals: Testing Three Competing Models." American Political Science Review 87, 1:61–73.

Isocrates. 1929. *Panathenaic Oration*. Translated by George Norlin. London: Loeb Classic Library.

Janis, Irving, and Leon Mann. 1977. *Decision Making*. New York: Free Press.

Kagan, Donald. 1969. *The Outbreak of the Peloponnesian War*. Ithaca, N.Y.: Cornell University Press.

———. 1971. *The Archidamian War*. Ithaca, N.Y.: Cornell University Press.

———. 1981. *The Peace of Nicias and the Sicilian Expedition*. Ithaca, N.Y.: Cornell University Press.

———. 1987. *The Fall of the Athenian Empire*. Ithaca, N.Y.: Cornell University Press.

Kant, Immanuel. 1970. *Kant's Political Writings*. Edited by Hans Reiss, translated by H. B. Nisbet. Oxford: Oxford University Press.

Kennedy, Paul. 1980. *The Rise of Anglo-German Antagonism*. London: Allen and Unwin.

Keohane, Robert O. 1983. "Theory of World Politics: Structural Realism and Beyond." In *Political Science: The State of the Discipline* ed. Ada Finifter, pp. 503–40. Washington, D.C.: American Political Science Association.

———, and Joseph S. Nye. 1977. *Power and Interdependence: World Politics in Transition*. Boston, Mass.: Little, Brown.

Keynes, John Maynard. 1919. *The Economic Consequences of the Peace*. London: Macmillan.

Kindleberger, Charles. 1973. *The World in Depression: 1929–1939*. Berkeley: University of California Press.

Knock, Thomas J. 1992. *To End All Wars: Woodrow Wilson and the Quest for a New World Order*. New York: Oxford University Press.

Kohn, George C. 1986. *Dictionary of Wars*. Garden City, N.Y.: Doubleday.

Kozyrev, Andrei. 1988. "Confidence and the Balance of Interests," *International Affairs* [Moscow] 1988, 11:3–12.

Krader, Lawrence. 1953. "Kinship Systems of the Altaic-Speaking Peoples of the Asiatic Steppe." Ph.D. dissertation, Harvard University.

Krader, Lawrence, and Ivor Wayne. 1955. *The Kazakhs: A Background Study for Psychological Warfare*. Washington, D.C.: George Washington University, Human Resources Research Office.

Kratochwil, Friedrich. 1991. *Rules, Norms and Decisions*. London: Cambridge University Press.

Labovitz, Sanford. 1970. "The Assignment of Numbers to Rank Order Categories." *American Sociological Review* 35, 3:515–24.

Lacour-Gayet, Robert. 1978. *A History of South Africa*. New York: Hastings House.

Lake, David. 1992. "Powerful Pacifists: Democratic States and War." *American Political Science Review* 86, 1:24–37.

Lambert, William, Leigh Triandis, and Margery Wolf. 1959. "Some Correlates of Beliefs in the Malevolence and Benevolence of Supernatural Beings: A Cross-Cultural Study." *Journal of Abnormal and Social Psychology* 58, 1:162–69.

Langer, William L. 1972. *An Encyclopedia of World History*. Boston, Mass.: Houghton Mifflin.

Larson, J. A. O. 1955. *Representative Government in Greek and Roman History*. Berkeley: University of California Press.

158 • References

Larson, J.A.O. 1968. *Greek Federal States: Their Institutions and History*. Oxford: Clarendon Press.
Lasswell, Harold D. 1941. "The Garrison State." *American Journal of Sociology* 96, 4:455–68.
Latcham, Richard E. 1909. "Ethnology of the Araucanos." *Journal of the Royal Anthropological Institute* 39:334–70.
Legon, R. P. 1968. "Megara and Mytilene," *Phoenix* 22, 3:200–225.
Leng, Russell. 1993. "Reciprocating Influence Strategies and Success in Interstate Crisis Bargaining." *Journal of Conflict Resolution* 37, 1:3–41.
Levy, Jack S. 1988. "Domestic Politics and War." *Journal of Interdisciplinary History* 18, 3:653–73.
———. 1989. "The Diversionary Theory of War: A Critique." In *Handbook of War Studies*, ed. Manus Midlarsky, pp. 259–88. Boston: Unwin Hyman.
Lewis-Beck, Michael. 1980. *Applied Regression: An Introduction*. Newbury Park, Calif.: Sage Publications.
Light, Margot. 1992. "Economic and Technical Assistance to the Former Soviet Union." In *The Collapse of the Soviet Empire: Managing the Regional Fall-out*, ed. Trevor Taylor, 1:58–75. London: Royal Institute of International Affairs.
Lintott, Andrew. 1982. *Violence, Civil Strife, and Revolution in the Classical City*. London: Croom Helm.
Lumsdaine, David. 1992. "The Moral Construction of Rationality in International Politics." Paper presented to the annual meeting of the American Political Science Association, Chicago, September.
———. 1993. *Moral Vision in International Politics: The Foreign Aid Regime, 1949–1989*. Princeton, N.J.: Princeton University Press.
Manicas, Peter. 1989. *War and Democracy*. London: Basil Blackwell.
Mansfield, Harvey, Jr. 1983. "On the Impersonality of the Modern State." *American Political Science Review* 77, 4:849–57.
Maoz, Zeev. 1989. "Joining the Club of Nations: Political Development and International Conflict, 1816–1976." *International Studies Quarterly* 33, 2: 199–231.
Maoz, Zeev, and Nasrin Abdolali. 1989. "Regime Types and International Conflict." *Journal of Conflict Resolution* 33, 1:3–35.
Maoz, Zeev, and Bruce Russett. 1992. "Alliance, Contiguity, Wealth, and Political Stability: Is the Lack of Conflict between Democracies a Statistical Artifact?" *International Interactions* 17, 3:245–68.
March, James, and Johan Olsen. 1984. "The New Institutionalism: Organizational Factors in Political Life." *American Political Science Review* 78, 3:734–49.
Markides, Kyriacos. 1977. *The Rise and Fall of the Cyprus Republic*. New Haven, Conn.: Yale University Press.
May, Ernest R. 1961. *Imperial Democracy: The Emergence of America as a Great Power*. New York: Harcourt, Brace & World.
McColm, R. Bruce, et al. 1992. *Freedom in the World: Political Rights and Civil Liberties 1991–92*. New York: Freedom House.
McGregor, M. F. 1956. "The Politics of the Historian Thucydides." *Phoenix* 10, 3:93–102.

McKim, Fred. 1936. *San Blas: An Account of the Cuna Indians of Panama. The Forbidden Land: Reconnaissance of Upper Bayano River.* Edited by Henry Wassen. Goteborg: Etnografiska Museet, 1947.

Mearsheimer, John. 1990. "Back to the Future: Instability in Europe after the Cold War." *International Security* 15, 1:5–56.

Meggitt, M. 1977. *Blood is Their Argument: Warfare among the Mae Enga Tribesmen of the New Guinea Highlands.* Palo Alto, Calif.: Mayfield.

Meiggs, Russell 1972. *The Athenian Empire.* Oxford: Clarendon Press.

Meritt, B. D., H. T. Wade-Gary, and M. F. McGregor. 1950. *The Athenian Tribute Lists*, vol. 3. Cambridge, Mass.: Harvard University Press.

Merritt, Richard L., and Dina A. Zinnes. 1991. "Democracies and War." In *On Measuring Democracy: Its Consequences and Concomitants*, ed. Alex Inkeles, pp. 207–34. New Brunswick, N.J.: Transaction Books.

Milner, Helen. 1988. *Resisting Protectionism.* Princeton, N.J.: Princeton University Press.

Mintz, Alex, and Nehemia Geva. 1993. "Why Don't Democracies Fight Each Other? An Experimental Assessment of the 'Political Incentive' Explanation." *Journal of Conflict Resolution* 37, 3.

Mintz, Alex, and Bruce Russett. 1992. "The Dual Economy and Israeli Use of Force." In *Defense, Welfare, and Growth*. ed. Steve Chan and Alex Mintz, pp. 179–97. London: Routledge.

Modelski, George. 1988. *Is America's Decline Inevitable?* Wassenaar: Netherlands Institute for Advanced Study.

Modelski, George, and William R. Thompson. 1988. *Sea Power in Global Politics, 1494–1993.* Seattle: University of Washington Press.

Morgan, T. Clifton, and Sally Howard Campbell. 1991. "Domestic Structure, Decisional Constraints, and War." *Journal of Conflict Resolution* 35, 2:187–211.

Morgan, T. Clifton, and Valerie Schwebach. 1992. "Take Two Democracies and Call Me in the Morning: A Prescription for Peace?" *International Interactions* 17, 4:305–20.

Morrison, J. S., and R. T. Williams. 1968. *Greek Oared Ships.* Cambridge, Mass.: Harvard University Press.

Most, Benjamin, and Harvey Starr. 1989. *Inquiry, Logic, and International Politics.* Columbia: University of South Carolina Press.

Moynihan, Daniel Patrick. 1990. *On the Law of Nations.* Cambridge, Mass.: Harvard University Press.

Mueller, John. 1989. *Retreat from Doomsday: The Obsolesence of Major War.* New York: Basic Books.

Murdock, George P. 1967. "Ethnographic Atlas: A Summary." *Ethnology* 6, 2:109–236.

Murdock, George P., and Douglas R. White. 1969. "Standard Cross-Cultural Sample." *Ethnology* 8, 4:329–69.

Murray, Shoon. 1993. "American Elites and the End of the Cold War." Ph.D. dissertation, Yale University.

Nelson, Joan M., with Stephanie Eglinton. 1992. *Encouraging Democracy: What Role for Conditioned Aid?* Washington, D.C.: Overseas Development Council.

Nincic, Miroslav, and Bruce Russett. 1979. "The Effect of Similarity and Interest on Attitudes toward Foreign Countries." *Public Opinion Quarterly* 33, 1:68–78.

Nordenskiold, Erland. 1938. *An Historical and Ethnological Survey of the Cuna Indians.* Arranged and edited by Henry Wassen. Goteborg: Goteborgs Museum, Etnografiska Avdelningen.

Nye, Joseph R. 1988. "Neorealism and Neoliberalism." *World Politics* 40, 2:235–51.

O'Connell, Robert L. 1989. *Of Arms and Men: A History of War, Weapons, and Aggression.* New York: Oxford University Press.

O'Donnell, Guillermo, Philippe Schmitter, and Laurence Whitehead. 1986. *Transitions from Authoritarian Rule.* Baltimore, Md.: Johns Hopkins University Press.

Olson, Mancur. 1965. *The Logic of Collective Action.* Cambridge, Mass.: Harvard University Press.

———. 1991. "Autocracy, Democracy, and Prosperity." Paper presented to the annual meeting of the American Political Science Association, San Francisco, August.

O'Neill, Barry. Forthcoming. *Symbols, Signals, and War.*

Oren, Ido. 1990. "The War-Proneness of Alliances." *Journal of Conflict Resolution* 34, 2:208–33.

Organski, A. F. K. 1968. *World Politics.* 2nd ed. New York: Knopf.

Ostrom, Charles W., and Brian Job. 1986. "The President and the Political Use of Force." *American Political Science Review* 80, 2:541–66.

Ostwald, Martin. 1986. *From Popular Sovereignty to the Sovereignty of Law.* Berkeley: University of California Press.

Otterbein, Keith F. 1970. *The Evolution of War: A Cross-Cultural Study.* New Haven, Conn.: HRAF Press.

Otterbein, Keith, and Charlotte Otterbein. 1965. "An Eye for an Eye, A Tooth for a Tooth: A Cross-Cultural Study of Feuding." *American Anthropologist* 67, 6:1470–1482.

Pastor, Robert A. 1987. *Condemned to Repetition: The United States and Nicaragua.* Princeton, N.J.: Princeton University Press.

Peffley, Jon, and Mark Hurwitz. 1992. "International Events and Foreign Policy Beliefs: Public Response to Changing Soviet-American Relations." *American Journal of Political Science* 36, 2:431–61.

Polachek, Solomon. 1980. "Conflict and Trade." *Journal of Conflict Resolution* 24, 1:55–78.

Pollins, Brian. 1989a. "Does Trade Still Follow the Flag?" *American Political Science Review* 83, 2:465–80.

———. 1989b. "Conflict, Cooperation, and Commerce: The Effect of International Political Interactions on Bilateral Trade Flows." *American Journal of Political Science* 33, 3:737–61.

Pope, Maurice. 1988. "Thucydides and Democracy." *Historia* 38, 3:276–96.

Poundstone, William. 1992. *Prisoner's Dilemma.* New York: Doubleday.

Prados, John. 1986. *Presidents' Secret Wars: CIA and Pentagon Covert Operations since World War II.* New York: Morrow.

Pseudo-Xenophon (The Old Oligarch). 1962. "The Constitution of the Athenians." In *The Greek Historians*, ed. Francis R. B. Godolphin, 2:633–43. New York: Russell and Russell.

Putnam, Robert 1988. "Diplomacy and Domestic Politics: The Logic of Two-Level Games." *International Organization* 42, 3:427–60.

Quinn, D. 1964. "Thucydides and the Unpopularity of the Athenian Empire." *Historia* 13:257–66.

Ray, James Lee. 1990. *Global Politics*. 4th ed. Boston, Mass.: Houghton Mifflin.

———. 1993. "Wars between Democracies: Rare or Non-Existent?" *International Interactions* 18, 3:251–76.

Reisman, W. Michael, and James E. Baker 1992. *Regulating Covert Action: Practices, Contexts, and Policies of Covert Coercion Abroad in International and American Law*. New Haven, Conn.: Yale University Press.

Richardson, Lewis Frye. 1961. *Statistics of Deadly Quarrels*. Chicago: Quadrangle Books.

Risse-Kappen, Thomas. Forthcoming. *Cooperation among Democracies: Norms, Transnational Relations, and the European Influence on U.S. Foreign Policy*.

Rock, Stephen R. 1989. *Why Peace Breaks Out: Great Power Rapprochment in Historical Perspective*. Chapel Hill: University of North Carolina Press.

Rokeach, Milton M. 1973. *The Nature of Human Values*. New York: Free Press.

Root, Elihu. 1917. "The Effect of Democracy on International Law." Presidential address to the annual meeting of the American Society of International Law, Washington, D.C., April 26.

Rosecrance, Richard. 1986. *The Rise of the Trading State*. New York: Basic.

Ross, Marc H. 1981. "Socioeconomic Complexity, Socialization, and Political Differentiation: A Cross-Cultural Study," *Ethos* 9:217–47.

———. 1983. "Political Decision-Making and Conflict: Additional Cross-Cultural Codes and Scales." *Ethnology* 22, 2:169–92.

———. 1988. "Political Organization and Political Participation: Exit, Voice, and Loyalty in Preindustrial Societies." *Comparative Politics* 21, 1:73–89.

Rotberg, Robert L. 1980. *Suffer the Future: Policy Choices in Southern Africa*. Cambridge, Mass.: Harvard University Press.

Rueschmeyer, Dietrich, Evelyne Huber Stephens, and John D. Stephens. 1992. *Capitalist Development and Democracy*. Chicago: University of Chicago Press.

Rummel, R. J. 1976. *Understanding Conflict and War: Vol. 2, The Conflict Helix*. Los Angeles, Calif.: Sage Publications.

———. 1979. *Understanding Conflict and War: Vol. 4, War, Power, and Peace*. Los Angeles, Calif.: Sage Publications.

———. 1981. *Understanding Conflict and War: Vol. 5, The Just Peace*. Los Angeles, Calif.: Sage Publications.

———. 1983. "Libertarianism and International Violence." *Journal of Conflict Resolution* 27, 1:27–71.

———. 1985. "Libertarian Propositions on Violence within and between Nations." *Journal of Conflict Resolution* 27, 1:419–55.

———. 1987. "A Catastrophe Theory Model of the Conflict Helix, with Tests." *Behavioral Science* 32, 4:241–66.

Russett, Bruce. 1963. *Community and Contention: Britain and America in the Twentieth Century.* Cambridge, Mass.: MIT Press.

———. 1967. *International Regions and the International System: A Study in Political Ecology.* Chicago: Rand McNally.

———. 1990. *Controlling the Sword: The Democratic Governance of National Security.* Cambridge, Mass.: Harvard University Press.

Russett, Bruce, and Gad Barzilai. 1991. "The Political Economy of Military Actions: Israel and the United States." In *The Political Economy of Military Spending in the United States,* ed. Alex Mintz. London: Unwin Hyman.

Russett, Bruce, and Elizabeth C. Hanson. 1975. *Interest and Ideology: The Foreign Policy Beliefs of American Businessmen.* New York: W. H. Freeman.

Russett, Bruce, and Harvey Starr. 1981. 1st ed. *World Politics: The Menu for Choice.* New York: W. H. Freeman.

———. 1992. 4th ed. *World Politics: The Menu for Choice.* New York: W. H. Freeman.

Russett, Bruce, and James S. Sutterlin. 1991. "The U.N. in a New World Order." *Foreign Affairs* 70, 2:69–83.

Rustow, Dankwart A. 1987. *Turkey: America's Forgotten Ally.* New York: Council on Foreign Relations.

Sabin, Philip A. G. 1991. "Athens, the United States, and Democratic 'Characteristics' in Foreign Policy." In *Hegemonic Rivalry: From Thucydides to the Nuclear Age,* ed. Richard Ned Lebow and Barry S. Straus, pp. 235–50. Boulder, Colo.: Westview Press.

Saikal, Amin. 1980. *The Rise and Fall of the Shah.* Princeton, N.J.: Princeton University Press.

Ste. Croix, G. E. M. de. 1954–55. "Character of the Athenian Empire." *Historia* 3:1–41.

———. 1972. *Origins of the Peloponnesian War.* London: Duckworth.

———. 1981. *The Class Struggle in the Ancient World.* Ithaca, N.Y.: Cornell University Press.

Sanderson, G. N. 1965. *England, Europe, and the Upper Nile, 1882–1899: A Study in the Partition of Africa.* Edinburgh: Edinburgh University Press.

Sartori, Giovanni. 1987. *The Theory of Democracy Revisited* Chatham, N.J.: Chatham House.

Schumpeter, Joseph. 1955. *Imperialism and Social Classes.* Cleveland, Ohio: World Publishing.

Schweller, Randall L. 1992. "Domestic Structure and Preventive War: Are Democracies More Pacific?" *World Politics* 44, 2:235–69.

Segall, Marshall H. 1983. "Aggression in Global Perspective: A Research Strategy." In *Aggression in Global Perspective,* ed. Arnold P. Goldstein and Marshall H. Segall, pp. 1–43. New York: Pergamon.

Senfft, Arno. 1903. *Die Marshall-Insulaner* [The Marshall Islanders]. In *Rechtsverhältnisse von eingeborenen Völkern in Afrika und Ozeanien,* ed. S. R. Steinmetz, pp. 12–30. Berlin: Verlag von Julius Springer. Translated in 1942 for the Yale Cross-Cultural Survey.

Shepherd, W. Geoffrey. 1986. *The Ultimate Deterrent.* New York: Praeger.

Singer, J. David. 1981. "Accounting for International War: The State of the Discipline." *Journal of Peace Research* 18, 1:1–18.

Singer, J. David, Stuart Bremer, and John Stuckey. 1972. "Capability Distribution, Uncertainty, and Major Power War, 1820–1965." In *Peace, War, and Numbers*, ed. Bruce Russett, pp. 19–48. Newbury Park, Calif.: Sage Publications.

Singer, J. David, and Melvin Small. 1968. "Alliance Aggregation and the Onset of War, 1816–1965." In *Quantitative International Politics* ed. J. David Singer, pp. 247–86. New York: Free Press.

Siverson, Randolph, and Juliann Emmons. 1991. "Birds of a Feather: Democratic Political Systems and Alliance Choices." *Journal of Conflict Resolution* 35, 2:285–306.

Skidmore, Thomas E. 1967. *Politics in Brazil: An Experiment in Democracy*. Oxford: Oxford University Press.

Small, Melvin, and J. David Singer. 1976. "The War-Proneness of Democratic Regimes." *Jerusalem Journal of International Relations* 1, 1:50–69.

———. 1982. *Resort to Arms: International and Civil Wars, 1816–1929*. Los Angeles: Sage Publications.

Smith, Michael Joseph. 1986. *International Realist Theory from Machiavelli to Kissinger*. Baton Rouge: Lousiana State University Press.

Snyder, Jack. 1991. *Myths of Empire: Domestic Politics and International Ambition*. Ithaca, N.Y.: Cornell University Press.

Spiro, Melford, and Roy D'Andrade. 1958. "A Cross-Cultural Study of Some Supernatural Beliefs." *American Anthropologist* 60, 3:456–566.

Spoehr, Alexander. 1949. *Majuro: A Village in the Marshall Islands*. Fieldiana, Anthropology, vol. 39. Chicago: Natural History Museum.

Starr, Harvey. 1991. "Democratic Dominoes: Diffusion Approaches to the Spread of Democracy." *Journal of Conflict Resolution* 35, 2:356–81.

———. 1992a. "Democracy and War: Choice, Learning, and Security Communities." *Journal of Peace Research* 29, 2:207–13.

———. 1992b. "Why Don't Democracies Fight One Another? Evaluating the Theory-Findings Feedback Loop." *Jerusalem Journal of International Relations* 14, 4:41–59.

Starr, Harvey, and Benjamin A. Most. 1976. "The Substance and Study of Borders in International Relations Research." *International Studies Quarterly* 20, 4:581–620.

Stearns, Monteagle, ed. 1992. *Entangled Allies: U.S. Policy toward Greece, Turkey, and Cyprus*. New York: Council on Foreign Relations.

Stein, Arthur, and Bruce Russett. 1990. "Evaluating War Outcomes and Consequences." In *Handbook of Political Conflict*, ed. Ted Robert Gurr, pp. 399–422. New York: Free Press.

Stepan, Alfred. 1971. *The Military in Politics: Changing Patterns in Brazil*. Princeton, N.J.: Princeton University Press.

Stohl, Michael. 1980. "The Nexus of Civil and International Conflict." In *Handbook of Political Conflict*, ed. Ted Robert Gurr, pp. 297–330. New York: Free Press.

———. 1984. "International Dimensions of State Terrorism." In *The State as Terrorist: The Dymanics of Governmental Violence and Repression*, ed. Michael Stohl and George Lopez. Westport, Conn.: Greenwood.

Stout, David B. 1947. *San Blas Cuna Acculturation: An Introduction*. New York: Viking Fund.

Strauss, Leo. 1963. *The City and Man.* Chicago: University of Chicago Press.

Summers, Robert, and Alan Heston. 1988. "A New Set of Comparisons of Real Product and Prices: Estimates for 130 Countries, 1950–1984." *Review of Income and Wealth* 34, 1:1–26.

Swanson, Guy E. 1959. *The Birth of the Gods.* Ann Arbor: University of Michigan Press.

Tamir, Yael. 1993. *Liberal Nationalism.* Princeton, N.J.: Princeton University Press.

Taylor, Charles L., and David Jodice. 1983. *World Handbook of Political and Social Indicators.* 3rd ed. New Haven, Conn.: Yale University Press.

Thomas, Raju C. 1986. *Indian Security Policy.* Princeton, N.J.: Princeton University Press.

Thucydides 1954/1972. *The Peloponnesian War.* Translated by Rex Warner. Harmondsworth: Penguin.

Tillema, Herbert K. 1991. *International Conflict Since 1945: A Bibliographic Handbook of Wars and Military Interventions.* Boulder, Colo.: Westview Press.

Tilly, Charles. 1990. *Coercion, Capital, and European States,* A.D. *990–1990.* Oxford: Basil Blackwell.

Titiev, Mischa. 1951. *Araucanian Culture in Transition: Occasional Contributions from the Museum of Anthropology of the University of Michigan.* Ann Arbor: University of Michigan Press.

Tocqueville, Alexis de. 1945. *Democracy in America.* 2 vols. New York: Knopf.

Treverton, Gregory F. 1987. *Covert Action: The Limits of Intervention in the Postwar World.* New York: Basic Books.

Tuden, Arthur, and Catherine Marshall. 1972. "Political Organization: Cross-Cultural Codes 4." In *Cross-Cultural Samples and Codes* ed. Herbert Barry III and Alice Schlegel, pp. 117–145. Pittsburgh, Pa.: University of Pittsburgh Press, 1980. Originally published in *Ethnology* 11, 4:436–64.

U.S. News and World Report. 1992. *Triumph without Victory: The Unreported History of the Persian Gulf War.* New York: Random House.

Vanhanen, Tatu. 1984. *The Emergence of Democracy: A Comparative Study of 119 States, 1850–1979.* Helsinki: Finnish Society of Sciences and Letters.

———. 1990. *The Process of Democratization: A Comparative Study of 147 States, 1980–88.* New York: Crane Russak.

Wallensteen, Peter. 1973. *Structure and War: On International Relations 1820–1968.* Stockholm: Raben & Sjogren.

Waltz, Kenneth. 1979. *Theory of International Relations.* Reading, Mass.: Addison Wesley.

Weart, Spencer. Forthcoming. *Never at War: Why Don't Democracies Fight One Another?*

Wedgewood, Camilla H. 1942. "Notes on the Marshall Islands," *Oceania* 13, 1:1–23.

Weede, Erich. 1983. "Extended Deterrence by Superpower Alliance." *Journal of Conflict Resolution* 27, 2:231–54.

———. 1984. "Democracy and War Involvement." *Journal of Conflict Resolution* 28, 4:649–64.

———. 1992. "Some Simple Calculations on Democracy and War Involvement." *Journal of Peace Research* 29, 4:377–83.

Wendt, Alexander. 1992. "Anarchy Is What States Make of It." *International Organization* 46, 2:391–425.

Whiting, John. 1969. "Effects of Climate on Certain Cultural Practices." In *Environment and Cultural Behavior: Ecological Studies in Cultural Anthropology* ed. A. Vayda, pp. 416–55. Garden City, N.Y.: Natural History Press.

Wilkinson, David. 1980. *Deadly Quarrels: Lewis F. Richardson and the Statistical Study of War*. Berkeley and Los Angeles: University of California Press.

Wittkopf, Eugene R. 1990. *Faces of Internationalism: Public Opinion and American Foreign Policy*. Durham, N.C.: Duke University Press.

Woodward, Bob. 1991. *The Commanders*. New York: Simon & Schuster.

Wright, Quincy. 1942. *A Study of War*. Chicago: University of Chicago Press.

Xenophon. 1964/1979. *A History of My Times*. Harmondsworth: Penguin.

Young, Oran R. 1980. "International Regimes: Problems of Concept Formation." *World Politics* 32, 3:331–56.

Zakaria, Fareed. 1992. "Realism and Domestic Politics: A Review Essay." *International Security* 17, 1:177–98.

Zinnes, Dina. 1980. "Why War? Evidence on the Outbreak of International Conflict." In *Handbook of Political Conflict*, ed. Ted Robert Gurr, pp. 331–60. New York: Free Press.

Index

Abdolali, Nasrin, 19, 22, 30, 77, 139n.1
Acanthus, 47
aid. *See* economic assistance; multilateral aid
Albrecht-Carrié, René, 8
Alker, Hayward R., Jr., 144n.22
Allen, H. C., 7
alliances: of Athens, 53–54, 58–62; in making peace, 27, 82, 85–87; post–World War II democratic, 73
Allison, Graham T., 132
Amphipolis, 47, 57, 62
anarchy principle, 24
Anglo-Saxonism, 6
anocratic states: Brazil, Chile, Guatemala, Indonesia, Nicaragua, and Iran as, 121–23; defined, 77; disputes among, 78–79; Third World states as, 86
Arab democracy, 134–35
Argos, 47, 48, 60
Aristotle: as data source, 45; definition of city, 48; on democracy in Syracuse, 54–55, 56; distinction between polity and democracy, 55
assistance. *See* economic assistance
Athens: city-state allies of, 54; as city-state meeting strict democracy criteria, 47; democracy in, 45–46, 54–55, 59; hegemonic discipline of, 53–54, 61; wars with democratic states, 54–58, 61–62; wars with Syracuse, 43, 49–50, 51, 54–56, 62
authoritarian states: perceived lack of democracy in, 32; perception of, 135. *See also* autocratic states
autocratic states: defined, 76–77; dichotomy between democracy and, 15; disputes with anocracies, 79; transnational linkages in, 26
autonomy: of Greek city-states, 48–50
Axelrod, Robert, 33
Azar, Edward, 82

Babst, Dean, 139n.1
Baker, James A., III, 10–11, 127–29, 131
Baker, James E., 122

Balfour, Arthur, 6
Banks, Arthur S., 19, 77
Barzilai, Gad, 29
Bates, Darrell, 8
Behr, Roy, 33
belief systems, 130–32
Berghahn, Volker, 19
Beschel, Robert P., 132
Bill, James A., 122
Black, Jan Knippers, 123
Boer War (1899), 17
Boulding, Kenneth, 42
Bradeen, D. W., 43
Brams, Steven J., 42
Brawley, Mark R., 141n.15
Brazil, 121–22
Brecher, Michael, 75
Bremer, Stuart A., 14, 19, 22, 27, 30, 74, 83, 86, 139n.1, 140nn. 2, 5, 9, and 10, 146n.12
Bueno de Mesquita, Bruce, 27, 28, 39, 40, 137, 139n.1, 140nn. 7 and 10, 141n.17, 146n.13
Burke, S. M., 20
Burley, Anne-Marie, 34
Bury, J. A., 141n.2
Bush, George: on democratic peace, 10–11, 128–29; on effect of change in Eastern Europe, 127–29; role of, in Desert Storm, 124–26

Campbell, A. E., 5
Campbell, Charles S., 5, 7
Campbell, Sally Howard, 145n.7
Carr, Raymond, 19
Chagnon, Napoleon Alphonseau, 103, 110
Chamberlain, Joseph, 6
Chan, Steve, 19, 139n.1
Chile, 121, 123
Christof, Horst, 9
citizenship: in Greek city-states, 45–46
civil rights, 15, 133–35
civil war: conditions for, 26, 133–34; in democracies, 14
Civil War, American, 16–17
Claude, Inis R., 83